Ech D0594602

Echo and Narcissus

**Women's Voices
in Classical Hollywood
Cinema**

Amy Lawrence

University of California Press

Berkeley / Los Angeles / Oxford

University of California Press
Berkeley and Los Angeles, California

University of California Press, Ltd.
Oxford, England

© 1991 by
The Regents of the University of California

Photos courtesy of the Academy of Motion Picture
Arts and Sciences, New York Public Library.

Lawrence, Amy.
    Echo and Narcissus : women's voices in classical
Hollywood cinema / Amy Lawrence.
      p.   cm.
    Includes bibliographical references and index.
    ISBN-0-520-07071-2.—ISBN 0-520-07082-8
(pbk.)
    1. Women in motion pictures.   2. Sex role in
motion pictures.   3. Motion pictures—
California—Los Angeles—History.   I. Title.
PN1995.9.W6L38   1991
791.43'652042—dc20   90-50903
                           CIP

Printed in the United States of America
9 8 7 6 5 4 3 2 1
The paper used in this publication meets the minimum
requirements of American National Standard for Information Sciences—Permanence of Paper for Printed Library Materials, ANSI Z39.48–1984. ∞

*For Herb, Terry,
and Fella*

Contents

Acknowledgments

I would like to thank Marsha Kinder, Beverle Houston, Michael Renov, and Michael Cody for their input during the earliest stages of this work. Much of Chapters 3 and 4 on the film *Rain* was written with the advice and encouragement of Daniel Dayan, to whom I am very grateful. Dennis Doros of Kino International was most generous in allowing me access to Kino's reconstruction of *Sadie Thompson*. Bob Drake and Michael Hanitchak helped with frame enlargements. I also want to thank Ernest Callenbach, Rick Altman, and Al LaValley for their careful readings of the manuscript, bracing suggestions, and kind advice. Much of the value of this work is due to their patient encouragement.

Parts of this work have appeared in various forms in other publications. Sections of Chapter 4 were published in the *USC Spectator* as "Feminine Discourse in *Blackmail*," 3, no. 2 (Fall 1983): 3–4, and "Sound and Feminism," 4, no. 1 (Fall 1984): 7–8, and I would like to thank the editors of the two issues, respectively, Gaylyn Studlar and Jon Wagner. "*Sorry, Wrong Number:* The Organizing Ear" was published in *Film Quarterly* 40, no. 2 (Winter 1986–87): 20–27; "The Pleasures of Echo" in the *Journal of Film and Video* 40, no. 4 (Fall 1988): 3–13; "*Rain:* Theorizing the Transitional Text" in the *Quarterly Review of Film and Video* 11, no. 4 (Spring 1990): 21–33. "Sound and Feminism in *Notorious*" was presented as a paper at the 1985 University Film and Video Association conference in Los Angeles, part of Chapter 1 was presented as "The Ideology of the Sound Reproduction Industry before the Twenties" at the 1987 Society for Cinema Studies conference in Montreal, and part of the work on *Miss Sadie Thompson* was presented at the 1988

UFVA/SCS conference at Bozeman, Montana, under the title "Sound/Spectacle/Silverman."

I would particularly like to thank Marsha Kinder for her unceasing support and encouragement, and the Critical Studies Department of USC's School of Cinema/Television.

Introduction

In *Metamorphoses,* book 3, Ovid tells the story of Echo and Narcissus. Echo has lost the power to speak, having been cursed for shielding a philandering god from his wife. She spies the handsome Narcissus in a forest. He spurns her even though she turns his words into declarations of love: "May I die before I give you power o'er me," he declares, and she replies, "I give you power o'er me." Rejected and desolate, she hides in caves, wasting away until "only her voice and her bones remain: then, only voice for they say that her bones were turned to stone." Narcissus is also cursed when an unsuccessful suitor asks the gods to make Narcissus feel the pain of unrequited love: "May he himself love, and not gain the thing he loves!" When Narcissus, tired from the hunt, lies near a pool, he sees his own reflection and falls so deeply in love he cannot be moved from the spot. He too pines away: "No thought of food or rest can draw him from the spot; but, stretched on the shaded grass, he gazes on that false image with eyes that cannot look their fill and through his own eyes perishes." Finally, "death sealed the eyes that marvelled at their master's beauty." [1]

The story of Narcissus is frequently used to describe the image's seductive power. However, in Ovid's original myth the story of Echo and Narcissus interweaves issues of sight and sound, vision and speech. In fact, it is the relationship between Echo and Narcissus that sets into play the series of oppositions the myth works through. Echo longs to speak to Narcissus but can only repeat his words; Narcissus gazes at his reflection in the water and becomes so enamored he drowns in his own image. Echo's story comes first in Ovid's tale because it is impossible to imagine Narcissus without accounting first for a series of crucial absences that make his consuming fascination with the image

1

possible. Narcissus begins by rejecting other people, women (Echo) and then men. But even when he is alone (watched by Echo) speech is the one thing that could break his absorption in the image, language the medium that could explain the image's status as reflection. It is only by eliminating the possibility of speech that Narcissus's immersion becomes logically possible. And so Echo fades away, unable to contact Narcissus once he ceases to speak, sound's absence established as a precondition for the image's irresistible allure.

The story of Echo and Narcissus is a cautionary tale warning against what is conceived of as the unnatural and dangerous separation of sound and image, woman and man, hearing and seeing—oppositions that are in many ways fundamental to the ways we think about film. Both Echo and Narcissus are ravished by perception, subjected to obstacles of expression or comprehension, and ultimately die from the missed connections.

Like the film viewer, Narcissus "sees" at one remove, seeing not what he loves directly but its reflection. Although the sound of a voice or the persuasiveness of language could correct Narcissus's misapprehension, in Ovid's tale sound, like vision, is equally subject to the dangerous disjunction between intention and execution, meaning and perception. Echo's speech has been fragmented. She has lost control of language (the ability to choose words) and cannot initiate sounds. She "could neither hold her peace when others spoke, nor yet begin to speak till others had addressed her." [2] Even the sound we hear when Echo speaks is not "Echo" but a representation of sound, not a person speaking but the acoustic reflection of a person. Like the reflection in the pool, an echo is defined by a fundamental absence: what we perceive is not an entity but an illusion, the reflection of what once was. In Ovid's story, sound and image already partake of the absence Christian Metz (1982, pp. 58–68) has argued is a key element in cinematic pleasure, the cinematic sign indicating not its presence but its absence, the sound and image apparatus eliciting desire for that which can never be grasped. In cinema, everything we hear and everything we see isn't *there* anymore. It is an echo and a reflection.

Although they are interdependent, the stories of Echo and Narcissus are not fully parallel. On the one hand, it seems Echo suffers more. (At least Narcissus sees his ardor returned.) More important, there is an implicit hierarchy in the myth (one that has been carried over to writing about film) wherein the image is depicted as more compelling than sound. This hierarchy becomes explicitly gendered in the course of the narrative. The man's tragic obsession with the image is more important than the woman's problems of expression, her death simply preparation for the grand climax of his death. Woman and sound are allied on the "weak side" of the story.

In classical Hollywood film and much that is written about it, the sound/ image hierarchy survives intact. The image is assumed to be the source of enchantment, "the dream screen," the object of the "all-perceiving Eye." Sound, like Echo, seems to fade away—if it is mentioned at all. The "gendering" of the image and the sound track has been a key issue in feminist film work, from the widely discussed "male gaze" of the camera to the postulation of "femininity" in theories of film music.[3] As in Ovid, the mutual dependence of sound/image is essential to cinema and, as with Echo, a woman's voice is at the heart of the matter.

In this book I shall attempt to disentangle certain issues of sound and gender by focusing on the representation of women's voices in classical Hollywood cinema. The term "woman's voice" used in this work condenses three issues: (1) the physical ability to make a sound, which is then reproduced through cinema/sound technology, (2) a woman's relationship to language or verbal discourse, (3) her possession of authorial point of view, as in the author's "voice." The first two are frequently and too easily collapsed in the term "speech." It is necessary to separate them because often the simple act of producing a sound is made impossible by the intensity of patriarchal pressures brought to bear on the women in the films I shall be discussing.

However, before we can understand the representation of women's voices in film, we have to understand the system in which these voices are placed. Sound in film is itself a kind of echo, re-presented and reproduced, never actually "there." Part of the ideology of sound reproduction from its beginnings has been the belief that the sound-recording apparatus constitutes a neutral, transparent conveyance of "real" sound, that it is "merely" a conduit or a medium. So it will be necessary first to briefly reexamine the ideology of sound reproduction from its inception.

The central subject of sound recording in the nineteenth century was the voice, reflecting a widespread urge to preserve the individual and the domestic scene through automatic mechanical reproduction apparatuses.[4] Yet ideological assumptions about the human voice—beliefs inextricable from sound's technology, uses, and marketing—have always been shot through with assumptions about gender. The "human" voice is always either male or female, and issues of *women's* speech have been central to controversies surrounding the development of all sound technologies, from the introduction of loudspeakers, which allowed women to speak to large public gatherings, to the advent of the telephone, radio, and the phonograph. It is the history of the phonograph, I argue, that most precisely comprises the prehistory of sound in film, because it is the phonograph's ability to record and play back sounds precisely the same way time and again that most closely parallels the cinematic image's perpetual reanimation of motion. Radio and telephone technology were fundamental to the creation and development of the phonograph (and the role of gender in the commercialization of each is quite marked), but both telephone and radio are concerned primarily with the *transmission* of sound. Where issues involving the radio and telephone industries overlap with the history of sound reproduction and ideologies of gender, they will be discussed in depth. Given the extensive prehistory of sound reproduction, it is clear that when women in film finally did speak, the technology that allowed them to be heard brought with it half a century's worth of ideological baggage.

It is important to remember that the experimentation and research necessary for the realization of sound *film* was merely an offshoot of the sound-reproduction industry as a whole. The sound industry grew parallel to the rising image industry and rivaled its competitor both as a business and as a popular cultural institution. When sound was connected with the image track in sound film, it brought with it its own history, markets, and ideology.

In Chapter 1 I focus specifically on how the ideology inherent in science and in the commercial models adapted to sell sound at the turn of the century influenced the development of sound technology. The early history of sound reproduction is a tangle of technological experiments, shifting marketing strategies, and questions about what the products of this technology were to be and how and to whom they were to be sold. Advertisements from early in the twentieth century suggest the range of pleasures the phonograph offered (constrained by what was thinkable, possible, and/or available to the public at a given time). More important, the commercial, legal, and scientific maneuverings surrounding sound reproduction in the late nineteenth century are indicative of ideological assumptions and pressures that in turn helped pre-construct the functions sound would be called upon to perform in film. I shall briefly show how the technological and commercial ideologies of the period, together with philosophical musings about sound and the voice common to the era, contributed to constructing a particular listener/subject and a particular way of inserting sound reproduction into culture.

Silent cinema had its own history of representing women's speech. In silent film, despite the privileging of the image, women were always represented as *speaking* subjects. By looking closely at a silent film that centers on a very vocal female character, we can see how the hierarchy of image over speech is constructed in silent film and how this privileging of the image affects the representation of women's voices. As an adaptation of a play based in turn on a famous short story, *Sadie Thompson* (1928) demonstrates the prose and theatrical narrative traditions that silent film could call upon in its representation of women. Genres such as melodrama place a high premium on women's speech as a means of achieving psychologically rounded characters, and yet I shall show how in *Sadie Thompson* the displacement of speech in favor of image has particularly insidious effects when the speaker is a woman.

The synchronization of voice and image ("talkies") exemplified sound film for producers and public alike and at first it seems that synchronized dialogue would present women's voices in a way fully equal with those of men. In *Rain* (1932) we see the opportunities opened up by the new combinations of sound, image, and dialogue—from the illusion of physical presence and visual depth the voice gives the image, to sound's ability to challenge the reduction of women to "spectacle" by providing "psychological backstories" that make

women characters rather than objects. But does the "technological equivalence" of sound film's presentation of women's and men's voices mean that
women's voices in sound film function in the same way as men's? How does
dialogue, now spoken rather than written, contribute to woman's ability to express her experience now that she is figured by both the image and the sound
track? Are women allowed to speak the truth about their experience as women
under patriarchy—to say how it actually feels to live the roles they have been
placed in? Or is the combined weight of the sound film's theatrical and silent
history too great?

The transition to sound film momentarily disrupted the traditional sound/
image hierarchy. The requirements of sound demanded that film producers re-
tool and rethink how films were made in order to accommodate the delicate
new technology. Within a few years (roughly 1928–31) sound films were established as the norm and the new methods of production fixed. In looking at
Rain (the sound remake of *Sadie Thompson*), I want to see whether the sig-
nificatory free-for-all of early sound films is still detectable once what might
be called the "classical sound film" has been established and whether the
more complex relationship between sound and image in this period allows
women's voices to come into their own.

As the films discussed in Chapter 4 show, the establishment of sound film
by no means instituted a system where women could speak on a level with
men. The space created for women's voices in the films of the 1940s is fraught
with tensions. While some of the fragmentation evident in these texts may be
attributable to the film noir genre (which has been defined by its susceptibility
to narrative fissures and crises in gender roles),[5] I argue that in these films
there is a disproportionate emphasis on women's voices as the *source* of textual anxiety.

In fact, when there is a crisis in the representation of women, it often manifests itself as a crisis in the representation of women's *voices*. This in turn is
often expressed through a representative (and *represented*) crisis in the sound
technology. Just as assumptions about women are expressed through the use
of visual and audio technology, when women challenge the status quo, the
technology frequently exposes itself in its effort to repress them. In these
films, ideology under pressure becomes technology under pressure. Consequently, in all of the films in Chapter 4 (and to a greater or lesser degree in
every work mentioned), the woman's natural ability to speak is interrupted,
made difficult, or conditioned to a suffocating degree *by sound technology
itself.* In *Blackmail, Notorious,* and *Miss Sadie Thompson,* it is the very recording process that fractures a woman's body and voice into irreconcilable
pieces. In *Blackmail* and parts of *Miss Sadie Thompson* the physical voice is
not even the actress's own, as sound and image literally piece together an
"ideal" woman.

In the suspense films of Chapter 4, women either talk too much or not at all. (Echo can "neither hold her peace . . . nor yet begin to speak.") Either way the main female character challenges the status quo through excess. Those who are silent (*Blackmail, The Spiral Staircase*) must be made to speak and those who talk too much must be silenced either by male characters (*Notorious*) or men abetted by the cinematic system (*Sorry, Wrong Number*). Telephones, phonographs, voice-overs and dubbing are foregrounded as sound technologies are marshaled to silence women and restore the primacy of patriarchy and the image.

The films in Chapter 4 also use women's voices to examine the relationship between sound and image. As an early sound film, *Blackmail* (1929) is a cinematic hybrid incorporating scenes shot silent and others recorded with sound. The film's suspense, turning on the *absence* of a woman's speech, can be seen as an interrogation of the moral force of sound film versus silents/ silence. In *Spiral Staircase*, the murderer is depicted as a pair of eyes distorting, then killing, the women they see. (The male gaze at its most punitive.) Whenever the eyes appear, they overwhelm the image track and make explicit the killer's obsession with woman's "lack"—characterized at its most chilling in a close-up of a woman with no mouth. Only in *Sorry, Wrong Number* does the woman's voice challenge the power of the eye to organize the cinematic system, seizing control of the narrative by means of hearing and speech.

In *The Acoustic Mirror*, Kaja Silverman argues that classical Hollywood cinema never truly allows women to speak anything other than their own oppression; women's voices are subjected at every point to either male or institutional control. The film noir is particularly fertile ground for examining both the challenges posed by women's voices and the attempts to silence them. Except for *Blackmail*, all of the films in Chapter 4 were made within a few years of each other (1946–48) and all can be inserted into the suspense or film noir genres. The musical, with its emphasis on harmony, humor, and integration, would seem to be the genre farthest removed from noir's obsession with anxiety and transgression (despite the fact that the golden age of the Hollywood musical in the 1950s was contemporaneous with later film noir). The films of the fifties demonstrate an institutional desire to recuperate the threat of the woman's voice. The chapter on the 1953 *Miss Sadie Thompson* will allow us to test some of Silverman's assertions and at the same time see how Sadie Thompson fares in stereo, Technicolor, and 3-D, as spectacle reemerges as a central factor in the representation of women in body and voice.

Sunset Boulevard (1950) is perhaps Hollywood's most direct (yet paradoxical) version of the story of Echo and Narcissus, with the genders tellingly reversed. The wisecracking noir narrator relates his attempts to stave off the encroaching madness of a female Narcissus. His voice, too, lingers on after he has died. And like Echo, he is unable to break Norma Desmond's narcissistic obsession with her silver screen image. Like the other films discussed, *Sunset Boulevard* poses a running commentary on sound film; however, as we shall see, when Echo becomes a man the sound/image hierarchy undergoes a radical shift. The woman's alliance with the image (Narcissus as ardent defender of silent cinema) brings her madness, not power. A new *sound* hierarchy is established in *Sunset Boulevard* as the synchronized voice of the woman is made subordinate to the disembodied voice of the male narrator.

The third kind of "woman's voice"—the authorial voice—combines issues of voice and speech as well as power. For a woman to possess the authorial voice in Hollywood films is rare, and *To Kill a Mockingbird,* the film I have chosen to illustrate the woman's authorial voice, was made in 1962, near what has been called the end of the classical period. Based on a best-selling novel by a woman, the film maintains the book's narrative point of view, seeing the story through the eyes of a six-year-old girl, and adds a voice-over narrator who is the child as an adult. *To Kill a Mockingbird* returns us perhaps more than any other film we've looked at to the voice as physical entity. How far can the charisma of a woman's voice on the sound track take us toward establishing a personal female subject within Hollywood film?

In film and mythology, Echo's voice is continually taken from her—by a jealous image frightened of her power, by a patriarchal system that wants to keep women silent. Is it possible for a woman to speak in classical Hollywood film? Can she be heard? Will Narcissus ever wake up and hear what Echo has to say?

The Pleasures of Echo: 1

The "Problem" of the Speaking Woman

In a standard history of cinema such as David Cook's *A History of Nar-rative Film*, the "prehistory" of cinema unfolds as a series of optical inventions, from photography and optical toys such as the zoetrope, thaumatrope, and the Phenakistascope, to Etienne-Jules Marey's "chronophotographic gun" and Eadweard Muybridge's "series photography."[1] However, equally relevant to the prehistory of *sound* cinema is the late nineteenth century's development of devices that could record sound. Cook himself argues that it was the phonograph that made the invention of cinema (as a technology and as a commercial medium) possible.[2]

In its pre-cinematic history, sound recording developed not only a set of technologies, but a set of ideological assumptions concerning what was to be recorded and what was to be sold. Particularly important to studies of sound in film is the process by which the *voice* became one of the principal subjects of sound recording. While other technologies were equally dependent on the reproduction of the voice (most important among them, radio and telephone), these media focused primarily on live transmission. It was recording, I argue, that formed the prehistory of sound film's acoustic dimension, and it was in the history of sound recording that the ideology of the voice, later transferred to cinema, evolved. That "the voice" was always implicitly a gendered one is obscured, unconsciously assumed, or actively covered over in the formulation of the technology and in the pronouncements of the period. And yet . . .

The pleasures of Echo are inevitably linked to issues of gender. The human voice is always either male or female and almost always recognized as such. The technology that reproduces the "human voice" at every point seeks to recreate men and women according to the standards of the day. For instance, an entire philosophy of Victorian gender relations can be read in the praises of the first telephone operators: "The dulcet tones of the feminine voice seem to exercise a soothing and calming effect upon the masculine mind, subduing irritation and suggesting gentleness of speech and demeanor."[3] Before the technology that could record sound was invented, the inventors, like the culture at large, already had ideas about what women's voices *meant*. When women's and men's voices were recorded for the first time, an entire lexicon of gender-specific cultural assumptions were recorded with them.

The last quarter of the nineteenth century saw massive social transformations wreaked by telephone and phonograph. Yet during the same period it was controversial for a woman to attempt to speak in public.[4] Throughout the development of sound-based media, from telephone to dictaphone, phonograph to radio, sound film to television, woman's place has been an issue argued in marketing reports, hiring practices, advertising strategies, in sound studios and in programming. And her "place" in sound media is measured by the presence of her voice. Whether the speakers occupied accepted roles as "invaluable" secretaries or receptionists, or were suffragists and early women radio announcers bucking the tide to effect change, women's voices were always inserted into a preexisting ideology that economically and politically predefined how the female voice was to be represented—or whether it would be heard at all.

When sound technology was incorporated into cinema, the reproduced voice brought with it a legacy of techniques of audio representation that had to be adapted by trial and error to cinema's already established conventions for constructing narrative. The difficult transition to "talkies" brought films not only speech but with it the issue or, more accurately, the "problem" of women's speech.

Feminist film analysis has focused over the past two decades on the issue of the visual representation of woman as spectacle or as object of the male gaze, fragmented and fetishized to reassure the male viewer's illusions of cohesiveness.[5] If, as Kaja Silverman suggests, classical cinema as a whole is constructed visually and acoustically to shore up a male subjectivity that is always at risk (Silverman 1988), then the woman's voice has a particular function within this system, one aimed not at her but at "him." Whether this bleak picture holds true for every representation of the speaking woman in classical film remains a question. However it is clear that it is possible to isolate the woman's voice as a recurring subject of sound film, one that frequently takes the shape of a problem or dilemma that must be resolved. For when women are disturbingly silent in Hollywood films, the texts force them to speak. Yet when they open their mouths, what often comes out is resistance—which must be suppressed. As I shall demonstrate, the "difficult" speaking woman refuses to be repressed, as films from the silent era to the early sixties struggle to put woman's voice in its place.

Is sound in Hollywood films *always* used paradoxically to "silence" women? Is it possible for a woman to speak in classical Hollywood cinema? If her voice, like her image, is constructed for a male eye and ear, in what sense can the women represented in Hollywood films be said to "speak," to articulate sounds, select words, and tell their own stories—stories women in the audience can recognize as their own?

Before examining the representation of woman's voice in film, it is necessary to locate the origins of the ideology of voice reproduction as it developed from the beginning of sound recording. In considering sound reproduction as a text in its own right I shall (1) discuss briefly why recording techniques that privilege the voice became central to recording before the turn of the century, (2) ask how sound recording that privileges the voice constructs the listener, and (3) try to define what kinds of pleasure the listener experiences as a *listener* rather than as an image-privileging "spectator." How each of these in turn is inflected by the presence of a gendered voice and a gendered listener makes up the remainder of the chapter.

Sound before Cinema

In an article written in 1878, Thomas Edison listed "ten ways in which his invention was to benefit mankind":

1. Letter writing and all kinds of dictation without the aid of a stenographer.
2. Phonographic books, which will speak to blind people without effort on their part.
3. The teaching of elocution.
4. Reproduction of music.
5. The "Family Record"—a registry of sayings, reminiscences, etc., by members of a family in their own voices, and of the last words of dying persons.
6. Music boxes and toys.
7. Clocks that should announce in articulate speech the time for going home, going to meals, etc.
8. The preservation of languages by exact reproduction of the manner of pronouncing.
9. Educational purposes; such as preserving the explanations made by a teacher . . .
10. Connection with the telephone, so as to make that instrument an auxiliary in the transmission of permanent and invaluable records instead of being the recipient of momentary and fleeting communication.

(Gelatt 1955, p. 29)

What is most noticeable in this list, besides Edison's prescience,[6] is that except for numbers 4 and 6 on the reproduction of music, nearly all of Edison's proposed uses for sound recording are linked to the reproduction of the voice—in elocution, pronunciation, preservation of family histories ("in their own voices"), dictation, lectures, and recording phone calls.[7] Thus, almost before the phonograph had been invented, its special mission as preserver of the voice was set out for it. The ideology of the apparatus to a great extent pre-existed the invention of the apparatus.

The first attempt to commercialize phonographic technology was located precisely between an emphasis on the technological nature of the apparatus and the goal of reproducing the voice. In January 1878, just months after Edison's first successful demonstration of the phonograph, "hundreds of machines were manufactured and a team of men was organized and trained to demonstrate the features of the phonograph to audiences across the nation."[8] These public demonstrations displayed the phonograph's overdetermination of wonders—as recorder, record player, scientific device, novelty, and entertainment medium. Its ability to record any sound and immediately reproduce it enabled the audience instantly to compare the fidelity of reproduction to performance. "The crowds came, listened with astonished incredulity to the phonograph's raucous croak, applauded it with gusto, and asked for more" (Gelatt 1955, p. 27).

However, at the same time, the "operators" would manipulate the sound in order to demonstrate the apparatus's control of the sounds it emitted. Early critics of the extremely popular novelty assailed the wilful distortions of sound committed by phonograph operators who varied their hand cranking of the apparatus to affect the pitch artificially—something never before possible (ibid., p. 27). By doing so, these traveling showmen instantly exposed any alleged neutrality of mechanical reproduction and, in effect, turned the apparatus itself into a text.[9] As Stephen Heath points out regarding the Lumières' comparable early film exhibitions, "what is promoted and sold is *the experience of the machine*," with discrete films (or recordings) merely "elements of the experience of the machine."[10] While cinema learned rather quickly to supplant the appeal of the apparatus's technological novelty with an unending series of ever-changing products (films), it took phonograph manufacturers a relatively long time to begin producing records as a lure for buyers, as I shall discuss below.

Because it was dependent on the inherently limited appeal of raw novelty, the period of phonograph exhibition, although initially highly lucrative, did not last.[11] A second, complementary, commercial tack—making rudimentary phonographs available for purchase and home use—was forced to confront the essential fragility of the tin-foil recording medium of Edison's first-generation cylinder machines, ending the so-called "phonograph craze of 1878" about six months after it started.[12]

After ten years of dormancy, the next attempt to commercialize sound recording focused on "the nation's business and government offices,"[13] with Edison and his competitors adopting the same marketing strategy—selling the phonograph as a dictating machine for business.[14] As with the telephone and telegraph (two words from which the name "phonograph" evolved and two industries made highly successful by their application to business and government concerns),[15] reliability of the equipment and the clear transmission of speech were paramount. Owing to various technical problems stemming primarily from the incompatibility of nonstandardized parts from competing phonograph manufacturers, the manufacturers' plans to make the phonograph an integral part of business, initiated in 1888, had dissolved by the early 1890s.

The capital required to enter the sound business was daunting. Because the sound industry was built first and foremost on the concept of selling machines, an investor needed a large amount of capital, a factory, a constant labor supply, plus raw materials such as wood (for the body), tin (for the amplifying horns), and equipment to form the recording cylinders or discs. When an investor named Seaman bought out the National Gramophone Company and changed its name to the National Gramophone Corporation in March of 1899, he needed to "raise the capitalization from $200,000 to $800,000," the historian Roland Gelatt notes (1955, p. 94).The next step was to set up a subsidiary to open a factory to produce the machines. A contemporary news account reported that Seaman's factory "expect[ed] to be able to commence deliveries" roughly six months after it started production (ibid.). The initial financial outlay, as well as the gap between investment and any potential profit, effectively locked out the small businessman.

Secondly, every time a company sold a phonograph, it lost a customer. While the cost of the machines was higher than say a ticket to a film or the theater, once a company made a sale there was no further potential source of profit. Selling replacement needles (a true demand) and blank cartridges or discs for home recording did not promise even cursory returns compared to the size of the investor's initial investment. These accessories, in fact, were practically given away. (As late as 1927 the Sears Catalogue was offering "five Silvertone records . . . needle assortment included" with every phonograph.)[16] In the sound industry, profits were slow in coming, and the ante was high. As long as the emphasis was on the machine and the machines stayed the same, there was limited potential for product turnover. Consequently the sound industry had to keep expanding its market until it hit saturation point, conceivably with everyone in America having a phonograph.

The phonograph's major function in the years between 1893 and 1914 was to provide *home-produced* entertainment in a manner similar to still photography; the subject matter recorded in both mediums was up to the consumer. Photography can thus be seen as another model for the phonograph industry. With still photography, the home use of sound reproduction had a preexistent ideology to key into and an industry to mimic in its advertising and suggestions of appropriate use. Amateurs bought their own equipment, which was simple enough for the average person to operate and maintain without advanced technical knowledge. Just as amateur photographers photographed what interested them personally (primarily members of their own families and their private surroundings), we find phonographs in ads of this period being sold on the basis of their ability to record the aural equivalent of photographs—the sounds of the domestic scene, the voices of loved ones. An ad for the $20 "Type AT Columbia Graphophone" in the 1906 Sears-Roebuck catalogue stresses

> *You Can Make Your Own Records* with this machine, as we furnish with each one the latest improved recorder, and *half the pleasure* in owning a graphophone is derived from record making. . . . You can put on a blank record [cylinder] and have any one sing or talk into the machine, and then keep this record indefinitely and reproduce it [i.e., play it back] as often as you care to. Just think of preserving the voice of each and every one in the family, and what a pleasure it would be to listen to these voices and reproduce these records in after years.[17]

The emphasis on "after years" (i.e., after the death of the subject), for instance, is a recurring image in (and argument for) early sound recording. The famous logo known as "His Master's Voice" is a queer exemplar of the connection made between sound recording and death. In early versions of the popular illustration of Nipper cocking a canine ear toward the flower-shaped horn of a Victrola, the faithful dog is depicted as sitting on a coffin. In some versions, the brass handles of the casket are clearly visible. Besides adding a decidedly morbid edge to the title, Nipper's placement on such a pedestal conveyed the comforting thought that a timely phonograph recording would allow your loved ones to continue to speak to you literally from beyond the grave.

The new strategy of selling phonographs as home entertainment underscores how, even in the initial forays into the marketplace, the selling of sound technology was geared toward exploiting perceived gender roles. The appeal to business with the ill-fated dictaphone was aimed at male stenographers and the businessmen of the period. The entrepreneurial "operators" who traveled the vaudeville circuit with the age's latest mechanical marvel were brothers of the era's traveling salesmen. Although none of the major histories of the early phonograph exhibitions mentions it, women do not seem to have been invited to take part, except as members of the audience. Illustrations of phonographs on stage in splendiferous concert halls universally feature a male operator taking bows nearby. The shift to home entertainment was accompanied by a new emphasis on the female consumer. Advertisements of the day stress aspects of sound technology thought to appeal to the lady of the house, such as ease of operation and the ability to record family sing-alongs and memorialize domestic life, while depicting her where they expect to find her, at home.

At the turn of the century, another important marketing shift took place, which helped alter the female consumer's role from an active one as preserver of the family to a passive one. The selling of prerecorded cylinders and discs was the first commercial adjunct to the selling of the phonographs themselves. The potential market for records was suggested on two fronts in the early 1890s: the phonograph parlor and the disc-playing Gramophone.

In 1890 an exhibitor named Louis Glass created the phonograph parlor, which allowed the public access to prerecorded subjects on a pay-per-listen basis. This popular form of exhibition was made possible by the "Graphophone's" reliance on "ear-tubes," necessary for hearing the quiet, but superior, sound quality of the improved cylinder machines. "Fixture[s] on the American scene in the 1890's,"[18] phonograph parlors repositioned the phonograph from the domestic to the public sphere and proved that people were willing to pay to hear voices other than their own and those of loved ones.

Before record production could become a major industry in its own right, however, it was necessary to find a reliable method of mass production. The reproduction of cylinders was time-consuming and difficult. Emile Berliner's disc-playing "Gramophone" had sound quality superior to the best cylinder machines. Louder and clearer, the sounds could be broadcast through a horn. The flat disc also had a marked advantage because producers could stamp an unlimited number of positives of a single performance from a metal negative.[19]

Manufacturers of the original cylinder recorders responded to competition from the disc player with ads that isolated the ideological crisis precipitated by the new sound technologies, at the heart of which lay the controversy over home production versus prerecording: whose voice does the listener want to hear?

> The [cylinder-playing] Graphophone does much more [than the Gramophone]; it repeats your voice; your friend's voice; songs sung to it or stories told to it. [The Gramophone can] reproduce only specially prepared cut-and-dried subjects. . . . Makers of machines limited by their mechanism to imperfect reproductions of specifically prepared records attempt to persuade intending purchasers that it is one of the merits of their invention that it will not make records of sound. Much of the pleasure, however, of a talking machine in the home is derived from its power of recording favorite musical selections, songs sung by loved ones, or the voices of friends.
>
> (Gelatt 1955, p. 90)

The Gramophone was eventually modified so that it *could* be used to record, but that was not until 1931, and as the historians Oliver Read and Walter Welch note, in the meantime "there had been virtually no attempt to sell home-recording equipment since the all-purpose cylinder machines of Edison of about 1906" (Read and Welch 1976, p. 290).

The popularity of prerecorded records became such that by 1907 Sears was openly using records to sell machines—a major reversal of the marketing techniques of the previous decades. An ad states that Sears will sell "a genuine Oxford machine for only $6.90 . . . simply as an accommodation to those who might . . . be unable to take advantage of this wonderful *record offer*." [20]

As the market for records continued to grow, there was a major shift in the subject matter being recorded. Originally in "the mid-Nineties, speaking records were in great vogue" (Gelatt 1955, p. 53). As late as 1909 the Sears Catalogue lists comedy skits with descriptions such as "Flanagan on a Farm—Irish character sketch," "Heinie—German dialect," or simply "Comic Rube Sketch." There is in addition an entire section of "Miscellaneous Talking Selections" including sixteen of "Uncle Josh Weatherby's Famous Laughing Stories." [21]

Recorded music's eventual eclipse of "talking records" can be seen as resulting from certain issues of ownership. "Value" in record-buying is popularly measured by repeatability: "How often does the purchaser listen to the same record?" This standard of value sets limits on the kind of material favored by early consumers. Narratives such as the short comic sketches above would exhaust their replay value as soon as one knew all the jokes and how the story ended. (Audio dramas would not truly flourish until radio days when "live-ness" dictated a "once only" policy for narratives.)

Music was seen as a more open-ended form, and as such, more acceptable under conditions of arguably limitless repetition. Subjects that lent themselves to repetition, like popular songs, would become the mainstay of a collection. This kind of popular music also fit in with other entertainment industries of the period that had already made themselves part of domestic culture—sheet music, piano rolls, music boxes with interchangeable metal discs, and so on.

It was with the adoption of a star system borrowed from opera that "fidelity" and the neutrality of sound reproduction became crucial issues in maintaining the indexical relationship between the star and the recording; what Walter Benjamin calls the "aura" of the work of art becomes the recorded "presence" of the artist. [22] Red Seal records (a European division of the gramophone manufacturer Victor Records) began recording opera singers in 1902. In much the way the adaptation of theatrical-length works would help transform cinema into a middle-class form that aspired to "high art," the recording of opera singers lent the phonograph the same "patina of high art" (Gelatt 1955, p. 129) as well as enabling the companies involved to charge middle-class prices. While ordinary records sold for as little as 14 to 35 cents each, Red Seal records sold for an astonishing $3–5 each (ibid., p. 148). Gelatt underscores the displacement of the machine by its product when he gushes that "the inventors and entrepreneurs played important and fascinating roles [in the development of sound recording], but their work would have little interest for us had it not been allied to the artistry of Caruso and Melba, Beecham and Casals" (ibid., p. 11).

The shift to classical music as privileged subject matter for phonograph records is formulated (particularly in Gelatt's account) according to the myth of the immigrant in America—with a definite Henry James twist.

> Emile Berliner's invention had arrived in Europe in 1898 a raw and uncultured immigrant, full of promise and inherent ability, but lacking polish and refinement, and denied access to the higher reaches of society. In seven years it had been transformed by the Old World which adopted it. The impact of European civilization had turned the gramophone into a musical instrument.
>
> (ibid., p. 129)

In their definitive history, *From Tinfoil to Stereo,* Read and Welch agree that an enthusiasm for recorded classical music was sweeping the country. The recordings that emanated from Europe, "most of them unavailable on domestically issued discs," catered to a "new class of record buyers" (Read and Welch 1976, p. 290).

The association of classical music and cultural status recurs in promotional material throughout the teens and twenties. The boxed centerpiece of a Sears ad in 1909 insists that its new Oxford Talking Machines are "not mere 'talking machines' but musical instruments of the highest order." It was such musicality, no doubt, that made possible the phonograph's success as a marker of class: "Today, the Waldorf-Astoria, New York City's most famous hotel, the mecca of wealth and fashion, entertains its guests at luncheon with a tapering tone arm talking machine." [23] Nearly every ad for phonographs in the 1927 Sears Catalogue features an endorsement from a prominent artist of the day. Patricia Ann Manners, "Star in 'The Student Prince,'" testifies that "the Truphonic Phonograph is certainly a great contribution to the art of *music.*" [24] The 1909 featured ad assures the potential customer that this model phonograph "brings to your own home the same musicians, the same great singers, the same entertainers, the same bands and orchestras that delight great audiences in our most famous theaters." [25] This appeal is on a national scale ("our" theaters) and openly class conscious (the "great" audiences in the big cities). Although these ads are for phonographs, the machine's value is clearly its ability to deliver recordings of classical music. Through listening to these records, the home listener gains equal stature with members of the upper class.

The shift to prerecorded music also affected how women's voices were seen in the period, particularly in their ability to compete with men's voices *as commodities.* Anne McKay notes that in a 1925 article on women's place in radio announcing, a dealer in phonograph records "reported that the public refused to buy recordings of women talking. Manufacturers lost several thousands of dollars, he wrote, before they learned that the public will not pay money to listen to the *talking* record of a woman's voice" (McKay 1988, p. 199; italics added).

Why a woman's speaking voice should prove so dramatically unpopular (which I am deducing from an admittedly limited amount of information on the subject) while women *singers* were by all indications as popular as men is at the same time mystifying and suggestive. One possible reason might be that singing was linked to an established tradition of theatrical performance, including music hall, vaudeville, and opera, where women were firmly entrenched. Advertisements for recordings by female opera stars certainly keyed into this perception. Another possible reason why women found a congenial audience as singers is that singing at the turn of the century was considered part of a young lady's "accomplishments" and as such a "decorative" feminine art. As will be shown later in relation to women radio announcers, a *speaking* woman puts herself in a position of authority—a definite breach of propriety. The controversy over the speaking woman was one that was to return with radio and that would never in effect be resolved throughout classical sound film—both points to be expanded upon later.

Ads of the day illustrate the move to obscure the function of the sound apparatus while promoting direct and unmediated access to the star. These ads are also early "mini-histories" of sound recording, framing the past so as to differentiate the "new and improved" products from their predecessors.

> The First Talking Machines and Records, crude in design and workmanship, were simply curiosities. . . . [but] great scientists, resourceful inventors, and skilled designers who foresaw [the phonograph's] possibilities were busily engaged in perfecting it. They perfected not only the machine itself, but they discovered and worked out new and better ways of making records.[26]

In the process of this rewriting, both the myths of science and art are invoked. Home recording is excised, replaced by the ideal of *professional* sound recording of *professional* artists.

However, the preservation, or more accurately, the creation of the illusion of an automatic correspondence between reality and mechanical reproduction required from the first a vigorous act of faith. From the first brief accounts of early sound reproduction in these ads and in promotional material for competing technologies, it is apparent that there was widespread contemporary awareness of "extra" sounds that signaled the detectable working of the apparatus. The ad above exposes the truth about early sound quality; "in those days," the copywriter avers, "the world was still marveling that a mere machine could actually talk and sing (even though it squeaked and scratched and wheezed)."[27] Frequently, comparisons with other models stress their "noise"—for instance, one attack cites the gramophone's "blasty whangdoodle noises," which presumably "are not desired by citizens of culture"

(Gelatt 1955, p. 91). These "flaws," characteristic of any kind of mechanical reproduction process, constantly bespoke the nature of the reproduction as a *mediated reconstruction* of sounds, yet they are marked as "not to be read" except in the past tense and then as signs of the failure of the apparatus. Static or noise or distortion of any kind was identified with the apparatus and not as part of the text.

The somewhat wishful insistence on the perfect fidelity of the new technology illustrates the desire to maintain the recorded voice as holding a special, essential connection to the individual—something stressed from Edison in 1878 to the Sears ad thirty years later.[28] With the shift to recording and a star system, the function of the machine was henceforth to be hidden, unobtrusive, while the "purity" of what was recorded, especially important in relation to the human voice, passed unimpeded and uninflected through the mechanism to the hearer.

The myth of what might be called the mechanical neutrality of sound recording has clearly been the dominant one in sound and film-sound recording. The urge to mask the function of the apparatus and to believe in the connection between the recorded and the real continues to the present day. In one of the most famous arguments in its favor, Jean-Louis Baudry has written that

> it is true that in cinema—as in the case of all talking-machines—one does not hear an image of the sounds but the sounds themselves. Even if the procedures for recording the sounds and playing them back deforms them, they are reproduced and not copied. Only their source of emission may partake of illusion; their reality cannot.
>
> (Baudry 1976, p. 110)

In his excellent article "The Acoustic Dimension," Tom Levin locates similar far-reaching statements throughout film theory (quoting examples from Christian Metz, Stanley Cavell, and Gerald Mast as well as Baudry) and concludes that

> while the critique of the cinematic [visual] technology has destroyed the myth of the "innocent" representation, the recognition that, as Jean-Louis Comolli puts it, "the most analogical representation of the world is still not, is never, its reduplication," does not seem to have been applied to the *acoustic* domain.[29]

Alan Williams uses a specifically technological approach in order to restore the consciousness of recorded sound as a reproduction. "To define sound as a thing 'in itself' requires omission of the material circumstances of production and reception of the sound" (Williams 1980, p. 52). Sound is defined, simply, as a disturbance of the air within a specific physical space. Every sound we hear is physically changed by the space in which we hear it. Williams asserts that our belief that we hear the same sound in two different spaces (a friend's voice, a recording of a concert we attended), is in fact a "(learned) process of ignoring . . . variations in favor of [holding onto our belief in] an identity posited as *necessary* to them" (ibid., p. 53). Hearing, in common with the other senses, is subject to ideology. In other words, "the represented is 'read' and thus always transformed by its representation" (Levin 1984, p. 55).

Recording practices also change sound fundamentally. As "microphones [are] more like ears than they are like rooms (they function as points and not as volume [in the spatial sense]), it is never the literal, original 'sound' that is reproduced in recording, but one perspective on it, a *sample*, a *reading* of it" (Williams 1980, p. 58). This "reading" is not done by the spectator but by the apparatus itself. Williams insists that

> in sound recording, as in image recording, the apparatus performs a significant perceptual work *for us*—isolating, intensifying, *analyzing* sonic and visual material. It gives an implied physical perspective on image or sound source, though not the full [actual conditions of] vision or hearing, but *the signs of* such a physical situation.
>
> (ibid., p. 58)

Thus, despite Baudry's contention, sound in film can be characterized as figurative; it is a sign signifying "sound," presenting us with the illusion of hearing while in actuality the apparatus of cinema "hears" for us, taking our place as Subject. "The consciousness at whose demand the world is remodeled is not 'ours,' but that implied by (and a virtual part of) the mechanism at work" (ibid., p. 59).

That "fidelity" is not a matter of increasingly sophisticated sound technology but of reader reception (or *deception*)—a reading of a reading—is made clear in David Alan Black's hypothesis "that the realism of [cinema and sound technology] may be traced not only (or even chiefly) to the immanent properties of their finished artifacts, but at least equally to a commercially generated realist longing constantly reinscribed in their popular reception."[30]

The desire to mistake acoustic realism for reality despite the extraordinarily complex techniques required to reproduce sound in film points toward a deep-rooted desire to naturalize (and thus obscure) ideology. The myth of "objective" sound reproduction ("mechanical neutrality") disguises the ideology of the apparatus, including (a) the ideology into which the apparatus is inserted, and (b) that which it promotes and organizes itself around. The first sound technology to fully exploit women's voices serves as a good example. Lana Rakow argues that "the history of the telephone cannot be told without accounting for the gender relations within which a telephone system developed. The telephone, in turn, was used to construct and maintain gender differences and hierarchies." Although the telephone apparatus treats all voices equally, nevertheless, as Rakow shows, "communications technologies in a gendered society are not gender-neutral" (Rakow 1988, pp. 224–25). The "dulcet tones" of women telephone operators, combined with severe restrictions on their speech to customers, worked to naturalize woman's place as a subservient, docile helpmeet, willing to assist anyone for the price of a call. Not only were "young, attractive and single women" employed for notoriously low pay, Rakow points out, "women's voices as commodities [were] bought to achieve just such an effect"—that is, the consolidation of the position of the male employer and his customers (ibid., pp. 211–17).

Sound-recording technology's relation to ideology is far more complex than that of telephone technology, particularly when it functions as part of a medium like classical cinema whose job is the construction of seductive fictions. But like telephone, radio, and other sound media, sound film's efforts to camouflage its materiality behind a myth of realism need to be strenuously deconstructed. Once we reinsert the conventions of film sound into their ideological and economic contexts, we can begin to examine (among other things) the implications for the representation of women's voices.

Another method for deconstructing the mythic "objectivity" of sound recording technology is a psychoanalytic analysis of the desire underlying the myth. In a construction that shifts the issue of cinema sound into the heart and vocabulary of psychoanalysis, Levin proposes we abandon "the uncritical phenomenological narrative which explains the technological history of cinema as the successive addition of 'real' movement and 'real' sound, [for] an alternative approach [that] would read this development in terms of a complicated alternation of *supplementation and lack*" (Levin 1984, p. 58)

As in Plato's cave, there is a constant play between the greatest illusion of realism and the simultaneous acknowledgment of fakery and artifice. "The cinema . . . in fact owes the success of its illusion not only to this catalogue of verisimilitude but to its artificiality" (ibid., p. 59). Quoting Jean-Louis Comolli, Levin advocates this approach over others because it

> takes seriously the mechanism of disavowal, recognising that any reality effect of any fiction "always depends on its self-designation as such, on the fact that its fictive character is human and recognized from the start, that it presents itself as an artificial arrangement, that it does not hide that it is above all an apparatus of deception."
>
> (ibid., quoting Comolli, "Machines of the Visible," p. 140)

From the time when audiences sat in rapt attention staring at *a machine,* listening to the artificial, mechanical reproduction of the voice of the man standing beside it, this awareness of the apparatus as such, of its unlimited ability to deceive (a potential inestimably aided by the listeners' pronounced willingness to suspend disbelief) was fundamental to its appeal. When a phonograph listener of 1898 gazed at a flat wax disc and murmured to himself, "That's Caruso," he was participating in a sophisticated form of make-believe.

This type of "play" openly demonstrates the listener/viewer's facility at a skill essential to subjectivity: the ability to construct "reality" or realism out of the most brazen artifice, to designate identity where logic would mandate difference.

These later arguments pertain to sound recording both inside and beyond cinema. However, as I outline below, the position of the listener is physically and psychologically different from that of the film viewer/film listener. Therefore, before we can theorize the powerful effects of a *sound* cinema, it will be necessary to speculate first on the specific pleasures offered by "merely" listening.

The Listener and the Voice

MILDRED: I like to hear you talk.

WALLY FAY: Yeah? So do I. Something about the sound of my own voice
             that fascinates me.

Mildred Pierce (1945)

With the transition to prerecorded cylinders and discs, the pleasure of recorded sound became focused on the voice of the other, a condition of listening pleasure equally true of cinema, because of its incorporation of the recorded voice, and radio. In order to clarify the significance of this transition for the voices of women, I shall briefly review the ways two prominent theorists have attempted to describe the appeal of listening.

As one of the few early film theorists to address the topic of sound-without-image (Dziga Vertov's sound experiments being the other major example), Rudolf Arnheim attests to the pleasure "pure" sound could offer, describing it in terms eerily resonant of Guy Rosolato's "sonorous envelope," but on a massive, even national scale (Rosolato 1974, p. 81). In his book *Radio*, written in Germany in 1936, Arnheim conjures up the image of the radio audience as an unseeing, eagerly listening mass, enthralled as their imaginations thrill to the bidding of a (benevolent) disembodied voice. Arnheim pursues this impossible figure to its logical conclusion, defining an ideal radio announcer/personality as a "bodiless" voice.

> It is very significant that certain expressive voices do not strike the naive listener as "the voice of somebody one doesn't see" and whose appearance can be speculated on, but rather transmit the experience of an absolutely complete personality.
>
> (Arnheim 1936, p. 142)[31]

In a chapter entitled "In Praise of Blindness: Emancipation from the Body," Arnheim argues that the recorded or transmitted voice has been "purged of the materiality of its source" (ibid.). In broadcasting as in record-ing, "Resonance is eliminated, out of a very proper feeling that the existence of the studio is not essential to the transmission and therefore has no place in the listener's consciousness. . . . The listener rather restricts himself to the reception of pure sound, which comes to him through the loudspeaker" (ibid., pp. 143, 142). The notable lack of spatial signifiers described in Arnheim's ideal radio broadcast enables him to construct the disembodied voice as an infinite one (comparable, as will be argued, to the infinity defined and filled by the voice of the mother). Not only does Arnheim wish to eliminate our awareness of space, but also of the body—and, consequently, gender.

Roland Barthes contradicts Arnheim by insisting on the voice's relation to the body, the voice as physical signifier. For Barthes, rather than being "pure sound," the "grain" of the voice signifies, first, the body. "The 'grain' is the body in the voice as it sings. . . . I am determined to listen to my relation with the body of the man *or* woman singing or playing and that relation is erotic" (Barthes 1977, p. 188; italics added). It should be noted that Barthes is deal-ing exclusively with recordings of singers and not with live performance. The possibilities of ownership, repetition, and control increase the potential identi-fication of the recorded voice as object and fetish.

Secondly, for Barthes, the voice exists in a constant, negotiated relation-ship to language. What he calls the "grain" is not merely a physical trace but "the very precise space . . . of *the encounter between a language and a voice*" (italics in original). Barthes aims to describe the effect of listening not to "the whole of music but simply . . . a part of vocal music." However, what he says regarding the space between the voice and language holds equally true for speech. Inasmuch as the speaking voice is involved in producing both lan-guage and sound, "the grain of the voice" is involved in "a dual production—of language and of music" (Barthes 1977, p. 181). When recorded, the voice, so often lost track of in the attempt to capture the meaning of the sounds artic-ulated, reemerges, becomes a capturable object, a source of pleasure separa-ble from its function within the symbolic field.

In Barthes' account, this awareness of the *sound* of the voice already cre-ates a space or distance between the voice and language. Referring to Julia Kristeva's work, he differentiates between her concepts of the "pheno-song," which covers "all the features which belong to the structure of the *language* being sung. . . . In short everything in the performance which is in the ser-vice of communication," and "the geno-song," which

> is the volume of the singing and speaking voice, the space where significations germinate "from within language and its very materiality"; it forms a signifying play having nothing to do with communication, representation (of feelings), ex-pression; it is that apex (or that depth) of production where the melody really works at the language—not at what it says, but the voluptuousness of its

> sounds-signifiers. . . . It is, in a very simple word but [one] which must be
> taken seriously, the *diction* of the language
>
> (Barthes 1977, pp. 182–83)

—or, what might be called the sound of the sound.

In this elevation of diction (defined in the *Random House College Dictionary* as "the accent, inflection, intonation, and *speech-sound quality* manifested by an individual speaker"),[32] Barthes goes so far as to differentiate between consonants and vowels. Consonants, in Barthes' reading, are on the side of the symbolic, setting limits, symbolizing restriction: "always prescribed as needing to be 'articulated', detached, emphasized *in order to fulfill the clarity of meaning*" (italics in original). Vowels, on the other hand, partake of the geno-song, encouraging the listener (as well as the singer or speaker) to dwell on a sound without limits: "There lay the 'truth' of language—not its functionality (clarity, expressivity, communication)," but instead its status as "pure" sound, as the place where one can discover the body in the grain of the voice. When sung properly, "the range of vowels received all the *signifiance* (which is meaning in its potential voluptuousness)." Barthes' preoccupation with voluptuousness reenforces the connection with the erotic—located in a specifically Oedipal place. He states, "Isn't it the truth of the voice to be hallucinated? isn't the entire space of the voice an infinite one?" (Barthes 1977, p. 184).[33] "Infinite space," as we shall see, is frequently invoked as a primary (fantasized) characteristic of the mother/infant bond, symbolized by the all-encompassing maternal voice. By invoking the fantasy of a boundless space, Barthes reintroduces the figure of the mother.

Mary Ann Doane also describes the voice as being at once language and that which exceeds language and leads us back, again, to the mother.

> The voice thus understood is *an interface of imaginary and symbolic*, pulling at once toward the signifying organization of language and its reduction of the range of vocal sounds to those it binds and codifies, and toward original and imaginary attachments, "representable in the fantasm by the body or by the corporeal mother, the child at her breast."
>
> (Doane 1985b, p. 171 [italics in original];
> quoting Rosolato 1974, p. 86)

What Barthes finally wants is a way to theorize the effect of the voice of the other on the listener, to give an "impossible account of an individual thrill that I constantly experience in listening to singing," and "to succeed in refining a certain 'aesthetics' of musical pleasure." Ultimately this new theory of listening "will certainly be individual . . . but in no way 'subjective' (it is not the psychological 'subject' in me who is listening; the climactic pleasure hoped for is not going to reinforce—to express—that subject but, on the contrary, to lose it)" (Barthes 1977, pp. 181, 188).

And one way to "lose" the subject, to flee the symbolic, the letter, the Law, is in pursuit of the presymbolic. While it is not actually possible to regain access to a condition before language, it is a frequent characteristic of cultural production to appeal to its vestigial traces, the lingering nostalgia for that time. Barthes' difference with Arnheim rests on Barthes' insistence on (1) positing a *male* subject and (2) wanting it both ways—wanting an infinite space inside the voice of the mother *and* an erotic relation to the "grain" of the voice, which always points back to the body. This seeming contradiction grows out of the fact that our construction of a presymbolic condition is "superimposed upon infancy from a subsequent temporal and spatial vantage" (Silverman 1988, p. 74). The fantasy of the maternal voice is invented in a post-Oedipal present and imposed on the past. Barthes wants to recapture the prelinguistic state where difference is abolished while keeping the erotics—the desire for the mother as woman, as difference—possible only for a post-Oedipal male subject.

As psychoanalytic theory has been of great significance to feminist film theory and to work on sound, it might be helpful now to briefly outline the Lacanian scenario of subjectivity to which I shall be referring throughout this work.

According to Lacan, the mirror stage provides the child's first awareness of itself as separate from its mother, the world, and, most crucially, itself. The progression toward subjectivity requires a series of separations and losses. What becomes separate is objectified (the mother, the figure of the Other onto which the child projects imaginary attributes, whatever is external) as the child defines what is internal (its self) in terms of its separation from these objects. As Silverman succinctly puts it, "to the degree that the object has been lost, the subject has been found" (ibid., p. 7). With the accession to language, the subject is subsumed into the symbolic. However, as the subject has been constructed around this "splitting," being cut off from what it was, it is haunted by a sense of loss, absence, or lack. "The object thus acquires from the very beginning the value of that without which the subject can never be whole or complete, and for which it consequently yearns" (ibid.). As I shall attempt to show, the process of listening isolates, intensifies, and crystalizes the subject's relationship to the other (present through the medium of the voice). Thus, the listening situation can become a crucible where the subject works through its relationship with the other and, in doing so, momentarily, and pleasurably, reconstructs a sense of wholeness.

As an invention, the phonograph provided unique new ways of listening and dramatically different relationships to the voice. Given the theory cited above, it is possible to posit a psychological reason for the shift away from home recording. The voice heard during playback is always the voice of the other—crucially, even when it is the listener's own. With home recording, the subject is forced to confront his/her voice wrenched from its internal echo of presubjective plenitude. Exposed, the subject's voice becomes comparable to the numerically limitless, but inherently *less important*, voices of others. It sounds too high (because heard for the first time outside the resonance of the cranium). It may sound monotonous and uninflected. It frequently sounds more like the voices of family members than oneself. The splitting of the subject is made unnervingly concrete when one is confronted with a playback of one's own voice. It is seldom a source of pleasure. Jean-Louis Comolli identifies the extreme care taken to preserve synchronization of the actor's voice and image in film as the sign of ideology at work, with dis-synchronization "scandalizing" one's sense of mastery and ownership (see Doane in Weis and Belton 1985, p. 58; Comolli 1972). How much more of an affront dissynchronization must be when the technologically externalized, "objectified" voice is one's own.

With the sound reproduction industry's shift to marketing prerecorded phonograph records (a move that effectively replaced or eliminated home recording),[34] the voice became openly and unproblematically that of the other, requiring a less drastic adjustment or fragmentation of the listening subject, and as such, could be substituted for other voices including, most crucially, that of the mother. The mother's actual voice is displaced to the realm of the "external" and "otherness" following the accession to language.[35] Through displacement, it becomes possible to substitute the voice of the other for the powerfully specific voice of the mother. Listening thus becomes an intimate affair, infinite in promise because keyed to an ancient desire, without calling to mind a possibly overwhelming and ambivalent relation to an actual parent.

In discussing what Silverman calls the "fantasy of the maternal voice," it becomes clear that the nature of the subject's relationship to the maternal voice is spatial. Rosolato's famous description of the mother's voice as a "sonorous envelope" surrounding the child identifies the voice as a place, a place to be, a space that is at once everywhere and nowhere.[36] The fantasmatic condition of existing within a place defined by the mother's voice can assume the form of either a terrifying miasma of non-meaning, from which the incipient subject struggles to escape through language, or a paradisiacal wholeness in which the child is blissfully united with the Mother. (Chion 1982 is Silverman's main example of the negative version of the fantasy.) The speaking subject recreates the mother's voice as "either cherished as an *objet (a)*—as what can make good all lacks—or despised and jettisoned as what is most abject, most culturally intolerable" (Silverman 1988, p. 86).

Sound reproduction, as I shall attempt to illustrate, is particularly suited to the fantasy of submission to the imaginary because of its unique ability to create a position for the listener as isolated, surrounded by sound but alone, and then to obliterate the subject's sense of alienation by re-merging subject and other. And it is "the fantasy of the maternal voice" that returns again and again as the model and locus of this imaginary operation.

Unlike in the mirror stage (where "here/there" and "internal/external" become clearly marked categories, because we can hear and speak at the same time), it is difficult in this phase, Silverman asserts, "to situate the voice, to know whether it is 'outside' or 'inside.' . . . Rosolato suggests [that the voice] can spill over from subject to object and object to subject, violating the bodily limits upon which classical subjectivity depends, and so smoothing the way for projection and introjection." In Silverman's view, "the child's economy is organized around incorporation" and "what is incorporated is the auditory field articulated by the maternal voice. The difficulty of establishing distance from the voice of the mother is suggested by its inclusion among Lacan's lost objects, or *objets (a)*, "those objects which are first to be distinguished from the subject's own self, and whose 'otherness' is never very strongly marked." The subject's difficulty in distinguishing between internal and external voices results from (1) the "double organization of the vocal/auditory system" (which has implications spanning the range of sound reproduction both in and outside cinema), and (2) attachment to the *objet (a)*, whose "loss assumes the proportions of an amputation," motivating fantasies of plenitude in regard to the voice, fantasies of recapturing and owning it as a fetish, since "once gone, the [lost object] comes to represent what can alone make good the subject's lack" (Silverman 1988, pp. 79, 80, 85).

The acoustic confusion of internal and external is not linked to the woman's voice per se. As Barthes illustrates, the voice we capture on recordings and choose to luxuriate in may be the most masculine basso profundo. If the "otherness" of the maternal voice, as *objet (a)*, is "never strongly marked" neither is its "difference." The "feminine" quality of the maternal voice, it could be argued, is one of the aspects projected onto it at a later stage, *after* the recognition of difference. The relation to the voice can be described in male/female terms, but the privileging of the female voice in the "fantasy of the maternal voice" is culturally conditioned. As Nancy Chodorow points out in *The Reproduction of Mothering*, "mothering" and "maternal" behavior are defined by a group of actions and are not inherent or gender-based.[37] By trying to occupy a fantasmatic space where the subject merges with the "object" or the "other," where "the boundary separating exteriority from interiority is blurred by [an] aural undecidability" (Silverman 1988, p. 79), the subject, whether male or female, seeks to escape or forfeit gendered subjectivity in an attempt to merge with an undifferentiated other.

The desire for non-subjectivity precedes issues of gender (the "symbolic castration" of the accession to language preceding the awareness of sexual difference) and manifests itself clinically in hypnosis. In the mirror stage, vision abets language and the voice in inscribing separation of self and other

Sound, especially as discussed here in reference to recordings and radio, can provide the illusion of repairing the split by reincorporating the other. The physical markers of hypnosis (the trance, insensitivity to pain, etc.) locate and reveal the symptoms of hysteria (the literal embodiment of psychic crises) in everyone as the body speaks an impossible desire. Hypnosis can be seen as clinical evidence of a persistent and unending confusion/confusability between inner and outer space, and as a sign of either gender's lingering, inherent desire to fuse with the voice of the other/mother, to dissolve what Lacan calls the "opposition between language and the phenomenal realm, . . . between meaning and life" (ibid., p. 8).

The confusion between subject and object in hypnosis is reiterated in clinical practice. Lawrence S. Kubie and Sydney Margolin have described the dissolution of the subject in response to the induction of a hypnotic state: "Once the subject is going 'under,' it is only in a purely geographical sense that the voice of the hypnotist is an influence from the outside. Subjectively it is experienced rather as an extension of the subject's own psychic process" (Kubie and Margolin 1944, p. 612). This condition is achieved through the classic methods of having the immobilized patient concentrate on repetitive visual stimuli (such as a metronome or swinging watch) as the hypnotist repeats various phrases.

> This simultaneous restriction both on the motor and sensory side reduces to a minimum the variegated sensory contrasts upon which Ego boundaries depend.
>
> It is the dissolution of Ego boundaries that gives the hypnotist his [sic] apparent "power"; because his "commands" do not operate as something reaching the subject from the outside, demanding submissiveness. To the subject they are his own thoughts and goals, a part of himself.
>
> (ibid., pp. 614, 612)

Such a condition is not restricted to classical hypnosis alone. Kubie and Margolin state that "such an obscuring of Ego boundaries, so dramatic in its manifestations when it is total, is frequently encountered in normal psychology as a partial phenomenon." In fact, their description of the efficacy of the techniques of the early hypnotists suggests the fundamental underlying appeal of listening to recorded sound through headphones. "The melodramatic maneuvers of the old-fashioned hypnotist" helped "*concentrate [the subject's] attention on one field of sensation and to withdraw attention from all others*" (ibid., pp. 613, 617; italics in original).

Hypnosis illustrates how the isolation of sound (and in cinema, sound and image) can return the immobilized spectator to the infinite space before the internal/external, self/other distinctions achieved with subjectivity. "This dissolution of the Ego boundaries creates a psychological state which is analogous to that brief period in early infancy in which the mother's breast in the mouth of the infant is psychologically a part of that infant far more than his own toes and hands, as much a part of the infant's Ego as is his own mouth" (ibid., p. 612).

The relinquishment of subjectivity, of the "I" as distinctly separate from the other, allows the individual to recover or recreate a pre-linguistic condition where s/he existed in an infinite space, united there with the mother and the body, *objets (a)* that the recorded voice momentarily returns to us.

A Woman's Voice

The theorization of listening pleasure is a necessary preliminary step to considering the issue explored in the remainder of this book—the representation of women's voices in classical Hollywood cinema. As I've shown, the ideology of sound recording eventually sought to hide the effects of the apparatus on the sound being recorded, particularly when that sound was the human voice. And yet a theme that resurfaces time and again in phonography, radio, and sound film is the persistent "problem" of recording, transmitting, or reproducing women's voices.

If we return to the very beginnings of sound technology with women's voices in mind, we find something at once obvious and rather startling: the basic ability to record the human voice was predicated on the ability to record the male voice. The original inventors were, of course, men, who recorded themselves. In news photographs, the introduction of new audio-technology is always performed surrounded by serious-looking gentlemen. A photograph of one of the early phonograph parlors shows over a dozen men hooked to ear-tubes, eager to hear the latest invention (Read and Welch 1976, p. 515). No women are present. Women *do* appear in ads, though. They are shown as consumers, and are often depicted as little girls demonstrating how simple it is to operate the equipment.[38]

The three major reasons given for the problems sound media encountered with women's voices are: the myth of woman's "naturally" less powerful voice, technical deficiencies, and what might be called, somewhat amorphously, "cultural distaste" for women's voices. Let us look at each in turn.

In her study of the social effects of electronic amplification on women's voices, Anne McKay rebuts the popular misperception that women cannot speak as loudly and clearly as men. Throughout the nineteenth century, as the pressures of various political movements caused social barriers against women speaking in public to fall, women began to emerge as powerful public speakers well before the advent of the loudspeaker. One woman, whose voice was reported as being "clear and musical, but not at all strong" was said to be able to address "five hundred or five thousand . . . making herself heard without strain or apparent effort" (McKay 1988, p. 190).[39]

"Experts" had long asserted that women suffer from a "natural vocal defi-

Edison's phonograph display at the Paris International Exposition, 1889

ciency . . . reinforced by custom and lack of training," and science had frequently been called upon to provide evidence to support this presumably
"natural" difference between genders. A series of experiments at Bell Laboratories in the twenties, for instance, mirrors the cultural assumptions of the
period. "The author [of the study's report] concludes that 'It thus appears that
nature has so designed woman's speech that it is always most effective when it
is of soft and well modulated tone.'" More recent experiments cited by
McKay suggest, however, that "physique may be far less important than ac-
culturation in producing gender-specific variations in speech." Scientists in
the seventies found that anatomical differences such as lung capacity were not
the major determining factor in "acoustic disparities" between men and
women. Instead, they found that "adult men and women modify their articulation of the same phonetic elements to produce acoustic signals that cor-
respond to the male-female archetypes. In other words, men tend to talk
as though they were bigger, and women as though they were smaller than
they actually may be" (Sachs et al. 1973, p. 75, in McKay 1988, pp. 187,
192, 193).

The "technical deficiency" explanation tends to center on problems associated with recording or transmitting women's voices owing to the fact that women's voices (whether because of physical determinants or by choice) are usually higher pitched than men's. A radio station manager in the twenties declared that "in no case does the female voice transmit as well as that of the man" (McKay 1988, p. 200).[40] In a technical manual on film sound recording written in 1929, the author asserts that the equipment "fails to some extent when a sound is characterized by the presence of high harmonics, for the diaphragm cannot vibrate rapidly enough to record them onto cylinders" (Cameron 1929, p. 80). And in 1928 a representative of Bell Laboratories told the *Scientific American,* with some finality, that "the speech characteristics of women, when changed to electrical impulses, do not blend with the electrical characteristics of our present day radio equipment" (McKay 1988, p. 203).[41]

Throughout the first half of this century, engineers were clearly working on ways to improve the reproduction and transmission of women's voices. David Bordwell, Janet Staiger, and Kristin Thompson (1985, p. 302) describe experiments in methods of sound recording designed to reproduce women's voices more favorably: "ultraviolet recording," for instance, "sought to eliminate the 'fuzzy high notes' and sibilants" said to be characteristic of women's voices, which, it was asserted at the time, would be "especially benefited" by the new technology. However, the Bell Laboratories authority quoted above makes it clear that the inadequacy of radio technology in regard to women's voices was not the result of mere technological chance. He asserts that "*the demand of the radio public* for radio equipment to meet *their* aural fancy had led to [the] design of equipment that impairs the reproduction of a soprano's voice" (McKay 1988, p. 203; italics added).[42] In other words, an already existing preference for low voices mandated equipment with a greater sensitivity to that range. As McKay concludes, "The ideal radio voice . . . was a baritone" (1988, p. 201).

The cultural distaste for women's voices noted earlier in relation to "talking records" was clearly still in effect in the twenties in regard to radio. One radio executive proclaimed "it is my opinion that women depend upon everything else but the voice for their appeal. Their voices are flat or shrill, and they are usually pitched far too high to be modulated correctly." He adds that women "don't seem able to become familiar with their audiences, to have that clubby feeling"—while another writer declared that the best reason "for the unpopularity of the woman's voice over the radio is that it usually has *too much* personality" (my italics). Whatever the reason, too little personality or too much, a woman columnist of the twenties reported that "a canvass of 5000 listeners [by station WJZ] resulted in a vote of 100 to 1 in favor of men as announcers." She admits "it is difficult to say why the public should be so unanimous about it," and eventually falls back on the failings of technology: "most receiving sets do not reproduce perfectly the higher notes. A man's voice 'takes' better." Besides, she adds, "it has more volume" (McKay 1988, pp. 200, 202).

Evidently the "problem" of the woman's voice is always a tangle of technological and economic exigencies, each suffused with ideological assumptions about woman's "place." McKay concludes "that when women used the new technology in support of the goals and activities of established institutions, they were applauded at best or ignored at worst. When they attempted to use it in ways that would lead to change in the traditional order and in women's customary roles, their right to use it at all was challenged" (ibid., p. 188).

In the following chapters I analyze a group of films that each construct woman's speech as a "problem." In all of these texts, the speaking woman disrupts the dominant order. The language she speaks is an affront to male authority and middle-class decorum; her very ability to make sounds is fraught with obstacles; and, in the final instance, the story she tells threatens to undermine the patriarchal order. As these films show, the "problem" of the speaking woman provokes increasingly severe methods of repression because she refuses to be silenced. Attempts to stop her from speaking rupture classical conventions of representation, however, and expose the way patriarchy uses language, image, sound, and narrative to construct and contain "woman." In the next two chapters I use literary methodologies to deconstruct the creation of woman's "voice" through words; analyze silent film's juxtaposition of language with visual conventions for depicting speaking women; and confront early sound film's striking potential for presenting women's speech—a potential that was to be compromised and subverted by the conventions of classical Hollywood cinema.

The question I seek to answer throughout this work is: "Can a woman ever be said to 'speak' in classical cinema?" And if she can, given all the technical and ideological limitations outlined above, what are her chances of being heard?

Gloria Swanson and Raoul Walsh in *Sadie Thompson*

Constructing a   2
Woman's Speech

Words and Images
"Miss Thompson" (1921),
Rain (1921), *Sadie Thompson* (1928)

Looking at a series of adaptations of a short story written in 1921 gives us an opportunity to analyze the way "woman" and her voice are constructed across a series of texts that themselves make the transition from silence to sound. In each of the works examined here, the character of the woman is the catalyst for the action. Her "character" and motivations are the subject of speculation and concern for others in the narrative. In the short story "Miss Thompson" and in the play *Rain*, Sadie Thompson's "language" or speech is foregrounded as a privileged way for the other characters and the reader/spectator to know "her." When the play was adapted to film in 1928's *Sadie Thompson*, language was displaced in favor of visual representation. However the dialogue from the play, while much reduced, is still prominent in the silent film. Therefore in addition to analyzing the function of language in constructing the character "Sadie Thompson," I raise the larger issue of how texts make allowances for other "voices." On a formal level, these would include other modes of representation—dialogue in silent film and the establishment of a hierarchy among dialogue, sound, and image in sound film. However, if sound itself is the other "voice" being introduced to silent cinema, what are the implications of associating sound, defined as a potentially disrupting force, and the woman through the presentation of her voice? In silent film, what are the implications for the woman's "voice" when her words are literally set apart, her ability to speak defined by the image?

Unlike the Maugham story, the play and the three films I shall be examining are average works and should not be considered artistically groundbreaking. Raoul Walsh's 1928 *Sadie Thompson* was perceived in its day as an entertaining vehicle for Gloria Swanson and for Walsh's own roughhouse, "masculine" comedy style. Lewis Milestone's *Rain* (1932) and the Curtis

Bernhardt adaptation *Miss Sadie Thompson* (1953) likewise do not stand out from other films of their periods or even within the arguably limited oeuvres of these particular directors. Representative of their eras in styles of filmmaking, use of sound, and the representation of women, these texts will serve to demonstrate a series of general propositions about the relationship of mode to the representation of women and women's speech.

In the movement from *Sadie Thompson* (1928) to *Rain* (1932) we can see how the conventions of classical silent cinema were challenged and forced to adapt to the presence of the sound-reproduction industry. Also present in these works is the pervasive influence of theater. While early sound film bears the alleged ignominy of flooding the screen with "non-cinematic" theatrical adaptations, silent cinema had never ceased adapting plays from the time of the Film d'Art movement onward. Producers were, in fact, always eager to turn to the stage for pre-sold material that promised to combine art with profit. The silent film *Sadie Thompson* and its sound remake *Rain* are both adaptations of John Colton and Clemence Randolph's play *Rain* (1921), which in turn is based on Somerset Maugham's short story "Miss Thompson" (1921). As each film claims descent from both play and story, we need a theoretical approach that will allow us to examine historical evolution, transformation within and between forms, and the relation between form and "subject matter," which in turn exerts pressures on, and is responsive to, formal change.

Summarizing the work of Marxist theorists, Fredric Jameson argues that every social formation or historical moment is made up of several overlapping modes of production, survivals of older methods now relegated to dependent positions (what Raymond Williams calls the "residual"), as well as anticipatory tendencies that point toward new methods yet to become standardized (the "emergent").[1] According to Bordwell, Staiger, and Thompson (1985), the project delineated by the classical Hollywood style is precisely to suppress or reabsorb signs of difference, to obscure historical change by reasserting a predominance of conventionalized forms within a given film as well as from text to text. In a highly conventionalized system, "emergent" or experimental modes of production and new styles are the rarely seen parameters of classical style. They keep the form fresh without ever shaking our confidence that we've been here before and will have no trouble "reading" the text.

Williams's discussion of hegemony, the dominant, residual, and emergent, is entirely in reference to social change, but it is helpful to appropriate his terminology in conceptualizing formal changes in cinematic style, keeping in mind the need to "find terms which recognize not only 'stages' and 'variations' but the internal dynamic relations of any actual process" (Williams 1977, p. 121). " 'The hegemonic,' " according to Williams,

> while by definition . . . always dominant . . . is never either total or exclusive. At any time, forms of alternative or directly oppositional politics and culture exist as significant elements in the society. . . . Any hegemonic process must be

especially alert and responsive to the alternatives and opposition which question or threaten its dominance. . . . The decisive hegemonic function is to control or transform or even incorporate

the oppositional or alternative elements that exist outside the dominant style (ibid., p. 113).

The precedence and subsequent coexistence of a multi-part sound industry (phonographs for recording blanks or playing prerecorded cylinders and discs; radio networks) constituted a potential challenge to the originally image-based industry of cinema. Radio threatened the economic base of cinema by drawing away its audience. Once the film industry chose to incorporate sound, sound recording posed a challenge to the formal system of signification within film texts by seeming to change the definition of "cinematic" to a style favoring speech over image. It then fell to the hegemony, here the dominant style, to incorporate or transform the threat posed by a wholesale switch to a sound-based system, and to make sure that the elements of sound that were used strengthened and reenforced the classical model.

Hollywood's classical project is by definition ahistorical, as it seeks to hide the materiality of cinema and obscure its signifying functions behind established conventions. In *Rain* (1932) the residual elements of silent film style, already five years out of date, are unusually prominent, disrupting the impression of a smooth "sound film" surface transparently "communicating" narrative information. Many transitional films (for instance, the half-silent, half-"talkie" films) suffer from an even more disturbing lack of consistency. Although much of the use of sound in *Rain* functions according to what were to become the classical conventions of the sound film, the film also demonstrates the new range of alternatives made possible by the cinematically emergent technology of sound.

All films to some extent juggle conventions formed in earlier eras. However, the varying modes of production visible in *Rain,* the antagonistic systems and styles, do not yet fit comfortably together. The older methods of the silent era clash visibly with newer methods, some that would become standard, others seldom to be seen after this transitional period. According to Williams, the "active presence" of these competing elements

is decisive, not only because they have to be included in any historical . . . analysis, but as forms which have had significant effect on the hegemonic process itself. That is to say, alternative political and cultural emphases [as well as the evolution of styles and processes of signification] . . . are important not only in themselves but as indicative features of what the hegemonic process has in practice had to work to control.

(Williams 1977, p. 113)

Accordingly any understanding of classical style has to take into account "the internal dynamic relations" between dominant conventions, residual and emergent, because "at any moment in the process, [these alternative and oppositional figures] are significant both in themselves and in what they reveal of the characteristics of the 'dominant'" (ibid., p. 122).

In his essay "Discourse in the Novel," Mikhail Bakhtin examines the novel as the form par excellence not only for revealing heteroglossia (Bakhtin's term for the dialogization of the many languages within a given language system) but as the one form that creates itself out of this multiplicity of languages and their interaction. Furthermore, every aspect of communication, being historically determined, shows traces of its determination. Bakhtin states that "verbal discourse is a social phenomenon—social throughout its entire range and in each and every one of its factors, from the sound image to the furthest reaches of abstract meaning" (1981, p. 259). He goes on to note that "proper theoretical recognition [needs to be] found for the specific feel for language and discourse that one gets in . . . the more complex artistic forms for the organization of contradiction, forms that orchestrate their themes by means of languages" (ibid., p. 275). "Discourse in the Novel" is his attempt to rectify this theoretical oversight.

However other forms of discourse besides prose and the novel will also, by necessity, reveal the workings of heteroglossia. Film is only tangentially a form that "orchestrates its themes by means of language," but cinema studies can expand the application of Bakhtin's concepts to other forms of artistic communication. In cinema, language (or verbal discourse) becomes only one of the modes of discourse in a complex of audio and visual forms, each vying for dominance. By examining the transformations of a specific short story (a prose work where "language" is the whole, but which in itself contains the interplay of many languages) as it is adapted into a play, a silent film, an early sound film, and a classical Hollywood musical, we can trace the displacement of verbal discourse in favor of other "languages," each in its own way a complex of languages passing through a historical evolution and serving a specific signifying function. With each change, the way woman is represented, here in the character of Sadie Thompson, undergoes changes reflecting the alteration in mode, style, and convention, as well as changes in the cultural position of women from the period of one adaptation to the next.

What makes cinema a potential example of heteroglossia beyond the fact of the multiple discourses simultaneously at work in a film is the dialogization of those discourses. Bakhtin notes that "the fundamental and wide-ranging significance" of the "dialogic nature of discourse . . . is still far from acknowledged" (ibid., p. 275). I shall argue that in early sound films the competing discourses—the image-based signifying system of silent film, the newly potent dialogue-based discourse from theater and radio drama, and the voices, music, sound effects, and ambient sound of the sound mix, each with its own power to signify—become dialogized as they struggle for dominance in the new cinematic form. The value of these transitional films lies precisely in their struggle, which the critical focus on classical films has ignored. Bakhtin admits that the "centralizing tendencies in the life of language have ignored this dialogized heteroglossia in which is [*sic*] embodied the centrifugal forces in the life of language" (ibid., p. 273). The same could be said of an evolving signifying system like cinema where signs of stylistic struggle are repressed in favor of a myth of a coherent, unified classical style.

Three areas of early sound film can be opened up when considered in terms of heteroglossia. First, dialogue is the most obvious and often the sole verbal discourse carried over in adaptations of literary works into films, yet because it stems from pre-cinematic sources, whether drama or prose, dialogue is seldom considered worthy of intensive examination in *cinema* studies. Dialogue, as well as being a chief carrier of narrative in sound film, performs a substantial narrative function in silent film and the change between the function(s) and placement of dialogue in silent film and in sound film is one of the major areas untheorized in the transition to sound.

Second, heteroglossia is characteristic of entire prose works and not merely of the dialogue of the characters. A character's "language"—that is, socio-cultural position—can "infest" and interpenetrate the author's discourse and open a dialogue with the other languages passing through the text. This, I would argue, is also possible in cinema, where the forms of "cinematic" communication surround and inform the spoken dialogue. Elements of mise-en-scène, editing, voice, sound effects, and music can all express, contradict, or reenforce a character's point of view or reveal its presence in scenes where the actor is not present (a musical theme often introduces a character in his/her absence). Point of view is thus not restricted to dialogue in novels or to subjective camera angles in film; it is closer to what Bakhtin terms the "struggle among socio-linguistic points of view" (here represented by elements in the image system versus the verbal/auditory system) and is not merely an "intra-language struggle between the individual wills or logical contradictions" (ibid., p. 273) among characters or within the narrative.

Third, by comparing various periods of cinematic history (classical silent film, early sound, and classical sound film) we can chart the evolution of the dominant hierarchical relationship between the languages within cinema. Through extreme industrial, technical and formal pressures, *Rain* in its very archaic, old-fashioned quality momentarily leaves bare the various functions of sound and image as the text suffers a temporary—historical—difficulty in hiding its enunciation. Through a combination of technological, cultural, and economic factors, the silent film hierarchy of languages is redefined as new conventions and a new hierarchy are formed.

As the substance of Maugham's story is subjected through a series of adaptations to the historically evolving properties of different media, it becomes possible for us to trace the effects of different systems on a single element—the representation of woman's voice. The potential for heteroglossia in a film's *form* then becomes particularly relevant to feminist analysis. The dominant conventions of cinema have traditionally been used to position woman within a very restricted number of patriarchal roles that deny her a voice. Once these conventions are broken and new forms become possible (for instance under the pressure to create a new signifying hierarchy in sound film), what was previously contained might break free. Traces of the truth of women's lives might, for example, be glimpsed through the cracks; a woman might snatch a fleeting opportunity to express her own experience in words that do not serve any patriarchal project.

However in any medium, whether short story, play, silent or sound film, a "voice" is the product of conventions of representation, and I shall first chart the way in which each of these forms constructs the speaking woman.

Somerset Maugham's short story "Miss Thompson" was first published in 1921. Later that year it was produced as a play on Broadway under the title by which it is now known, *Rain*. (The story was subsequently reprinted under the title "Rain," reflecting the popularity of the play.) Written by John Colton and Clemence Randolph, the play was very successful and made a star of Jeanne Eagels, the actress who played Sadie Thompson. It has been filmed three times.[2] The 1928 silent version stars Gloria Swanson (who also produced) and Raoul Walsh, who directed and helped write the screenplay. In 1932 Joseph Schenck, who had distributed the silent version for Swanson through United Artists, chose the property for a sound remake to serve as a vehicle for Joan Crawford. This version was directed by Lewis Milestone, who had established himself as a pioneering director of sound films with *All Quiet on the Western Front* (1930) and *The Front Page* in 1931. This version was not commercially successful (it was the only film version that did not make money or garner critical praise for its star). The story was not adapted again until 1953, when it became *Miss Sadie Thompson* and provided a starring role for Rita Hayworth (abetted by color and the new 3-D process), supported by Jose Ferrer and Aldo Ray, and directed by Curtis Bernhardt.

Each of the films claims to be based solely or in part on the original story. Owing to legal complications, the 1928 version declares itself to be entirely based on the original, while the 1932 film credits the story, the play, and un-specified additional script work by Maxwell Anderson. However, it is impor-tant to keep in mind that it is the play that forms the foundation of all the major film versions. In order to appreciate the importance of the changes made by Colton and Randolph and carried over into the films, it will be neces-sary to look at the story at some length, in regard both to heteroglossia within the prose form and how it relates to the characters and their subsequent real-izations in dramatic and cinematic form.

The story concerns several people forced by quarantine to spend two weeks together on a South Sea island. Dr. Macphail and his wife meet the Reverend Alfred Davidson and Mrs. Davidson (who are missionaries in the Pacific) on a ship bound for the island of Apia. When they stop in the port of Pago Pago, they are informed that no ship will be leaving for two weeks and that they must stay at the island's only inn. There they find that another passenger from the ship, Sadie Thompson, has also taken a room. Hearing loud music and men's voices coming from her room, Davidson realizes that she is a prostitute from Honolulu and exhorts her regarding her evil ways. He is thrown out of her room by some sailors. After this, Davidson alternately prays for her soul, condemns her wickedness to Macphail, and demands of the island's governor that she be deported on moral grounds. Afraid of being returned to San Francisco, where a prison sentence awaits her, and under a great deal of mental stress, Sadie repents and becomes totally dependent on Reverend Davidson, who has persuaded her to go back to San Francisco as punishment for her sins. The night before she is to leave, Davidson goes to pray with her; the next morning he is found on the beach, having cut his own throat. Back at the inn, Dr. Macphail discovers Sadie, dressed vulgarly and playing her phonograph loudly. When Macphail, horrified, insists she turn off the music out of respect for the dead man and his widow, she screams at him that men are all alike, "filthy pigs."

Any summary of a literary or cinematic work inevitably ends up privileging the diegesis over the structure. Just as form is inseparable from "content" and is essential to the creation of any meaning a work might have, it is impossible to discuss heteroglossia through plot summary. One of the most interesting things about Maugham's story is that most of the action takes place "offstage"—the story is built around absences and enigmas, which are in turn re-presented to Dr. Macphail, who functions as a witness within the text. Dr. Macphail hears noises and deduces that Davidson has been thrown out of Sadie's room by the sailors. He is told that Davidson has been to see the governor, that Davidson has bad dreams and prays for Sadie's soul, that Sadie has later repented. Most important, it is through him that we are given to understand what has led to Davidson's death (something never made explicit in any of the versions of the story). Everything we learn is filtered through Macphail, our observer and the author's representative of objectivity and accurate perception.

Macphail is presented as a doctor. By profession he is thus an educated, disinterested observer, a purveyor of "scientific" discourse, a moderator between the excesses of Sadie and Davidson. His relation to excess is noted early on, when he is eager to see some native cases of elephantiasis. However it is the exaggerated and perverted emotional extremes that become the bulk of the story's action, and that are diagnosed as such by the doctor.

Maugham describes Macphail initially as "precise and rather pedantic" (Maugham 1967, p. 412; page numbers given below refer to this edition). "He spoke with a Scots accent" (cultural connotations of pragmatic Scotsmen) "in a very low, quiet voice" (p. 412)—again connoting moderation. He appreciates, at first, the "good" qualities in both Sadie and Davidson. He admires her "effrontery" (p. 420) in bargaining for her room and is in awe of Davidson's physical courage (p. 423). He is portrayed as kind, asking his wife to speak to Sadie because "she's all alone here, and it seems rather unkind to ignore her" (p. 427). His easygoing nature betrays "misgiving" when Davidson's fanatic discipline tries to impose itself (p. 428), and he has a sense of humor (p. 433).

The most prominent thing about Macphail is his reticence. When the innkeeper appeals to Macphail about Davidson pressuring him to evict Sadie Thompson, Maugham writes, "Dr. Macphail did not want to commit himself" (p. 435). When Sadie pleads with him to intervene with the governor on her behalf, Macphail "had the shy man's resentment at being forced out into the open" when confronted about it by Davidson (p. 441). Later he openly states, "I think one does better to mind one's own business" (p. 441). Macphail's role as observer requires him to stay out of the conflict in order to maintain his aura of "objectivity" and disinterest. When Macphail does begin to take sides, his earlier reserving of judgment suggests that his eventual choice will be the inevitable and appropriate one. Earlier, when he heard of Davidson's techniques for compelling the natives to abide by the church's mores, "What he heard shocked him, but he hesitated to express his disapproval" (pp. 424–25). But later Macphail begins to speak out against Davidson, his relativistic moral stand, a beacon of liberal pluralism, placed in opposition to Davidson's absolutist one. Davidson disparages the governor for not deporting Sadie. Macphail says, "I suppose that means he won't do exactly what you want" (p. 437). Davidson retorts with the language of common sense and the transparency of the "one true path": "I want him to do what is right." And when Davidson argues that Macphail wouldn't hesitate to amputate in a case of gangrene, Macphail counters, "gangrene is a matter of fact"—speaking the irrefutability of empirical science, confronting Davidson's monologic discourse of the sacred with the empiricism underlying liberalism.

Macphail's reservation of judgment merely prepares the reader for his eventual decision to step in and take charge of the action at the climax of the story. When Davidson's body is found on the beach, Macphail is called to determine the cause of death. Here every word Macphail says is grounded in his medical authority; as Maugham says, "He was not a man to lose his head in an emergency" (p. 452). The trader is superstitious about having a corpse taken to his inn. Macphail replies "sharply": "You'll do what the authorities say" (p. 452). Macphail (directing the course of the narrative) instructs his wife to break the news to Mrs. Davidson, and it is Macphail who confronts the resurrected whore-ish incarnation of Sadie, assailing her for "playing ragtime loud and harsh" (p. 454).

Macphail's perceptions guide the author's description for the rest of the story. "Dr. Macphail was outraged. He pushed past the woman into her room. 'What the devil are you doing?' he cried." His confusion about the meaning of her actions shows Maugham's use of the hermeneutic code to both inform the reader and create a need to know, a question that needs to be answered. This is repeated when Sadie callously tells Macphail, "can that stuff with

me," and he replies, "What do you mean?" Maugham repeats this as well:
" 'What do you mean?' he cried. 'What do you mean?' " (p. 455).

> She gathered herself together. No one could describe the scorn of her expression
> or the contemptuous hatred she put into her answer.
>   "You men! You filthy, dirty pigs! You're all the same, all of you. Pigs! Pigs!"
> Dr. Macphail gasped. He understood.
>
> (p. 455)

The story ends this way with Macphail's understanding substituting (and supposedly being sufficient) for the reader's understanding. In fact, the enigma of "what happened between Sadie and Davidson?" is still open. In place of an explanation, the text suggests that "common sense" will make it clear by asserting that if our moderate, objective reader-figure Dr. Macphail understands, then whatever we choose to fill in the blank will probably be the "right" choice. Maugham depends instead on inference. (This is made ham-fistedly clear in the play—the trader and Sergeant O'Hara are outside Sadie's door when they hear the loud music and exchange these lines: "What do you infer?" "I don't infer anything.") The clues offered by Sadie's non-response response are based on late Victorian cultural assumptions about the language of prostitutes (men only want one thing—"You're all the same") and the Victorian equating of male sexuality with animal (as opposed to spiritual) "instincts," ("Pigs!"), and its accompanying assumption that sexuality is "filthy, dirty." (Ironically, this puritanical and Victorian disgust with sexuality is the one view Sadie and Reverend Davidson share, revealing that they are in fact at opposite poles in the same discourse of good and evil. It is the inability of either to compromise, a problem endemic to the discourse of the sacred, that destroys them.)

What Macphail observes that so horrifies him is the revelation of a naturalist discourse, so vicious and untamed by either the sacred or the liberal light of reason that it threatens to overwhelm all that goes before it. The secular pluralism Macphail represents is powerless to intervene, for the fanaticism of Davidson and the violence of Sadie are antithetical—there is no middle ground.

The use of Macphail is a strategy employed to suppress heteroglossia, the chaos that would ensue if Sadie and Davidson were left alone to fight to the death for dominance. By distancing the reader through a more comfortable identification with the good doctor, Maugham (himself an M.D.) provides the reader with a "safe" position, knowledge of the extremity (the great chasm existing between classes and genders and its potential to shatter the world), while providing a safety net in the conservative reenforcement of a non-extreme, middle language from which to view the others. By creating and foregrounding the doctor's discourse, characterized as reliable and therefore close to denotative or "realist," Maugham urges on us a point of view "everyone" can agree is better than either of the "extreme" views—in other words, a centralized, unitary language. The words of Sadie and Davidson, their cultural positions, "are completely denied any authorial intentions: the author does not express *himself* (as the author of the word)—rather, he *exhibits* them as a unique speech-thing, they function for him as something completely reified" (Bakhtin 1981, p. 299). He places Macphail's language as the superior choice in a language hierarchy and seeks to separate the reader from any possible identification with Sadie or Davidson.

The most salient difference between the story and the play is the replacement of Macphail with a character/participant, Sergeant O'Hara, and the attempt to reconcile and smooth out the oppositions delineated by Sadie and Davidson. The play dramatizes almost every one of the scenes "reported" to Macphail in the story: the confrontation with the sailors in Sadie's room, her discussions with Davidson. (Her conversion is reported in the play but dramatized in all of the film versions.) The only scene always left unrepresented is the final one between Sadie and Davidson. This is both the climax of the story and the ultimate taboo, but in the play it is displaced by a supposedly "greater" event—Sadie's acceptance of O'Hara's marriage proposal. Sadie and Davidson remain structured as a series of oppositions based on class and gender: Davidson as authority (religious, military, political), and as a man with physical and vocal superiority. Sadie is sub-working-class, "vulgar," without political power, exploited and female. Davidson's views on sex are puritanical (the conversion of sexual energy into work results in profit), the supposed opposite of Sadie's, who exploits sex for direct access to cash, exposing the work ethic as an exchange of sex for money. Sadie's and Davidson's names are virtual inversions of each other, the initials of which indicate their positions as representatives of the Marcusian bipolar opposites, eros and thanatos, or Sex and Death (the sexual woman and the puritanical minister, the prostitute and the suicide). Or as Barthes might have it, "S/D." O'Hara is at every point inserted as the middle ground between their antithetical positions. It is through O'Hara that Sadie is reconciled to men and middle-class monogamy. Macphail is phased out.

Sergeant O'Hara becomes so important in the play that in the introduction to the published version of the play, Ludwig Lewisohn defines the major conflict as being between Davidson and O'Hara. "It is O'Hara who saves Sadie" (Colton and Randolph 1936, p. xi). This is a misreading of the play, because what "frees" Sadie from Davidson's influence is what happens between the two of them before he kills himself. O'Hara functions in the same way Macphail does, as the observer who eventually takes sides, and like Macphail he is identified with reliability. When he is introduced in the play by Quartermaster Bates, his main attribute is that he "flies straight" (Colton and Randolph 1936, p. 11). But instead of being in Macphail's disinterested position, O'Hara is placed *between* Sadie and Davidson. His language is a combination of authority (the marines) and slang (Sadie's refutation of authority). His class standing is between Davidson's (he's not as educated or "respectable") but above Sadie's (holding with the cultural assumption that men should marry "down" a little and bring the woman "up"). But, principally, O'Hara is able to marry Sadie and propose a refuge in Australia, portrayed as an idyllic place where men and women can marry and live in a class-free society. In effect, the religious, dictatorial male authority of Davidson is refuted by a figure of democratic pluralism who can actively create a male and female utopia based on similar goals and a truce by consensus.

The introduction of O'Hara creates certain strains near the end of the play, where the full chasm between Sadie and Davidson becomes most apparent. When Sadie wrathfully denounces all men as "filthy, dirty pigs," the text struggles through O'Hara to patch things up again as quickly as possible. The stage directions have Sadie's "voice black with loathing":

> You men—you're all alike. [Hoarsely] Pigs! Pigs! I wouldn't trust one of you! [She turns quickly toward O'Hara] No offense to you in that last remark, old pardner. [She pauses.] And I'm going to Sydney if that invitation of yours still holds good.
>
> (Colton and Randolph 1936, p. 241;
> brackets in original)

In the interests of reconciliation and recuperation, she is forced *instantly* to modify what was originally an out-of-control and heartfelt blanket condemnation. The psychological likelihood of such loathing melting in the presence of "Mr. Right" is a gap the text is willing to live with. In the face of pluralism, both holiness and naturalism disappear.

The play's urge to reconcile everything and everybody extends to Davidson's strict, puritanical wife. Although a key figure in labeling Sadie as morally objectionable and beyond the pale in both the play and the story, at the end of the play Mrs. Davidson has a change of heart only slightly less sudden than Sadie's. As Sadie and O'Hara are preparing to leave arm in arm for the boat for Sydney, Mrs. Davidson returns from having identified her husband's body on the beach. She looks up at Sadie and says, "I understand, Miss Thompson.—I'm sorry for him and I'm sorry for you" (Colton and Randolph 1936, p. 241). This line preserves (if displaces) the story's famous last line ("He understood.") and completes the conversion of the play's characters so that now everyone sides with Sadie, no matter how improbably.

One can see how great a transformation this is when comparing it to the end of the story. There, as Dr. and Mrs. Macphail escort Mrs. Davidson back from the beach, they find Sadie all dressed up again, "the flaunting queen that they had known at first" (Maugham 1967, p. 454).

> As they came in she broke into a loud, jeering laugh; and then, when Mrs. Davidson involuntarily stopped, she collected the spittle in her mouth and spat. Mrs. Davidson cowered back, and two red spots rose suddenly to her cheeks

> Then, covering her face with her hands, she broke away and ran quickly up the stairs.
>
> (pp. 454–55)

That Mrs. Davidson, whose "anger almost suffocated her" (p. 432) when she thought of Sadie earlier, should suddenly feel sympathy for her is hard to make psychologically persuasive, although Colton and Randolph try to ease us into the change with an added scene of Mrs. Davidson expressing doubts about her strictly celibate marriage. But it *is* absolutely necessary in order to attest (indirectly) to the rightness of Sadie marrying O'Hara (covering up the gulf of oppositions that had existed between Sadie and Davidson).

The main conflict that drives the story, play, and films is the one personified by Sadie Thompson and Reverend Davidson. This conflict is an "intra-language" dialogue, exposing the contradiction at the core of the sacred discourse. Sin is the engine that makes religion move in Western culture, the problem the sacred purports to solve and without which it would be unnecessary. Without hell, heaven would be meaningless. Bakhtin argues that drama cannot fully embody heteroglossia precisely because it is built of intra-language dialogue, although he also admits that this form "has hardly been studied linguistically or stylistically up to the present day" either (Bakhtin 1981, p. 273).

> The internal dialogism of authentic prose discourse, which grows organically out of a stratified heteroglot language, cannot fundamentally be dramatized or dramatically resolved (brought to an authentic end); it cannot ultimately be fitted into the frame of any manifest dialogue, into the frame of a conversation between persons; it is not ultimately divisible into verbal exchanges possessing precisely marked boundaries.
>
> (ibid., p. 326)

Although dialogue is used within the novel, heteroglossia is greater than that small portion of the novel expressed in the dialogue alone.

> True, even in the novel heteroglossia is by and large always personified, incarnated in individual human figures, with disagreements and oppositions individualized. But such oppositions of individual wills and minds are submerged in *social* heteroglossia, they are reconceptualized through it.
>
> (ibid.)

These "languages," represented by characters or not, exceed dialogue and begin to interact with each other *across* the text, infiltrating the author's discourse after the specific characters linked with a particular language are out of the "scene." It is this free play of languages, this dialogue between languages, as opposed to characters, that makes heteroglossia so rich, so present in every part of the novel.

"A speaking person's discourse in the novel [is] not merely transmitted or reproduced [as in drama]; it is, precisely, *artistically represented* and thus—in contrast to drama—it is represented *by means of* (authorial) *discourse*" (ibid., p. 332; italics in original). Within the authorial discourse, a word or sentence becomes "double-voiced," serving "two speakers at the same time and express[ing] simultaneously two different intentions: the direct intention of the character who is speaking and the refracted intention of the author" (ibid., p. 324).

With the displacement of an identifiable "author figure" in drama, double-voiced discourse must be contained almost completely in dialogue. The characters must always speak doubly, must always convey the author's intentions about what they say as they say it. They must (if distanced from the author's intentions) condemn themselves out of their own mouths, while simultaneously being true to their own discourse. Although Bakhtin admits that a form of double-voicedness exists in the rhetorical and poetic genres (where he places drama), he feels that "it is not fertilized by a deep-rooted connection with the forces of historical becoming that serve to stratify language" (ibid., p. 325). In other words, by aspiring to a closed, monologic universe (which Bakhtin finds typical of poetic genres), a narrower, closed system is presented, one that represses the complexity of society, language, and their historical evolution.

But any character in a drama is a complex of social and historical "evidence," all interacting to inform the audience of the class, cultural, educational, ethnic, religious background, and gender of the character in his/her "process of becoming." All of these languages speak to each other and situate themselves in relation to the other languages within any segment of character dialogue. Any part of dialogue from one character to another also situates its complex of languages in relation to another character's complex mix of linguistic and historical/social affiliations and enmities.

Bakhtin feels that "oppositions between individuals are only surface upheavals of the untamed elements in social heteroglossia, surface manifestations of those elements that play *on* such individual oppositions, make them contradictory, saturate their consciousness and discourses with a more fundamental speech diversity (ibid., p. 326). Since characters in drama are types selected from a pool of already determined characteristics provided by a specific culture at a specific time, I would argue they represent not merely individual conflicts but social ones. The "surface upheavals" embodied in dialogue are, as Bakhtin notes, legible symptoms of deeper issues. Not all characters have access to all languages in a given society, therefore there is a strong potential for social/historical conflict each time a character speaks, that is, each time anyone is forced to define him or her self from a limited set of predetermined and determining linguistic choices. In a dialogue, each character's choices are also in potential conflict with the social and historical determinants indicated by the language choices of the other characters.

It is necessary to consider the question of the relationship between hetero-glossia and dialogue in such depth because most of the time the dialogue (and a few stage directions) is all that is preserved of dramatic "texts." In order to understand the full embodiment of heteroglossia in a drama, one would ideally need the dramatic performance: acting, lighting, stage direction, the behavior of extras, costumes, and the audience. These other "languages" are the as-pects of the dramatic form that have the potential to become dialogized, inter-acting with the dialogue as the dialogue interacts and repositions itself in rela-tion to them. This requires a drastic repositioning of the play's author. The actor's distance from the character would assume as much importance as the writer's. The ability to reify, to parody, to distance oneself from the words of a character *while speaking them* would create another register unique to the pro-duction as a whole, and one not to be found in the published script. The posi-tion of the author thus exists across the text, fragmented and dissolved, as one more language engaged in dialogue with all the others. Heteroglossia needs a complete form, not the transcript provided by a published version of a play, in order to be traced out in its full complexity. The complete dramatic text (exist-ing in performance) is ephemeral and therefore difficult to analyze. Cinema, which also radically repositions the author, provides us with a complete ar-tifact for study, as does the novel. But rather than passing over dramatic dia-logue, I would like to look at it in some detail in order to understand how *much* social and historical specificity it holds. When we appreciate the lin-guistic diversity of dialogue alone—"those socio-ideological cultural hori-zons (big and little) that open up behind heteroglot languages" (ibid., p. 299)—we shall be better able to appreciate dialogue's re-positioning within the larger complex of cinema as a whole, both silent and sound.

The languages that form the character of Sadie in "Miss Thompson" vary greatly from those that create "Sadie" in Colton and Randolph's *Rain,* which supplied almost all of the dialogue in the 1932 film and much of what remains in the 1928 silent version. The issues surrounding Sadie, defining her, and working through her, are softened to a great extent in the play and a look at the languages used by and about Sadie will show how this ideological shift is made.

Maugham's Sadie is a remnant of the Victorian stereotype of the prostitute. She is from the "lower depths," carrying almost exclusively negative con-notations of a sub-working-class position. She is described as "quite willing to gossip" and her voice is "hoarse" and usually "jeering" (Maugham 1967, pp. 427, 420, 454). In need of the doctor's help, "she gave Macphail an in-gratiating smile," and in apologizing to Davidson, "she stepped toward him with a movement that was horribly cringing" (p. 445). ("Ingratiating" and "horribly cringing" have an almost Dickensian flavor, reminiscent of Uriah Heep trying in a distastefully false way to "make up to his betters.") Sadie is inarticulate and uneducated. When she is upset she speaks "a torrent of insult, foul and insolent" (p. 438)—insolence being the refusal of someone on the lower end of a power relation to accept his or her "place." Elsewhere Sadie gives vent to "an inarticulate cry of rage" (p. 439) and "a torrent of confused supplication [as] the tears coursed down her painted cheeks" (p. 445).

Physically Maugham seems disgusted with Miss Thompson. "Her shiny white boots with their high heels, her *fat legs bulging* over the tops of them, were strange things on that exotic scene" (p. 427; italics added). When she becomes ill worrying about Davidson, there is no sympathy, but rather continuing distaste. "Macphail noticed that her skin was yellow and muddy under her powder and her eyes were heavy" (p. 440). "Her hair, as a rule so elaborately arranged, was tumbling untidily over her neck"; her clothes are "unfresh and bedraggled" (p. 444). When she has broken down under pressure from Davidson, Maugham has Macphail observe that "she had not troubled to dress herself, but wore a *dirty* dressing gown, and her hair was tied in a *sluttish* knot. She had given her face a dab with a wet towel, but it was all *swollen* and *creased* with crying. She looked a *drab*" (p. 448; italics added).

Compare this unappealing physical detail to the introduction of Sadie by Colton and Randolph:

> Miss Thompson is a slim, blondish young woman, very pretty, very cheery, very rakish. She has a tip tilted nose and merry eyes. She walks easily without self-consciousness. There is something of the grace of a wild animal in her movements, something primitive perhaps, even as her clothes suggest savage and untutored response to cut and color.
>
> (Colton and Randolph 1936, p. 26)

The lack of self-consciousness absolves Sadie from being guilty of any calculated attempt to offend or oppose the dominant order. Anything "animal" or "savage" about her is modified by being linked to "grace" or deflected to her clothes. Colton and Randolph's description is altogether one of youthful high spirits and innocence, an attractive construction especially when contrasted with Maugham's vulgar drab.

Part of what Colton and Randolph are doing in their massive revision of the character of Sadie Thompson—besides making the main character likable—is turning her into a fetish. Annette Kuhn summarizes the process of fetishization this way:

> In the social-historical context of the patriarchal family, it is argued, the body of the mother begins to signify the threat of castration and powerlessness. . . . [The resulting anxiety for the male] may be dealt with by turning woman, or the figure of woman, into a fetish: that is, by disavowing and defusing the castratory aspects of the image by making them their opposite through idealizing the image.
>
> (Kuhn 1982, p. 61)

According to Laura Mulvey, this fetishized object "becomes reassuring rather than dangerous" (Mulvey 1975, p. 14). The fearful viciousness of Maugham's Sadie, the jeering, exultant hoyden "red in tooth and claw," is replaced by a cutie-pie, a prototype for the upcoming flapper who has plenty of "it." The horror of the castrating "bad mother" who flaunts her sexuality disappears, denied and obscured by the pointedly "young" Miss Thompson. In making this journey from slut to slim, cheery, and rakish, Sadie is also repositioned from upholding a pole in the sacred discourse to standing firmly within the bourgeois world of melodrama and psychoanalysis.[3]

The difference in conception of the two characters is epitomized in language, particularly in their dialogue. Sadie's dialogue in the story is reified and never infiltrates Macphail's (or the author's) descriptions. The play's conception of Sadie is different because its conception of class is different; it is more complicated and therefore the use of language is more complex. In his introduction to the play, Ludwig Lewisohn writes, "Sadie is lifted from mere suffering to action. The drama required that she be not left passive, no mere object, but that she, too, be in herself a source of interest and energy" (Colton and Randolph 1936, pp. viii–ix). What is intriguing about this description of Sadie, besides the writer's own rather strange syntax, is his tone of amazement that Sadie should be an active character, a potential subject and not just an object of contention between O'Hara and Davidson. For our purposes, it will be most illuminating to analyze the way this impression of an "active" and "interesting" character is created entirely through her speech, speech that was to become a major point of controversy for all subsequent adaptations.

Maugham's Sadie curses and uses slang expressions in ways that convey her coarseness. "The feller's tryin' to soak me for a dollar and a half a day for the meanest sized room" (p. 420) and " 'Don't try to pull that stuff with me,' said Miss Thompson. 'We'll settle this right now. You get a dollar a day for the room and not one bean more' " (p. 420). Her grammar also shows the class status of an outsider. Shouting at Davidson: " 'You done it,' she shrieked. 'You can't kid me. You done it' " (p. 438). " 'Do you think I want to stay on in this poor imitation of a burg? I don't look no busher, do I?' " (p. 439). Along with the previously noted "inarticulateness," Sadie's language marks her, sets her apart from everyone else in the story. If this Sadie is comparable to an animal, it is to a dumb animal; if she is unselfconscious, it is because she is too low in class to be aware of how vulgar, how far outside of bourgeois norms, she really is. A significant part of what sets her irrevocably outside of society's norms is her use of language, and so language itself becomes an issue, one that is carried over and elaborated upon in the play.

Sadie in Colton and Randolph's *Rain* speaks more interestingly than any of the other characters; this is part of what makes "Sadie" the starring (and star-making) role it is. Linguistic complexity—sudden changes in style, unexpected words and word usage, an awareness of language and distancing herself from her own language—makes Sadie's speech unpredictable and fascinating. The constant mixture of tones and languages in later or "better" plays often passes for psychological realism giving the impression of background for a character, a lived past, and "untold depths" of experience and feeling. Although it does not blend smoothly into a "psychological realism" here, Sadie's extremely varied use of a number of languages (both within a language system and quoting French, Japanese, and British forms) creates a foundation of adaptability that will be transformed into psychological malleability later (underscoring her conversion under Davidson and her proposed new life in Australia with O'Hara).

The following speech occurs early in the play when Sadie first enters the inn following a sudden rainstorm.

> Christ on the mountaintop! That was sudden—and me in the only decent togs I've got to my name. Put that stuff down anywhere, boys. [Holds up her hat] Behold—the Wreck of the Hesperus! H'm—that plume has waved its last— farewell, pretty one—farewell—I guess any idea of me looking neat and chipper when I get to Apia is shot to pieces, eh, what?

To separate the languages out of this, let's look at it phrase by phrase.

"Christ on the mountaintop!"

> This illustrates the issue of "bad" language, the use of a moderately shocking biblical reference to express a conception of "the ultimate" (*Christ, mountaintop,* and the exclamation point). The ejaculation also expresses frustration and ruefulness as seen in the follow-up, "That was sudden." (In the 1932 *Rain* the phrase "Moses on the mountaintop" was substituted. This is directly traceable to the Production Code, which forbad exactly this usage of "Christ." "Moses on the mountain" seems to have caught on as an acceptable film substitute because it is used again in the 1937 *Nothing Sacred.*)

"That was sudden."

> Coupled with the preceding phrase, this modifies the shock value by emphasizing that it was unpremeditated, thereby preserving Sadie's innocence and unself-consciousness.

"—and me in the only decent togs to my name."

> Further justification with connotations of poverty. Expresses Sadie's sense of humor and ability to accept a joke that is "on her." Comments on nature, fate, and bad luck, as well as on Sadie's ability to survive and adapt.

"Put that stuff down anywhere, boys."

> Casual, informal way of relating to others seen in the lack of a more formally polite "Would you" or "Please put that" or other niceties mandated by etiquette. "Boys" shows her ease at making acquaintances and familiarity with the marines.

"Behold—"

> Here she is referring to her soaked hat. The dash implies a pause afterward. This is because simply stating "Behold" is in itself a reference to Shakespearean or classical drama signifying a knowledge of "high culture." (Maugham's Sadie would *never* be capable of pronouncing "Behold.")

"—the Wreck of the Hesperus!"

Longfellow's poem "The Wreck of the Hesperus" is associated with nineteenth-century theatrical melodrama. Historically, it connotes the educational policy of having schoolchildren memorize and recite epic dramatic poems. All of this indicates an "All-American" public school education for Sadie, implying that she was brought up in this turn-of-the-century, literature-privileging society. Sadie instantly steps up in class, becoming an average petit bourgeois American girl of standard education who has fallen on hard times. (Sadie's education is implied elsewhere when she speaks of someone's "fine Spencerian hand," referring to a course of instruction in penmanship, using an archaic meaning of "hand," and again, distancing herself from the phrases she uses by making them so florid.) Because Sadie has "fallen," she can be redeemed, restored to her prior social status, the class in which she was raised. Marriage to O'Hara is appropriate because he has similar class mobility. As an enlisted man he has worked his way up to sergeant, which is the highest rank available without being a commissioned officer, and he is about to become a small businessman in partnership with his ex-army buddy. These are "poor but honest" petit bourgeois aspirations to middle-class status.

"—that plume has waved its last—"

Nineteenth-century rhetorical formations along with connotations of patriotic songs and slogans ("Oh say, does that Star-Spangled Banner yet wave . . . ?"). "Waved its last" calls to mind "breathed its last"—a euphemism for "died."

"farewell, pretty one—farewell"

Reminiscent of nineteenth-century melodrama and Dickensian elegies (Paul Dombey, Little Nell).

"I guess any idea of me looking neat and chipper when I get to Apia is shot to pieces, eh, what?"

"Shot to pieces": military. "Neat and chipper" and "eh, what?" are British expressions and point to Sadie's varied background, travel, experience, meeting a lot of people who speak in many ways. Combined with the above nineteenth-century theatrical and literary allusions, this expresses intelligence, the ability to pick up new languages (literally, too, for her next line is in Japanese which she then translates into English). This exaggerated fluency also suggests that Sadie has "been around."

In the story, Sadie is in a class-based trap. In the play, she's freer, more resilient, in part because by positioning herself *within* a variety of languages she is able to distance herself from the negative and restricting class connotations of one specific language. This defines and illustrates her freedom. It is when she loses the ability to distance herself from language (particularly from the language of others), when she succumbs to the authoritarian language of Davidson, that she seems trapped and needs to be rescued; her escape comes from being able to regain her distance and once again mock the religious discourse she obediently mouthed when converted.

"It is precisely the diversity of speech, and not the unity of a normative shared language, that is the ground of style," Bakhtin observes (1981, p. 308). He means "diversity of speech" within a prose *text,* but nonetheless we can see here how the same may apply to a single character. Those with "a normative shared language," like the Davidsons, are embodiments of a language that seeks to efface its determinations and claim its discourse as the "right" (natural) one. Sadie, on the other hand, can be described as having style, demonstrating a range of vocabulary that indicates knowledge of many discourses and usages, her awareness of her position in regard to all of them, and her exercising a choice among them every time she speaks. Specifically, Sadie has a comic style.

Bakhtin defines comic style thus: "Comic style (of the English sort) is based . . . on the stratification of common language and on the possibilities available for isolating from these strata, to one degree or another, one's own intentions, without ever completely merging with them" (ibid , p. 308). When Sadie uses class-ified, "educated" terms, she separates them out as phoney, reified, and reflects them back on themselves in order to expose their pretentiousness as well as the dominant class's attempt to impose them as signifiers of "culture" (high culture), as the normative language of the high-culture-aspiring middle class.

The reification and ridicule of these terms can be seen as a form of rebellion, as a refusal of "their" discourse and its dominance. Julia Kristeva, whose work on language in the novel forms a complement to Bakhtin's, notes that "on the omnified stage of carnival, language parodies and relativizes itself, repudiating its role in representation; in so doing, it provokes laughter but remains incapable of detaching itself from representation" (Kristeva 1980, p. 79). Sadie may assert a comic distance from language(s), but she is enslaved by one and eventually beguiled by another (that of O'Hara and marriage). The fact that she does use the languages that are ultimately used against her reveals the limits of her range, the fact that she acts from within a culture that has already defined how far she can go. Kristeva's continuation of that thought applies resonantly to Sadie's place in *Rain* as a whole: the history of language in carnival "is the history of the struggle against Christianity and its representation; this means an explanation of language (of sexuality and death) [Sadie and Davidson], a consecration of ambivalence [what happens between them] and of 'vice'"—here the celebration of the "whore" at the expense of a centralized monologic religion, until she is recuperated into the middle class through marriage (ibid.).

The following exchange shows Sadie openly parodying religion, the culture of Victorian literature and melodrama, and the ways in which each seeks to position her:

[Hears voices] Methinks I hear the winds of religion whistling down the chimney! [with mock trepidation] Whereat the low hussy frolics off to buy her dinner!

(Colton and Randolph 1936, p. 97)

The pragmatic finish deflates the archaic rhetoric of "methinks" and "whereat," while the dark melodrama of "the low hussy" clashes with the pastoral "frolics off."

> [To Dr. Macphail before she leaves] Life just teems with quiet fun, don't it?
>
> (Colton and Randolph 1936, p. 97)

The ungrammatical "Don't it?" more closely reflects the grammatical insouciance of the British upper class in this period (à la Dorothy L. Sayers's Lord Peter Wimsey) than the uneducated status of Maugham's Sadie.

Parody may not be able to break free from representation, but "carnivalesque discourse breaks through the laws of language censored by grammar and semantics and at the same time, is a social and political protest. There is no *equivalence, but rather identity* between challenging official linguistic codes and challenging official law" (Kristeva 1980, p. 65). Sadie's language throughout the play is clearly oppositional as she rejects any single language as whole, normative, or transparent. Her essentially comic tone is one of the elements that makes us identify with her and regret her submission to Davidson. While Colton and Randolph actively insert comic elements into the first part of the play, they do not use Sadie's comic discourse subversively, resorting instead to melodrama for Sadie's confrontation with Davidson and her ultimate recuperation.

Davidson is the exemplification of unitary language in the play, as is Maugham in the story through his validation of Macphail's speech at the expense of the other characters' language. Bakhtin describes how the working of unitary language is inherently opposed to Sadie's challenges. "Thus a unitary language gives expression to forces *working toward concrete verbal and ideological unification and centralization,* which develop in vital connection with the processes of socio-political and cultural centralization" (Bakhtin 1981, p. 271; italics added). Davidson's language goes hand in hand with his work as a missionary, his imposition of Anglo-American Protestant beliefs on the native population and his fellow travelers.

> The victory of one reigning language (dialect) over the others, the supplanting of languages, their enslavement, the process of illuminating them with the True Word, the incorporation of barbarians and lower social strata into a unitary language of culture and truth, the canonization of ideological systems. . . . All these . . . give expression to the same centripetal forces in socio-linguistic and ideological life.
>
> (ibid.)

And Davidson is their representative, the spokesman for religion (as a minister), politics (his mission, he points out to the governor, has many friends in Washington), the military (in the film *Rain* he is described as an official inspector of navy morals), and as a man ("You may be big and you may be strong," Sadie at one point argues before attacking his superior position).

Davidson's language is very controlled; there are few contractions, the syntax is careful and perfectly balanced. He speaks in complete sentences and does not use slang, giving the impression that *his* language is transparent and not subject to historical change. All languages must bend to his. In dialogue with Sadie we can see how their positioning themselves with regard to language (plural and distanced for Sadie, wholly at one with the only "true" language for Davidson) makes it almost impossible for them to communicate. Their first discussion (Colton and Randolph 1936, pp. 114–16) is built on misunderstandings and miscues.

SADIE: You want to see me?

DAVIDSON: Yes, I want to talk to you, Miss Thompson.

He takes her blunt question and submits it to the rules of grammar and etiquette.

SADIE: I'm eating my supper. [Her mouth is full of banana.]

She opposes his polite form with fact, rudely implying the inconvenience of his visit.

DAVIDSON: I'll wait until you're through.

Connotations: he is patient. The use of contractions implies his reasonableness, his willingness to recognize her needs.

SADIE: Oh, the supper can stand by if it's important.

"Stand by," nautical, to wait.

DAVIDSON: It is important, very important.

Again he uses her phrase as if they are in sync, showing his willingness to use her language, implying they will see things the same way.

[continued] Sadie Thompson, I have brought you out here to make you a gift—the most precious gift life can offer you.

Use of her full name signals the beginning of a speech, a set form. Religious discourse.

SADIE: [uncertainly] You want to give me something?

She substitutes a practical meaning for a spiritual one.

DAVIDSON: Yes—I want to give you something.

Uses her words.

SADIE: I guess I'm not following you—

Her incomprehension mildly implies *his* inadequacy at expressing himself.

DAVIDSON: The gift I offer is free.

Continuing the religious metaphor regardless of her "confusion" or rejection.

SADIE: I'm glad of that—I'm pretty short on cash.

Again substituting the practical for the spiritual.

DAVIDSON: The gift I'm offering you is the infinite mercy of our Lord, Jesus Christ.

He reveals the religious meaning of his ruling metaphor. The standard use of "our" suggests the centralizing tendency of both Davidson and all religious institutions. By repeating forms of the phrase "the gift I offer you," Davidson implies that this expanded version was always contained in embryo in the earlier ones, as if he has been making a set speech without any real regard for the presence of his listener.

SADIE: Just what is the idea, Rev. Davidson—making me these presents?

Kristeva notes how "the dialogism of [Menippean discourse's] words is practical philosophy doing battle against idealism and religious metaphysics" (Kristeva 1980, p. 83). Sadie's intensely practical concern for her dinner and her negative cash flow continue to outweigh Davidson's spiritual discourse. Later in the scene, as this miscommunication becomes apparent, each begins to interpret the intentions underlying the other's words. (Their interpretations are for the most part positive; if they were negative, the conversation would end.)

SADIE: You mean right by me, Reverend Davidson—and I sure am grateful. . . .

DAVIDSON: You are mistaking me—but I do not think wilfully.

SADIE: They all told me you were sore, but I just couldn't think a man as big as you would hold a grudge over a little misunderstanding.

Later in the scene Davidson spells out the "two paths" Sadie can take, either accepting his "gift" of submission or being destroyed. Sadie's opposition clearly fits Kristeva's description of "politically and socially disturbing" Menippean satire. "Menippean discourse tends towards the scandalous and eccentric in language. The 'inopportune' expression, with its cynical frankness, its desecration of the sacred and its attack on etiquette, is quite characteristic" (ibid., pp. 82, 83).

DAVIDSON: The devil in you is strong, poor Sadie Thompson. Evil has claimed you as its own.

He positions her according to his own discourse.

SADIE: You take care of your own evil, and I'll take care of mine.

She now uses his words against him, rejecting his power to position her.

I know what you want!

> Reveals understanding in place of earlier confusion. Asserts that she holds the key, the hidden meaning of his "gift."

You want another scalp to hand to the Lord.

> Displaying Kristeva's "inopportune" cynicism and frankness as well as the desecration of the sacred.

Well, you don't get mine, old tit-bit!

> —And the attack on etiquette.

DAVIDSON: Lord! Hear Thou my prayer for this lost sister

> He counters with the full power of religious discourse, speaking directly to God and closing her out of the conversation.

—close Thy ears to her wild and heedless words.

> Rejecting her discourse as being beyond the pale—which it is, and intentionally so.

When Sadie gives in under pressure and tries to consciously adapt herself to his language in order to negotiate with Davidson and avoid prison, her language shows the difficulty of synthesizing two such opposing discourses:

> Not all words for just anyone submit equally easily to the appropriation, to this seizure and transformation into private property: many words stubbornly resist, others remain alien, sound foreign in the mouth of the one who appropriated them and who now speaks them; they cannot be assimilated into this context and fall out of it; it is as if they put themselves in quotation marks against the will of the speaker.
>
> (Bakhtin 1981, p. 294)

SADIE: Reverend Davidson—wait a minute! Reverend Davidson—you're right.—I am a bad woman, but I want to be good, only I don't know how—So you let me stay here with you, then you can tell me what to do, and no matter what it is I'm going to do it for you.

> Here, "bad" and "good" stand out along with "only I don't know how," a faux-naïf expression of dependence meant to elicit a protective response. Davidson speaks in such global simplicities; Sadie can't. It "feels" wrong. She isn't necessarily lying—that's too simplistic. What she's doing is trying to embody a discourse she doesn't believe, her words putting "themselves in quotation marks" regardless of whether that is her actual intention.

DAVIDSON: No, you can't stay here—You've got to go back to San Francisco— You've got to serve your time.

> Again the repetition: "You can't," "You've got to—," "You've got to—."

SADIE: You mean to say if I repent and I want to be good—I still have to go to the penitentiary?

> She tries to use the same simple sentence structures and short words in order to give an impression of artless simplicity and sincerity. Shows an effort to understand ("You mean") and then uses two of "his" terms ("repent" and "be good") before reaching the part that directly concerns her.

When Sadie finds that negotiations haven't worked, that total capitulation is all Davidson will accept, she reverts to her own original position in regard to language in all its multiplicity and variety. Davidson tells her that she has to go to jail whether or not she is guilty of the charge.

SADIE: Innocent or guilty? What kind of a God are you talking about? Where's your mercy? Ah, no, Rev. Davidson, I guess that repentance stuff is off.

DAVIDSON: Was it ever on, Miss Thompson?

SADIE: Whether it was or not, it's off now! The way you figure out God, he's nothing but a cop.

DAVIDSON: You've got to go back to San Francisco!

> Retorts with the "law," straight and simple.

SADIE: Straight orders from your private heaven, eh? Ah, no, Rev. Davidson, your God and me could never be shipmates,

> Naval reference domesticates religious discourse.

and the next time you talk to Him—you tell Him this for me—Sadie Thompson is on her way to Hell!

> She takes his biggest threat and changes it into a positive assertion, a personal choice, deflating it and taking possession of the religious discourse.

In dialogue, the speaker anticipates the response of the listener and at the same time positions the listener's possible responses. For instance, when Davidson speaks to Sadie, he positions her as either a brazen sinner or a potentially repentant one, a "poor lost soul." There are no other positions from which she can answer; if she did, Davidson would not recognize or acknowledge the response. Monologic discourse typical of a centralized language like Davidson's reduces the number of positions it recognizes and from which it will allow itself to be addressed. When Davidson says to Sadie, "My poor lost child, what happened the other day is of no importance. Do you imagine what you or those sailors said to me made any difference?" (Colton and Randolph 1936, p. 122), he is making it clear that their words are literally as if unsaid because authority such as he represents cannot be addressed in that way— he/it doesn't hear it.

"In any actual dialogue the rejoinder also leads such a double life: it is structured and conceptualized in the context of the dialogue as a whole, which consists of its own utterances ('own' from the point of view of the speaker) and of alien utterances (those of the partner)," Bakhtin says (1981, p. 284). But some utterances are more alien than others because of class contiguity or other differences in status. O'Hara, in an intermediate position with regards to Sadie and Davidson, is able to position himself vis-à-vis language in a way that is more open to the many possible rejoinders of the partner. When O'Hara speaks three different languages in one sentence (say, slang, official marine jargon, and deference to authority), he positions Sadie in an equally complex way; his freedom of speech allows her to respond in any of the languages he has used or any contiguous language (her street slang in response to his marine slang, her "Christ on the mountaintop!" to his "holy bilge-water"). O'Hara's dialogues with Sadie show not only their individual wills but the historical position of their classes; which classes can speak to each other, and which languages are reconcilable, as opposed to those that are irredeemably opposed. Sadie cannot speak to Davidson unless she completely submits. O'Hara can speak to Davidson, but as an inferior to a superior. As a mid-level officer in the strictly hierarchized military, O'Hara's ability to yield to rank is a necessary part of his daily life. Around Davidson, O'Hara controls his language. In all the subsequent versions, when Sadie begins to curse Davidson, it is O'Hara who tries to shut her up.

Although O'Hara recognizes Davidson's higher status, he is closer to Sadie. He can speak the codified language of the military, "speak" it in his dress, posture, and gestures. At the same time he undermines it with slang, specifically *army* slang. The oppositional stance of slang is very close to Sadie's opposition to almost all authority, and in their dialogues we see how they are able to negotiate a common ground.

The invention of O'Hara softens the story's "fight to the death" conflict between Sadie and Davidson's inimical historical positions. If the ruling class cannot tolerate the exploited working class, there is the middle rank of sergeant ("Tim O'Hara," Irish immigrant, a group making its way up from the ghetto into the petite bourgeoisie through jobs as priests, police, and members of the armed forces throughout the 1920s and 1930s). If religious authority cannot tolerate a sexual woman exploiting her exploited position, O'Hara can accept her sexuality and contain it by offering her a less controversial position as wife (but unlike Davidson, he gives her a choice rather than insisting on submission). If Davidson elicits Sadie's virulent attack on all men, O'Hara is there to make her immediately modify her position to *some* men. O'Hara as a construct attests to the redemptive powers of the middle class, mediating harsher "Old World" distinctions of class and church, softening sexual antagonisms by forgoing the double standard, and doing it all within the forms of democratic pluralism, repeatedly asking Sadie what *she* wants. The reconciliation O'Hara seeks with Sadie is closer to Bakhtin's description of prose:

"The unity of a literary language is not a unity of a single, closed language system, but is rather a highly specific unity of several 'languages' that have *established contact and mutual recognition*" (ibid., p. 295).

Although drama as a system cannot be fully analyzed (because the other codes or languages are "missing" and changeable), film provides a complete text with all the interrelationships *within* the text fixed and available for analysis. In discussing the differences between cinema and theater, Christian Metz states that "because the reflection (the signifier) is *recorded*" in cinema, as opposed to being live in theater, it "is hence no longer capable of change" (Metz 1982, p. 68; see, in general, pp. 63–68). It merely awaits the spectator/ listener's reading to constitute it, as we shall do here.

Sadie Thompson (1928) is the silent film adaptation of the play *Rain*. The play was high on a list of works banned by Will Hays as inherently immoral and not to be adapted to the screen under any circumstances. Gloria Swanson in her autobiography relates how she gained Hays's permission to adapt a *story* about a minister and a prostitute if she agreed to change the minister to a plain Mr. Hays agreed and she set about buying the rights to the story (and the play as well, for legal reasons). She attained those rights cheaply because, she asserts, "we would not be using the play, which was supposedly the valuable property, to concoct the script" (Swanson 1980, p. 303; see, in general, pp. 297–314). This is clearly not true, as the film closely follows the play in structure, in all of the dialogue titles, and most prominently in the presence of the character of Sergeant O'Hara, an invention of the playwrights, Colton and Randolph.

Dialogue is the only part of drama that lasts, that precedes and succeeds the ephemeral production and each individual performance, but in silent film dialogue and verbal discourse as a whole are drastically limited. As we shall see, this has consequences for Sadie and for the representation of women's voices in general. Dialogue as a form brings with it all the patriarchal assumptions of language. Silent film's reduction of dialogue in favor of visual communication offers a way out of the ideological strictures of pure language. However, the consequences for the representation of women are, as we shall see, decidedly mixed.

Sadie Thompson convincingly illustrates to what extent verbal discourse has been reduced in the effort to establish film as a monologic (visual) system. As previously noted, the idea that film should be primarily visual is a myth and not a "natural" result or expression of any cinematic essence. Silent films are constructed, particularly in classical Hollywood narrative films, to promote the image as the primary bearer of meaning. Because it was seldom possible to provide an intelligible narrative out of images alone, it became necessary to incorporate verbal discourse in the form of titles while segregating it, setting it apart as an "inferior" language system.

In the urge to centralize language, other languages must be either entirely suppressed or marked, set apart as belonging to "a" discourse versus "the" essential and transparent discourse of the dominant language. Just as hegemony is never total and has gaps and the traces of what it seeks to suppress, the impulse to make film a monologic system fails (except in the few historically overemphasized titleless silent films).[4] In place of a monologic system, silent film substitutes a hierarchy: the "invisible" discourse of the image, with conventions of editing that hide themselves as the story "constructs itself" (eyeline match, invisible editing, cutting on movement) while other languages (verbal discourse, music) are set apart, not "part" of the text but "other," visible as discourse. One scene in *Sadie Thompson* when compared with the play shows the extent to which verbal discourse is made secondary to the visual discourse and the implications for the representation of woman's "voice."

After Sadie receives the letter from the governor telling her she must return to San Francisco, she and O'Hara run into Reverend Davidson (here "Mr." Davidson as described above). Sadie, furious, begins to curse him and tell him off. In the story Sadie becomes so frustrated, "she gave an inarticulate cry of rage and flung out of the room" (Maugham 1967, p. 439). In the play, this confrontation becomes a major scene, with thirteen dialogue exchanges covering three pages. The silent film maintains the position and prominence of the scene while retaining only four lines of dialogue in a scene that runs for about three minutes. This is all the more striking because one of the subjects of the scene is language itself, specifically Sadie's "bad" language, or profanity.

The scene consists of twenty-seven shots and five dialogue titles. Of the twenty-seven shots, *twenty-one* are of Sadie talking, five are reaction shots of Davidson or of Mrs. Davidson and Mrs. Macphail *listening* to Sadie, and one is of Davidson speaking. In effect we have a visualization of a tirade where the dynamism and energy of the emotional outburst is communicated through the editing, the acting, and the mise-en-scène. It is nonstop talk where the words don't matter.

In the first shot, Sadie and O'Hara, moving left, encounter Davidson coming up the stairs of the porch, moving right. He passes them by, but Sadie turns to Davidson and begins to speak. He exits right. She follows. In the next shot Davidson is crossing the main room and Sadie enters screen left, following him. She confronts him again until O'Hara steps between them (shot 2). Davidson again exits right and Sadie again follows him, with O'Hara in pursuit, leaving an empty frame. In shot 3, Sadie traps Davidson with his back to a staircase. Close-up of Sadie and the first dialogue title: "You dirty squealer. What lies did you tell the governor about me this time?" (condensing the following lines from the play, "You low down skunk, what have you been saying to the Governor about me?" and "filling the Governor up with a lot of filthy lies about me" [Colton and Randolph 1936, pp. 145, 146]).

The first four shots of the scene are all cut on movement in classical silent film editing style. There is no camera movement. Cutting on action and on the "look" of the characters makes the visual discourse invisible. The narrative

Shot 2

constructs itself from within as it effaces its own construction. The sense of relentless pursuit is conveyed through the repetition of movement to the right. In each shot Davidson faces Sadie as if to listen but always buckles under the (visualized) verbal onslaught and flees. The shots are filled with constant motion, especially from Sadie and Davidson, with O'Hara as an observer (one literally in Sadie's corner). The constant motion stands in for the stream of words we don't hear.

The one aspect of a silent film that cannot be completely hidden by editing techniques is the introduction of the second discursive system, verbal discourse. Shot 4, the close-up of Sadie talking, and the title that follows it show one of the ways silent film works to contain the limited verbal discourse within the privileged visual system. Sadie in close-up looks offscreen right and rapidly moves her lips. Cut to the title, "You dirty squealer. . . ." Cut back to the same close-up of Sadie completing the words of the title in pantomime (". . . to the Governor about me?").

The shot / title / (same) shot structure is one of the ways silent films made dialogue titles comprehensible *as dialogue*. An S/T/S structure fits the dialogue as much as possible into the image while obscuring (as much as possible) the work of the author. In earlier silent films, titles that described a mood or an action or that set the scene were clearly the work of the author/producer/filmmaker or the exhibitor. With the exact shot of a speaker bracketing a title (and the frequently "readable" mouthing of the words before and after the title), it is the image that triggers and contains the title, the words generated by the image and retroactively attributed to it. The image speaks the words. The opposite could easily be said of the earlier form where the title would lead into and pre-define the image. The words are reified as words and their interruptive power only keeps them more separate, "lesser" in their communicative ability than the smooth enveloping visual narrative.

Sadie Thompson is late in the silent period (1928) and consequently doesn't need to slavishly follow the S/T/S form for intelligibility; it can use more sophisticated forms, usually a shot 1 / title / shot 2 (speaker/title/listener) structure.

In shot 4 following the title, O'Hara steps in front of Sadie and she pushes him aside to continue her abuse of Davidson. Davidson in medium close-up holds up his hand and visibly says, "Enough!" Cut to title 2: "It was my duty to have you deported." Cut back to Sadie as in shot 4. We no longer need the bookend effect of identical shots surrounding the title. Once Davidson has begun to speak (making clear who is speaking the title), we can return to a shot of the listener and understand that (s)he is hearing the remainder of the title we just saw. In keeping with this, after a few moments of "listening," Sadie begins to curse even more heatedly, presumably in response to the title she just "heard."

Shot 7 is a long shot of O'Hara, Sadie, and Davidson (facing her with his back to the stairs). He exits right and she follows. Shot 8: Sadie enters, throwing off O'Hara's arm, and faces Davidson on the right, with Mrs. Davidson and Mrs. Macphail on the far right behind him. Title 3: "Was I doing you any harm, you bloodthirsty buzzard. Was I?" The way this title is "fixed" as coming from Sadie is by having Sadie be the only figure moving in this shot. Everyone else is static. She points her arm at full length at Davidson, shakes her hair and throws back her cape. This could be called an S1/T/S1a structure. After the title we return to the speaker, Sadie, but in a reframed shot taken from a different angle. The new shot is a medium close-up of Sadie. This shot becomes in turn the beginning of a new sequence, grounding the upcoming title, title 4: "Who gave *you* the right to pass judgment on *me*, you psalm-singing louse." Return to shot 9 (the close-up of Sadie) still speaking. Title 5: "You'd tear your own mother's heart if she didn't agree with you, and call it saving her soul."[5]

The string of dialogue titles (titles 3–5) is built into an alternating structure of titles and shots of the speaker—S1/T3/S1a (shot 1 with slight variation) / T4/S1a/T5/S2. After she says title 5, we return not to the close-up of Sadie but to a new long shot (shot 10) of O'Hara on the left and Sadie in the center yelling and pointing at Davidson on the right. This is the silent film's visual representation of a harangue—nonstop dialogue with no listener represented. Having three consecutive titles gives the impression of a lengthy diatribe while actually containing only four short sentences. The titles also are never literally consecutive; three "pages" of words on black background, one after the other, would lose the dynamic close-up of Sadie, her facial expressions, her hair flying, and her violent gestures. Besides, we must always be reminded that *Sadie speaks*—this is more important than what she says.

After the flurry of titles 3, 4, and 5, there are no more dialogue titles, even though Sadie talks continuously for the next sixteen shots. It is in these shots that the *image* of Sadie talking overwhelms and *improves* upon dialogue itself. Through the narrative we are given the impression that we don't want to know the words themselves, that we "get the gist of it," pure meaning, and understand what she means better than words could express. This is the hierarchy of languages in silent cinema, the image advanced as superior to words,

10   11

12   13

more true to verbal expression than words themselves could be—a hierarchy
that was to be profoundly challenged by early sound cinema.

In shot 10 (the long shot described above) Sadie climbs up on the chair
between her and Davidson and points her finger at him. Shot 11: Davidson, in
heavily shadowed light, looks disturbed, eyeline match suggests he looks at
her. Shot 12: Sadie speaking vigorously and shaking her hand as O'Hara in
soft focus behind her tries to pull her away. Shot 13: The two ladies cover their
ears presumably in horror at what they *hear*. They exit left. Shot 14: Long
shot as the ladies cross left in the foreground. Shot 15: Mrs. Davidson and
Mrs. Macphail enter from the right and cross left out on the porch. Mrs. Macphail turns however to look back in the direction from which they have come
and the camera cuts on her look. Shot 16: The earlier long shot with Sadie on
the chair gesturing toward Davidson. O'Hara reaches around her with his arm.
Shot 17: Close-up of Sadie with O'Hara's hand reaching in and covering her
mouth.[6] In the original stage directions, he pulls at her arm and finally she "is
pulled out of the scene by O'Hara" (Colton and Randolph 1936, p. 148).

As Sadie pulls herself away from O'Hara, still talking, we cut to shot 18,
of Davidson shielding his eyes (connoting stress, possibly prayer, in a nice

14   16

17

echo of Sadie with a hand over her mouth). Shot 19: Close-up of Sadie trying to free herself to speak. Shot 20: O'Hara drags her off the chair and out of the shot to the left, reversing the direction of their initial pursuit of Davidson. Shot 21: Long shot of the porch as O'Hara drags her to the left, her feet trailing, as Sadie continues yelling and gesturing with her arms. Shot 22: Close-up of Sadie yelling. Shot 23: Mrs. Davidson and Mrs. Macphail again cover their ears in shock and retreat right. Shot 24: O'Hara helps Sadie to her feet and she agrees to stop attacking Davidson, although she has one final word, extending her arm toward the right "at" Davidson. She and O'Hara turn left. Shot 25: They walk down the stairs and into the courtyard.

Thematically, the exhilaration of Sadie standing up to Davidson is tempered by O'Hara, who clearly marks off when she has "gone too far." It is also O'Hara who makes the episode comic by literally stopping her mouth and dragging her out of the scene. Here, he leads the couple instead of following Sadie. Her feet dragging in front of her is visual slapstick and reduces her outrage and oppositional stance to an eccentric, comic one.

Noël Burch argues that in Western film, "speech, the Word, was an intangible, ineradicable presence *inside* the diegesis"—its presentation on inter-

18   19

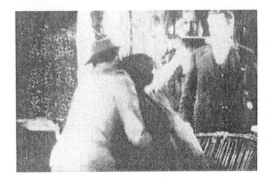

20   21

ruptive title cards signaled only "the parenthetic suspension (not the acknowledgment) of representation" (Burch 1979, p. 78). As we have seen in *Sadie
Thompson*, speech itself is presented as *in* the image and it is to the images
that the titles refer, supporting and strengthening them in their creation of the
diegetic world rather than presenting an equal verbal and/or auditory field
that, with the images, could become a multilinguistic, heteroglossic, dialogized form.

The displacement of verbal language by the image in silent film was not
inevitable; nor was the use of title cards, so graphically distinct from the visual flow of the narrative-bearing image, the only choice available. In Burch's
description of the *benshi* who spoke throughout the projection of silent films
in Japan, we see the verbal presentation of a simultaneous field of signification, parallel, but in no way inferior, to that of the image. In fact, according to
Burch, the narration of the *benshi* took precedence in both narrative and performance over the image. "We may, in fact, consider the *benshi*'s entire discourse as a *reading* of the diegesis which was thereby designated as such and
which thereby ceased to function as diegesis and became what it had in fact

22a

22b

22c   24

never ceased to be, *a field of signs.*" Speech was also positioned differently. "Speech was indeed explicitly absent, since it was *removed*, put to one side; the voice was there, but detached from the images themselves, images in which the actors were thereby all the more mute and were confined, moreover, in many instances, to remarkably static visual renderings of the scenes unfolding through the *voice.*" Because of the *benshi*, "the image was purged of speech" (Burch 1979, pp. 79, 78).

The other possible languages of silent film, music and sound effects, were kept so thoroughly "outside" of what was defined as the "text" (the image track and interspersed titles) that there was no felt need to control them in exhibition (they were merely indicated in "cue sheets" suggesting well-known musical numbers to accompany certain scenes and possible effects for specific actions). Consequently much of this "supplementary" material has been lost to history, in part because of lack of concern for its preservation. Film historians presenting *Battleship Potemkin* or *Metropolis* or *Napoleon* evidently feel no qualms at substituting a newly written score in place of the original. This lack of shame has extended as far as *sound* films; *Alexander*

Nevski (1938) has, for example, been exhibited with its carefully recorded music track excised and replaced by a live orchestra.[7] The assumption of music as ornamental, "outside" the text, thus becomes a self-fulfilling prophecy—the silent film text is reduced to the celluloid strip.

Without a preserved score or cue sheet, it is not possible to analyze the interaction of the score and the image in *Sadie Thompson*. Briefly though, silent film music tended to present a continuous wash of sound whose purpose was to guide the viewer emotionally, indicating the tone (suspenseful, humorous, romantic, etc.) of a scene. The constant auditory *presence*, especially in a silent film with a live orchestra, wraps the audience in a mood, and smooths over any gaps or interruptions in the visual text, the transition to titles or the abruptness of cuts. Noël Burch and Walter Kerr point out the difficulty of watching silent films silent, the unpredictable rhythms of the editing and the "weakness of the diegetic effect."[8] The emotional effect of the music is preserved in sound films as is the privileging of the image. The sound film, however, had to work out new methods for "containing" and subordinating voices and dialogue—for instance, the voice of a woman who doesn't know her place.

Although silent film representation is vastly different from either the theater or prose, the results are fundamentally the same when we consider Sadie's speech. As we have seen, over and above the narrative's restriction of women to dramas of sexual conflict resolved by a climactic marriage, the silent film's system of visual representation found analogous methods for limiting a female character's ability to speak as a subject.

In *Sadie Thompson,* the figure of the woman can be dynamic, forceful, and impressive. In the "tirade" outlined above, Sadie's "speech" exceeds the dialogue and is transferred to the image. In that scene, Sadie's fury seems to control even the filmic enunciation, with the camera and editing striving to "keep up." However, her power (synonymous with her rebellious point of view— her outspokenness) is literally contained by the men in the text. O'Hara stops her mouth when he considers she's had her say. Davidson converts her energy in denouncing the system that oppresses her into whole-hearted endorsement of her own repression. Sadie's relationship to her "voice" in the play is at every point restricted by the languages she is forced to adopt from the men around her, "freedom" being submission to the "right" language of egalitarian marriage. The cinematic system, which had seemed to conform itself to Sadie's point of view, also yields to O'Hara's hand. We *see,* when she is converted, that Sadie does not know what she is saying—that her expression of her own experience is confused. Rather than visually stating Sadie's expressed peace, the camera presents a wide-eyed, hypnotized "drab." In place of Sadie's absolute trust of Davidson, we are given Davidson's lustful vision, which Sadie does not see.

The cinematic system reveals the limits of the woman's understanding,

Lionel Barrymore and Gloria Swanson in *Sadie Thompson*

which leads to her propensity to be victimized. The film, like the play, positions O'Hara as the agent of the correct way of seeing *and* speaking. With O'Hara, we "see through" Davidson. He authorizes our view of Sadie as worthwhile. And he speaks the right language.

In *Sadie Thompson*, "woman's speech" remains subject to every system (narrative, language, image) that simultaneously constructs and contains her. The question to be asked next is whether the addition of sound—bringing with it its own prescriptions on how and when a woman should speak—will in any way challenge the obstacles placed between woman and her voice, woman and her vision, woman as speaker/author of her own experience.

"I was born hootched."

Constructing a Woman's Speech 3

Sound Film
Rain (1932)

As we have seen in previous chapters, cinematic representation does not come "ideology free." The visual representation of women in silent film—itself problematic in terms of spectacle and woman as object of the male gaze—is always joined to narrative that brings with it an extended pedigree of literary and dramatic assumptions about woman. Sound technology itself was also fully inscribed within patriarchal ideology, its very invention replete with prescriptions about a speaking woman's "place" typical of its day. As illustrated by Bordwell, Staiger, and Thompson (1985), it was classical sound cinema's goal to find equivalencies in sound to reenforce the ideals of visual cinema as soon as possible. That is why if we are to have any hope of finding a break in the hegemony of classical style (silent or sound), a time when a woman's voice could be her own, we must look closely at a limited period in American film history when the conventions of cinematic representation were for a time in crisis. (Outside of this period, works that constitute a radical break with classical style are restricted to the output of a few brave experimentalists.)

To continue the project begun in the last chapter, the major question to be addressed now is this: "Does the breakdown of established silent film conventions in the transitional period provide gaps in the representation of women that can be read progressively?" To put it another way, to what extent does the dialogization of these modes of representation make it possible to "hear" the voices of women at this historical moment? Does the very struggle to construct new hierarchies between image, dialogue, and sound track make possible, for a moment, the recognition of cinema's efforts simultaneously to represent and contain women and their voices as objects of representation in sound film?

In the transition to sound film, the classical cinematic hierarchy is upset. *Rain*, directed by Lewis Milestone and produced by Joseph M. Schenck for United Artists, shows the visual discourses of silent film fighting to regain their earlier dominant position, while the theatrical or dialogue-based discourse is simultaneously present and operating at full force. *Rain* offers us an opportunity to chart the efforts of the transitional period to negotiate a new classical, transparent form for sound film.

The work of the text is everywhere apparent in *Rain* in the play between insufficiency and excess. By varying from previously set norms defined by the conventions of silent film, the excessive quality of the camera work and the insufficiency of preparation in the editing (leading to jarring cuts, "unmotivated" camera moves, "odd" angles, etc.) stand out and declare their enunciative function. Conventions that had become naturalized in the earlier cinematic hierarchy are altered or abandoned.

In the transition to sound film, new conventions had to be established in full view of the audience. A possible cause for the cinematic institution's tolerance of such visible disarray can be seen in the industry's need to continue churning out product despite the fact that conventions for the construction of sound/image narratives had not yet been fixed. Seen in this light, *Rain*'s status as an adaptation of a play, a short story, and a remake of a silent film becomes not just a pedigree but a strategy. In order to maintain the necessary level of popular intelligibility, *Rain* and the many other remakes and adaptations of the era summon earlier forms to shore up their ability to signify and to stave off the fragmentation caused by attempts to incorporate sound.

Julia Kristeva argues that a "dynamic notion of reading as a relationship between reader and text . . . implies that no texts, 'mainstream' or otherwise, bear specific *a priori* meanings in and for themselves" (Kristeva 1980, p. 12). At its most fragmented, *Rain* illustrates a cinematic version of the centrifugal forces of "dialogized heteroglossia" (Bakhtin 1981, p. 273) where languages (here systems of signification) are flung away from a center, their differences emphasized as chances of mutual recognition and cooperation become more and more remote. Because of its very stylistic inconsistency, *Rain* is an ideal text to indicate the range of experimentation conducted before the classical style was recovered and reconstituted. The value of a text like *Rain* lies precisely in its struggle, its revelation of the historical determinations that influence the preference for a given signifying system over another in a given period, here made clear in the comparison of the silent and sound versions.

Because of the primacy of the struggle to form a new classical style that would "invisibly" incorporate sound, women in sound film could not be inserted directly back into the roles and styles of representation conventionalized in silent film. The examination of "woman and her voice" in cinema thus requires a combination of formal analysis of the use of sound and a feminist analysis of representation. My analysis of *Rain* will thus alternate shot-by-shot close textual analysis with summaries of scenes. The major part of the analysis corresponds to the first act of the play and four other scenes or sequences I find illuminating on the subject of woman and/or her voice. This is an admittedly arbitrary approach, and in its defense I can only cite Roland Barthes: "The text, in its mass, is comparable to a sky, at once flat and smooth, deep, without edges and without landmarks . . . The commentator traces through the text certain zones of reading, in order to observe therein the migration of meanings, the outcropping of codes, the passage of citations" (Barthes 1974, p. 14).[1]

Another methodological issue worth noting is the separation of the film text in terms of shots. The shot is a measurement applicable solely to the image track. It has been a point of sound editing to overlap the cut (see Doane's "Ideology and the Practice of Sound Editing and Mixing" in Weis and Belton 1985).[2] Music has also traditionally been used to smooth transitions between shots and scenes with sound effects acting as a binder of spatial and temporal continuity within a scene. As providing a seamless flow of sound has been one of the strongest principles of sound editors, using the shot as a marker disregards the true entry and exit point of sounds. Nevertheless, using shots as markers does allow a practical breaking point to which the ebb and flow of sounds can be referred, therefore it will be retained—with these reservations—in the shot-by-shot sections of the analysis.

Because 1932 is rather late for an "early" sound film, *Rain* also defines itself in relation to the earliest sound films. This is especially noticeable in mostly negative ways, primarily in an almost compulsive urge to move the camera in order to avoid presenting a great deal of dialogue from a static camera position. In terms of discussing the contribution of sound and the conveyance of narrative information during a long take, the beginning and the end of a shot become virtually useless as reference points. Sounds begin and end somewhere in the middle of a take, some takes in *Rain* lasting as long as six minutes. In those instances, we shall need to propose new sound and dialogue-based methods for analyzing the content of a shot, redefining a shot as an audio/visual unit.

The importance of the long take in the representation of women is one that I do not think has been addressed. In the long takes as used in *Rain* it initially seems not only possible but probable that women speaking synchronized dialogue while walking side by side with men in a continuous take are at last equal holders of cinematic space. Whether or not that turns out to be the case is one of the key questions this analysis will seek to answer.

Introductory Montage and the Opening Scene

The opening minutes of the film, made up of roughly three segments, introduce a competition among signifying systems culminating in the dramatic entrance of the figure of the woman, Sadie Thompson. In the opening montage, the silent film hierarchy appears to have been lifted whole from an earlier era. We see clouds moving overhead. A drop falls in a puddle and ripples form. Another drop falls in the sand on a beach with shells lying around. Drops splash on the diagonal lines formed by boards. The clouds continue to mass.

As the montage of rain falling on various surfaces proceeds, we hear the symphonic score from the titles. Except during the titles and credits, *Rain* uses all forms of music sparingly. During the "rain montage" there is no attempt at synchronous sound effects.

Throughout the course of the film these tropical montages (all strongly reminiscent of Flaherty's *Moana* [1926]) will reappear at specific points. What might be called the (silent-) cinematic discourse is consistently summoned to oppose the emergence of the theatrical discourse at *its* strongest. At the ends of acts 1 and 2, each clearly preserved, the camera pulls back, revealing the set as a set, the actors pronouncing famous lines, and an approximation of the proscenium appears at the top of the frame. Such obtrusive theatricality is immediately contradicted by the outdoorsiness of sunrises, natives hauling in nets, montage-style editing versus camera movement, asynchronous singing and symphonic music versus the careful sync and formalism of the acting in the preceding scene.

In the opening scenes, however, the silent-style montage leads effortlessly into a flawless example of what was to become the classical hierarchy of sound film. As a close-up of a rain barrel dissolves into a long shot of a rain-swept, muddy path, the sound of falling rain gradually rises on the sound track. The score fades away. After a moment we hear men singing. It is impossible at first to determine whether or not their voices are part of the physical space "offscreen" or non-diegetic. Aurally, the singing is a little lower than the volume of the rain, which helps place it "in" rather than "under" the scene as well as giving it a quality of distance in relation to the image. When a group of soldiers marches into the frame from behind the camera, the spatial depth added to the image by sound effects and offscreen voices is emphasized.

The soldiers sing about being tricked into the Marine Corps with promises of paradisiacal islands as we see them marching in the mud and rain. Unlike in silent films such as *The Big Parade* (1926) where title cards with musical notes drawn on them are intercut with close-ups of various soldiers "singing" as they march, the sound film doesn't have to construct the "effect" of singing. Instead, sound allows for continuous spatial and temporal progress while the ironic commentary is built in, the counterpoint between the two registers contained within one shot.

Tracking shots alternate close-ups of individual singers with shots of boots marching, intercut with long shots that replay the question of diegetic versus non-diegetic sound. Once more we see an unidentified gray exterior of rain-beaten palm trees, held a couple of beats before the men appear. As the marines enter the frame, the camera begins to track right, framing them through the horizontal slats of a fence. As they come to a halt at the end of the song, a sergeant gives an order. Two men step out of line and join him. They begin the dialogue. In a striking shot in depth, we see a large ship in the distance (the subject of their conversation) and hear its horn. The three marines reverse direction and the camera tracks left to follow them.

The aural balance of the sound track, between the song and the continuing rain, the fading of the rain as the dialogue begins, and the visual balance of having the characters "lead" the camera in order to diegetically motivate the camera movement all give the effect of a much later period and are in fact reminiscent of John Ford and Raoul Walsh service films of the late 1930s. The long take and moving shot exalt the image while allowing for uncut sound and a rather complicated sound mix. The human figures are placed in an audio and a visual continuum, the foregrounding of the action classically effacing the enunciation.

In another nice integration of silent and sound techniques, the marines announce they are going to fetch the local store-owner, Horn (Guy Kibbee) and take him to the ship we see in the distance. With the mention of Horn, we cut to a sign identifying Horn's "General Store." The camera smoothly tilts down from the sign to reveal the veranda of a tropical inn and, in an effect of depth, a child running out of the store toward the camera. The child falls and cries, and a large woman in tropical dress lumbers after it, scolding. She bends over to pick up the boy and falls herself. The marines, bringing with them their characteristic camera movement, lift the child up and hoist Ameena (Mary Shaw) onto a chair. Ameena and Sergeant O'Hara (William Gargan) in a medium long shot joke about her husband Horn. The other marines carry Horn out as the camera dollies back to accommodate them. Throughout the scene, camera movement and stasis alternate fluidly while the dialogue unselfconsciously establishes character and short-term narrative goals that link the island's inhabitants with the ship.

However, this classical sound style effortlessly sets up a cruel joke on the text's "other" woman. A large woman with long black hair and a prominent mole on her cheek, Ameena's appearance contradicts Hollywood and European standards of glamour. As a half-asleep Horn is carted onto the veranda, he drunkenly asks where he is. In an extreme close-up, Ameena turns to face the camera and answers, "Home." The "joke" rests on our deducing that his wife's appearance is the direct cause of Horn's drunken lethargy: "If that was *my* wife. . . ." As an insert in the midst of fluid tracking and long shots, the close-up stands out, bearing the unspoken weight of several kinds of prejudice. Exhibited for our derision as a South Sea islander, but more particularly as a woman, Ameena is nailed on looks. The flawless integration of sound and image shows how woman can be positioned as the center of a scene while ruthlessly excluded as its subject. (When the film was edited to seventy seven minutes, presumably in order to fit a double bill, the character of Ameena was cut almost entirely.) This pattern of woman as disruption will be repeated for the next two women we meet and will find its most elaborate expression in the introduction of Sadie.

What is perhaps most striking about *Rain* as a text is that once it has achieved what will become the "correct" balance between image, camera movement, and the layers of the sound track, it promptly abandons this hierarchy and continues to experiment with different possible hierarchies between sound, dialogue, and image. It is the lack of any sense of progress from scene to scene that lends *Rain* its archaic quality, exposing its bricolage of old and new conventions.

The hybrid nature of the earliest attempts to join sound and image is most readily apparent in the partial talkies of the late twenties, especially in films with silent dramatic scenes and interjected musical numbers. However the continuing hybrid nature of later transitional films is less well noted. Bakhtin defines the function of hybridization in the novel as "a mixture of two social languages within the limits of a single utterance, an encounter, within the arena of an utterance, between two different linguistic consciousnesses, separated from one another by an epoch, by social differentiation or by some other factor." Although Bakhtin feels that it must be conscious and intentionally done in order to be artistically significant in the novel, he adds that even "unintentional, unconscious hybridization is one of the most important modes in the historical life and evolution of all languages. We may even say that language and languages change historically primarily by means of hybridization" (Bakhtin 1981, p. 358).

Both of the director Lewis Milestone's earlier, and notably successful, sound films were equally hybrid in construction. *All Quiet on the Western Front* (1930), which was seen as an early model for reclaiming the "cinematic" from the staginess of other films of the period, did so through the use of silently filmed and edited scenes with non-synchronous sound tracks applied over them. *The Front Page* (1931) forfeited the location montage of the earlier film in favor of a constantly moving camera and the rapid-fire dialogue and dramatic construction of the theatrical adaptation. However, both of these films exhibit *internally* consistent rules, something remarkably absent in *Rain*. By 1932 the half-measures of the earlier films were being rejected in favor of a search for a stable hierarchy of the relation of image to dialogue to sound that could be employed in all scenes with the transparency of enunciation typical of silent narratives.

Rain's sudden breakdown of any consistently employed system of signification cannot be attributed to simple incompetence on the part of the director (as he managed the "correct" construction in one scene and would again in later ones) or to difficulties with the primitive technology. By this time many sound films with more "advanced" and consistently employed conventions for binding sound and image had already appeared—for example, *Blackmail* (1929), *Applause* (1929), *M* (1930), and *The Blue Angel* (1930). The "proper" hierarchy of the marching scene and others proves that Milestone (using the director's name as shorthand for the industrial, technological, and cultural struggles rampant in all films of the period) knew *how* to organize the various registers of sound film. What the unpredictable and unconventionalized experimentation in other scenes suggests is that this particular hierarchy was not yet privileged. Bordwell, Staiger, and Thompson describe the philosophy that determined the eventual canonization of a certain hierarchy of registers in what they term the "image-sound analogy," where "the recording of speech is modeled upon the way cinematography records visible material and the treatment of music and sound effects is modeled upon the editing and laboratory work applied to the visual track" (1985, p. 301). *Rain* shows the range of possibilities still being juggled in 1932.

The Ship

After the marines march away with Horn, there is a cut to the interior of a cruise ship. On several visual planes, we see passengers dressed in 1920s clothes standing in line and we hear tinny music, "crowd noises" made up of murmuring voices and laughter, and pursers calling, "Have your passports ready, please." We cut to a close-up of a handbag as a woman's hands search through it and take out a passport. She extends the passport (with the word *Passport* written on it) directly toward the camera. A man's hand enters from the lower portion of the frame and takes it. The camera tilts down as if in a point-of-view shot and reads the name on the card as the man points with a pencil "Mrs. . . . Robert . . . Macphail." On the sound track we hear a woman's voice: "Let me see. You want my passport, don't you?" As the customs agent points to her name, the woman's voice continues: "My husband and I usually use the same passport. We have separate ones this time, in case I should wish to visit the other islands while he's working."

The use of voice-over combined with a close-up of a card with the character's name on it is a hybrid of filmic conventions from two different periods combined in a single shot. In the silent film *Sadie Thompson*, the characters are introduced in a strikingly similar manner. A sailor approaches Dr. Macphail and Mr. and Mrs. Davidson and requests that they sign his "travel diary." Each writes something "characteristic," which we read (Davidson about evil, Macphail about tolerance) and signs his or her name. In this way, their personalities are directly linked to their names while avoiding the use of an overt and disruptive title card. In *Rain*, it is the voice that is first linked to the name through sound film's ability to let us hear the character speak while showing us something else.

At the end of the passport shot there is a dramatic swish pan to the right. In a medium shot we see a young woman standing across a table from a customs agent. The use of the swish pan as a transition is one of the oddest choices made in the film and illustrates a breakdown within the image system due to an overreliance on the sound track. The continuity of voice (from the woman speaking about joint passports to this woman's speech about the rain) does not sufficiently establish that the figure we see is the same woman who stood directly in front of the camera in the previous shot. Not knowing to what extent sound could be depended upon to convey a sense of spatial continuity to the audience, the image system neglects some of its earlier rules for creating a coherent space in favor of confusing experimentation.

A swish pan (also known as a zip pan or a flash pan) automatically implies directionality. The image within the pan is blurred, but the streaks move in a specific direction. The camera's tilt in the earlier shot indicated that we were facing Mrs. Macphail, and that it needed only to tilt back up to locate the speaker, consequently the sudden pan to the right to a woman standing silent disorients us. If it is the same woman, she has suddenly moved several feet in space with no visual or audio indication of it (such as her hands moving out of the shot or a voice saying, "Step to your right, please.") The change in screen position of the customs agent is similarly puzzling. His hands were directly in front of the camera, as in a classical point-of-view shot, and now we pan right and find him in effect sitting next to himself. The dissection of character into name (conveyed by graphics), voice-type (male/female, mellifluous/grating, intelligent/foolish), and image (hands/body) contributes to the incoherence of character identification.

Throughout *Rain,* examples of similarly confusing constructions will be traceable to this play between insufficiency and excess. In the original establishing shot of the interior of the ship, close examination of the crowded shot shows *two* customs agents sitting side by side. Mrs. Macphail, chatting away, has in fact moved from her original position in front of the first agent (and the camera) to the position we discover her in, standing before the second man. Her movement, like the second customs agent's receiving the passport, occurs offscreen. The second time we see this shot sequence (for the introduction of Mrs. Davidson), the first customs agent clearly hands the passport offscreen to someone on his right.

Although the image seems to depend on the sound track for connecting the passport shot to the shot following the swish pan, it refuses to let dialogue carry simple narrative information such as the name of the characters. It would be simpler and quicker to have the woman look into the camera as she hands over her passport and say, "I'm Mrs. Macphail." However the visual construction of graphics, pan, *then* image—at the same time more insistent and more confusing—maintains the precedence of the image and of silent film conventions for character identification, while sound is relegated to background filigree or to a function it cannot easily perform (connecting characters in space regardless of the work of the image). This formula for introducing characters, though time-consuming and cumbersome, will be followed for Mrs. Macphail, Mrs. Davidson, Dr. Macphail, and Mr. Davidson, with little elision.

David Wills suggests that "excess, finally, is always about the means or economy by which the Same accommodates, appropriates, or represses the Other; by which difference is and isn't," (1986, p. 35) and this construction not only points to the conflict between image-systems and sound but, fittingly, to the representation of the women. The smoothly flowing opening scenes on the island are interrupted by the fragmented, chaotic world onboard the ship, a disorganized, disconnected place to which we are incoherently introduced by two women.

Despite the fact that she is the first character introduced, Mrs. Macphail doesn't *have* any character. She mindlessly parrots the other characters' prejudices. Her dialogue can be accurately described as foolish prattle; even the nearly unidentified character of the customs agent is allowed in effect to have the last word in their exchange. She gazes into the distance and muses, "I wonder why it should rain. Doesn't it ever stop?" The officer responds "Yes, ma'am?" as if he purposely hasn't been listening. Insulted and confused, Mrs. Macphail takes her passport and turns away.

In her series of introductory shots, Mrs. Davidson (Beulah Bondi) is effectively introduced as a rude, inconsiderate woman, as well as an inefficient one who criticizes others for what the image reveals are her own failings. When we see the second woman's hands (Mrs. Davidson's), we see the customs man's hand reach in and wait for the passport. A woman's high voice states, "A little more efficiency and we wouldn't be kept waiting so long," as she fiddles with her purse. Here the film does take advantage of the asynchronization of shot and sound track, ironically contradicting her words with the cultural stereotype about women and their messy purses.

Mrs. Davidson also allows the text to make use of stereotypes associated with women's voices. Before we see her, her shrill and monotonous voice is defining her as unattractive and prudish. Mrs. Davidson's voice type was established in Maugham's original story. "The most remarkable thing about her was her voice, high metallic, and without inflection; it fell on the ear with a hard monotony, irritating to the nerves like the pitiless clamour of the pneumatic drill" (Maugham 1967, pp. 413–14). When we see her, it is not surprising to find her a middle-aged woman wearing a floppy, shapeless hat and glasses. She stands adjusting her hair as the agent waits, holding her passport out to her. She makes no move to take it, saying officiously, "Thank you, just put it down, please."

In contrast, the introduction of Dr. Macphail is neat and quick. We begin immediately with the name-bearing card in the agent's hand, pointing to the name "Dr. Macphail." Macphail addresses the men by their proper titles

("By the way, officer . . .") and they exchange "witty" repartee about the islands (as opposed to the curt dismissal of Mrs. Macphail), establishing the men as equals. The issue of pronunciation is also introduced, in its own way calling attention to the possible contradiction between image and sound track. "Pago Pago" which we see written on the passport cards is pronounced "Ponga Ponga." In story, theater, or silent film, this apparent discrepancy would not be an issue. Here it is demonstrated and unexplained.

When Davidson is introduced, there is no small talk. The card reads "Mr. Alfred Davidson." After the swish pan, the officer says, "Welcome to Pago Pago, Mr. Davidson," the first exchange that allows a character to be identified aurally as well as graphically. Davidson's voice is culturally identified as being typical of a minister, while the "Mr." on his passport and in the dialogue insists on his unaffiliated status. Nevertheless, his voice, posture, bow tie, and careful enunciation define him as a preacher. (Maugham also mentions Davidson's "deep, ringing voice" [1967, p. 422].) Shortly afterward, when he informs the others that a quarantine will keep them on the island, Walter Huston's enunciation of the line, "It may mean a delay of several days," complete with the rhyme of "may," "delay" and "days," and the elongation of "sev-er-al" calls attention to Davidson's oratorical expertise and is the sort of elocution-ary bravura that identifies a nineteenth-century public speaker.

After Davidson is introduced, the text undergoes a crisis in point of view. In the background, framed by Davidson and the customs agent, a man dressed in white ascends a dark, curving staircase spanned by an arch. As he reaches the top, we can just see his legs turn left as he exits the frame and his partial reflection comes into view in a mirror on the right of the stairs. This begins a series of looks that will float around a confused, insufficiently established space.

Mrs. Davidson (who has mounted the stairs during Macphail's introduc-tion) turns and looks down. Mr. Davidson says, "Thank you" and goes to the stairs. As Mrs. Davidson begins down the stairs, walking toward the right of the frame, the camera pans with her. However, as the camera pans horizon-tally, Mrs. Davidson moves progressively downward and disappears from the bottom of the frame. The pan continues without a subject until it rests on the mirrored wall *behind* the back of Mrs. Davidson's head. Mr. Davidson's re-flection enters this odd two-shot from the right. Dr. Macphail in a low angle shot approaches a railing and looks down to the left. Already, his position in space is impossible to fix. According to the layout of the ship, as will even-tually become clear, Macphail is on the right at the top of the stairs, despite the fact that we saw him turn to the left earlier. If he is on the right, though, his gaze is not at the mirrored shot presented to the audience but at the physi-cal figures of Mr. and Mrs. Davidson, which remain unrepresented—we never see them occupy the space Macphail is seeing. As Davidson reaches the top of the stairs to announce their quarantine on the island, there is a reaction shot of Macphail standing on the left of the stairs, looking at Davidson screen right. This shot would require an offscreen shift in position as insufficiently indicated as that of Mrs. Macphail during the passport scene.

When all of the characters are standing at the top of the stairs in a small waiting room, the text recreates one of the static long takes for which early sound cinema was rightly or wrongly notorious. This shot's tribute to sound lies in its conceding major narrative information for the first time to the verbal discourse. As the camera looks on from a distance, the characters stand around, their bodies artificially posed facing the camera. Davidson, the principal speaker, stands with his back to the camera so that even the visual pleasure of reading lips (so salient in silent film close-ups) is lost, leaving only the recognition of his voice to tell us "who is speaking." Even this shot, however, leads to a breakdown in visual point of view. We see a shot of men marching past an open window. Davidson, his back turned to the camera, says, "There's Mr. Horn now." There is a repeat of the previous shot (a literal demonstration of déjà vu) and this time we see Horn pass. Contradicting the silent film convention of having a look key a cut to a subjective point-of-view shot, here Davidson's look is completely unrepresented visually because his back is turned. It is only the dialogue that tells us he has seen something and retroactively authorizes the first shot through the window. At the end of the scene, Davidson leaves the group and Macphail turns to watch him go. The cut to a close-up of Macphail is a mistake In cutting continuity, jumping stage line 180 degrees, from Macphail's back to his face, in order to accommodate his look.

The reason the text doesn't completely fall apart is to a great extent because the sound functions as a backup system, binding together this highly problematic series of cuts. Despite visual fragmentation, the dialogue flows, exchanged by characters as if they were in a coherent space, maintaining a minimum of intelligibility at the narrative level. The continuation of the same sound effects at a stable volume among these shots connects them in space and time even if it cannot specify where the characters are in relation to each other or maintain consistency in their relation to the camera.

The above breakdown of rules governing the image alerts us to an uncertainty about how sound functions in relation to the image. The consistency of sound effects from shot to shot within a scene is followed throughout *Rain* even though, as the scene above shows, it is not sufficient to make up for visual incoherence. The sound track's "coherence of causality, space, and time" (Bordwell, Staiger, and Thompson 1985, p. 304) seemed to offer the filmmakers at this moment in history the chance to free the image system from its obedience to those same principles. Milestone et al. did not "forget" classical rules of construction; they merely abandoned them, feeling—wrongly— that other methods, specifically sound track construction, would serve as well. We see in this the indication of a potential and radical break with classical paradigms, provoked and made possible by sound.

The text immediately compensates for the confused editing of these scenes by restoring the absolute coincidence of sound and image in another uncut traveling shot of Horn and the marines as they stroll along the outside deck discussing Davidson. Such bravura tracking movements provide the reassurance of unqualified spatial and temporal continuity both aurally and visually. The result is a form of realism more technical than dramatic, synchronization displayed as an end in itself. Compared with the preceding scene, the camera's movement stands as a signifier of the "cinematic" (versus the theatrical or early sound film style). It also reenforces the presentation of the marines as a liberating force.

The dialogue between Horn and Sergeant O'Hara establishes Davidson as *not* a missionary while speaking strictly in terms that refer to missionaries: "They'll break your back to save your soul." Instead, Davidson becomes a "professional reformer" with the presumably civilian/political post of "investigator of navy conditions." The political is excised with the next line—"He wields more influence in the South Seas than the sun, the planets, and the American government"—leaving Davidson as an independent operator rather than the representative of either church or party.

As the camera dollies back to keep the group at a constant distance, the sound of music and voices below deck, so prominent early in the scene/shot, is left behind. The "tinny" ragtime, which had been loudest in the first establishing shot of the ship's interior, then quieter at the top of the stairs and barely heard on the walkway, provides an aural transition that maintains the spatial relationship of each setting to the previous one. As the marines march on, they again supply a diegetic source of music, singing, "The worst is yet to come, the worst is yet to come." A muted horn mockingly underscores them as jazz intrudes on the sound track and threatens to drown them out. The camera stops in its tracks as a body comes flying out of a doorway and lands at the feet of the marines.

The conflicting musical discourses are a powerful auditory introduction to a new force within the narrative. The jazz theme's relationship to the image is once more difficult to determine. The competition in volume between the singing (initially louder) and the jazz (ultimately louder) suggests it is diegetic, however "movie music" could serve the same function just as easily. After all, the marines never register any awareness of it—it is the dramatic entrance of Bates, the ship's quartermaster, that gets their attention. In this scene the source of the music is insufficiently delineated and it is only the period's and the rest of the film's hesitance to use non-diegetic music that mitigates the assumption that this is standard or classical background music.

Historically, *Rain* occupies a position halfway between the earliest sound films' painstaking accounting for any sound on the track and classical sound film's use of the wash of the non-diegetic score. The indeterminacy of the music on the sound track (the low volume of the ragtime, the half-hearted visual presentation of possible sources) is part of the transitional phase. A cause is supplied for nearly all of the music in the text, but it is not stressed. When Macphail looks down from the top of the stairs at the Davidsons, there is a loudspeaker in the corner of the frame that could be playing the music on the ship. After we meet Sadie and enter her cabin, we see a phonograph that may or may not have been playing the jazz we heard.

The introduction of Sadie demonstrates what will become the classical way to create and maintain a space by tying together a montage of looks with over-lapping dialogue, voice-over, and background music—a style, as we shall see, with particular implications for the representation of women. A shot-by-shot description will show the close coordination of the various parts working together rather than at odds. As Bates's exaggerated motto about the British lion (spoken with a pronounced British accent) continues, an enigma is estab-lished regarding what it is everyone sees that (a) has the power to excite them all, (b) has the strength to throw Bates out on *his* tail, (c) presents such a threat to imperial masculine power (a castrating woman?), and (d) is related to that music.

Shot 1:   Bates pushes his hat back. "Now look here. You may take the British lion by the tail—"

Shot 2:   O'Hara smiles (at Bates) then suddenly turns his head to the right. Bates in voice over: "—you may twist it—"

Shot 3:   Second marine quickly looks right. Bates: "—you may jerk it—"

Shot 4:   Horn grins and slyly looks to the side and mouths "Oh!" Bates: "—you may yank it—"

Shot 5:   Third marine looking right smiles and looks appraisingly up and down. Bates: "—you may tie it in a—"

Shot 6:   A heavily jewelled hand reaches into the frame and grips the side of the doorway. Bates: "—big bow knot—"

Shot 7:   Another jewelled hand, the left one, reaches out to the other side of the door. Bates: "But dash it all—"

Shot 8:   A foot wearing mesh stockings and a shoe with a big bow on it steps into the frame and touches the floor. Bates: "—you can't—"

Shot 9:   The other foot steps into the shot and steps down beside the first. As the music plays, the woman turns her ankle on the beat, giv-ing the impression of dancing. Bates: "—pull it out by the roots! I say!"

Sadie's entrance is in terms of metonymy in the image and on the sound track. Her jewelled hands and stockings all stand in for the prostitute as "fancy woman," "vulgar" and excessive. The montage in itself is an excess,

"Now look here. You may take the British lion by the tail . . ."

". . . you may twist it . . ."

". . . you may jerk it . . ."

". . . you may yank it . . ."

". . . you may tie it in a . . ."

". . . big bow knot . . ."

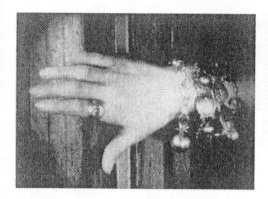

"But dash it all . . ."

". . . you can't . . ."

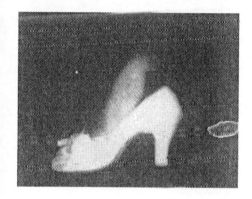

". . . pull it out by the roots! I say!"

fragmenting the woman's body, taking her apart in a way that correlates to the looks of the men in the previous montage. The major project of the film will be the task of reconstituting Sadie as a "whole" woman, something that can, according to the values of the narrative, only be achieved through marriage. Sadie needs to be turned from spectacle into subject, but a subject who is ultimately positioned firmly within patriarchal terms. The question of the woman's body is at the heart of the text: the conflict between Sadie and Davidson, which reaches its climax offstage and offscreen and reduces (or epitomizes) their conflict as a sexual one. Sadie, as a representative of opposition to the dominant order, is most disruptive not as a member of an exploited subclass but as a woman.

Although the narrative resolves the "problem" of the sexual woman through the recuperation of Sadie into marriage, the condition of the text itself allows it to be interrogated from a feminist perspective. Sadie's oppositional stance in dialogue, voice, posture, dress, and so on, infiltrates the codes of editing, helping the spectator read them for what they are, and revealing the fragmentation of the woman in response to the male gaze. Annette Kuhn,

summarizing theories of a "feminine text" (those of Kristeva and Hélène Cixous in particular), locates exactly this sort of decentered spectator position as central to a potential feminist/feminine art.

> The feminine text would disrupt, challenge, question and put its reader-subjects into process. In providing a challenge to situations in which the process of signification is not foregrounded, as is the case—it is argued—in dominant texts, in masculine discourse, the feminine would be subversive of such discourse, would constitute a disturbance to dominant modes of representation and thus to the dominant cultural order.
>
> (Kuhn 1982, p. 13)

As a partially open text—that is to say, one that is for many reasons unable to provide the transparent signification of the traditional classical text—*Rain* enables the reader/viewer to take a more consciously active position toward constructing meaning and repositions the spectator/auditor as a producer instead of a consumer. Its processes of signification are revealed through excess and through insufficiently instituting the new conventions of the emerging classical sound film.

Shot 10:   The climax of the "Sadie montage" is an empty frame. After a pause, Sadie *leans* into the frame. She wears a feathered hat, a huge necklace and smokes a cigarette. Bates offscreen: "—can't you take a joke?" We hear the men laughing. Sadie does not smile. The music again reaches the "wah wah" muted trumpet phrase as Sadie's face remains immobile, low in the frame. Bates: "Hello, lads!"

As Wills points out in connection with Godard's *Prenom: Carmen*, "The figure of the woman is obliged to bear the internal contradictions of a system in crisis" (1986, p. 33). In the first shot of Sadie, she has no voice and is defined in relation to the hierarchy of silent cinema—the image and music.

She is her image, defiantly made up of parts, and "her" music. Each gives her some control while always placing her in a negotiated position in relation to the hostility of language. She can turn the music on or off (late in the film this will be a point of conflict with O'Hara) just as she chooses her extravagant costume. At the same time, the music that substitutes for her voice serves as commentary on the text, typing her. We do not yet know whether Sadie is playing her gramophone, leaving the music to be read as the text's, a point of view distanced from Sadie's. And although Sadie might choose her clothes, she has no control over the montage that fractures her image. She is fetishized by the fragmenting visuals and the music, which distills her "essence" into a blues number.

The relation of woman and montage has been well examined by feminists (Kuhn, Mulvey, Johnston, Bergstrom et al.), but the relationship of the woman to music is equally complex. "Sadie's music" is fetishized and as such can stand in for her. Wills addresses this audio/visual interaction, arguing that through music "the economy of representation is both articulated and disrupted": music "provides a difference against which the visual can define itself while at the same time participating with the visual in the same field of possible representations" (ibid., p. 42). I would argue that music and image are not in the "same field," however, as we see here in *Rain*. The music *can* be harnessed to serve the same narrative and cultural function within the text that the image does. Nevertheless the woman's relation to the music is quickly problematized as Sadie moves to assert her will through control of the apparatus. Even in this first scene, there is an excess in the music, a quality that exceeds the narrative and the image and that cannot simply be read as approval or deprecation. The jazz number has connotations of sex and heat ("low-down" and "dirty") and carries jazz's affiliation with a black culture here stereotyped as being closer to "animal instincts" than the repressed middle-class Protestant culture represented by Davidson and the Macphails. Acoustically, the most recognizable motif in the instrumental number is a muted trumpet announcing itself with a "wah wah wahhh."

The energy and also the volume of the music give it a rush that's invigorating after the downbeat symphonic opening music or the inconsequential tune played under the passport scene. This is not to put forward an audio essentialism (sound as automatically "more" than the image in some kind of transcendent way); what I am trying to avoid is the assumption of an image/sound analogy or of sound as always an image-function substitute (see Bordwell, Staiger, and Thompson 1985, pp. 301–4, and Metz 1985, pp. 154–61). Even when fitted into the pattern of image-system functions from silent film, sound (music, voice, effects) exceeds its function and model.

Bates addresses the marines, saying, "Boys, I want you to meet Thompson. Sadie, meet the boys!" We cut to a medium long shot of Sadie from head to waist as she leans against the doorjamb, her left arm extended out to the other side. She smiles ruefully and gives a small salute: "Boys."

Crawford's voice is very low on her first line, approximating the husky or hoarse quality Maugham describes, and at odds with the high "feminine" voices of Mrs. Macphail and Mrs. Davidson. Such a low voice contrasted with the exaggerated femininity of appearance (jewels, hat, heels) suggests androgyny. As Richard Dyer hypothesizes in *Stars*, the star's persona works to reconcile various cultural contradictions.[3] These are worked out both in the narrative and in the space between image and voice. Many female stars of the 1930s are fetishized for their low voices, a trait combined with a tendency to portray characters with masculine as well as feminine traits (and clothes). Dietrich (especially when singing), Crawford later in the decade, Garbo (*Anna Christie, Queen Christina*), Lauren Bacall in *To Have and Have Not*— all sported glamorous, ambiguous images and low voices noted by critics and fans.

While low voices were particularly apt for fetishizing, and thus controlling, the always potentially disruptive representation of women, high-pitched "feminine" voices were frequently caricatured as suitable for comic parts (Betty Boop, squeaky "baby doll" voices) or, as with Mrs. Davidson, for puritanical "battle-axes." Certain technological innovations during the 1930s were seen as improving the recording of women's voices, which had been considered "problematic" and even inadequate for the recording apparatus. Crawford's voice is not only low, but it also is the sort of "faceless" voice, lacking distinguishing characteristics such as an accent, that was favored by Hollywood at this time (Marie 1980, esp. p. 221 n.3).

Later, when the Davidsons and the Macphails are gathered in the main room of the inn, we are again made aware of the connection between Sadie and music. Sadie has already had a set-to with Mrs. Davidson over some wild dancing on the Sabbath, presented in a dizzying 360-degree pan. As Davidson sets forth a "program of recreation" for their forced stay on the island, we hear "The Wabash Blues" start up in a room offscreen. Mrs. Davidson explains that Sadie is a common woman who was also on the ship and will be staying at the inn with them. As the music plays loudly, Davidson shows signs of distraction.

Thematically, the music acts as a signifier of Sadie's sexuality and is her power to disrupt. Her sexuality *is* the disruption of the patriarchal authority established to contain it. The music broadcasts to everyone within hearing that she is available and not contained. Unlike her voice, which fades in and out depending on whether the men in the room are talking, the music has a constant presence, floating through all the conversations and beyond the confines of its immediate geographic setting. Davidson is so keenly aware of her presence, through the music, that he can't concentrate. Here Sadie begins to assert control of the music on the film's sound track. Whether or not she can play it becomes the original conflict between her and Davidson, and upon being freed from his control, she returns to the music, brazen and loud. Only when she is

Woman and sound technology in silent film (*Sadie Thompson*)

about to accept the marriage proposal from O'Hara does she agree to turn it off.

As it does in both the play and the short story, Davidson's fight with the marines in Sadie's room takes place "offstage." As such, it marks a return to theatrical discourse. Sitting with his wife and the Macphails, Davidson suddenly proclaims, "She's out of Iwelei!" (pronounced "evil lay," the text's code word for the red-light district of Honolulu) and storms "off" into Sadie's room. We hear the scuffle between Davidson and the marines and hear the needle being dragged off the record. The music stops and Davidson is thrown out back into the image/set.

Humiliated after the scuffle, Davidson exits by walking slowly up the long flight of stairs against the back wall. Mrs. Macphail asks Mrs. Davidson what Mr. Davidson is going to do. Mrs. Davidson, standing on the stairs, announces portentously, "I don't know what he'll do. But I wouldn't be in that girl's shoes for anything in the world." The camera pulls back to reveal the entire set. The *Ordoona*'s horn sounds in the distance.

While the ship's horn reminds us of the film's access to real locations in its offscreen space, the image at the same time closes us off from that fundamentally cinematic space. The shot of the set reveals the painful spatial limitations of the theatrical while adhering to them. Most of the offscreen space indicated in the rest of the film by sound effects (fog horns, the sound of rain) works to close the characters in—a narrative excuse to keep them within these spatial limits. Offscreen sound merely recreates its role as offstage sound in scenes such as these.

Both the sound, the backward movement of the camera, and the last line of dialogue (as well as the way it is spoken) distinctively mark this as a closing point, and it is in fact the end of act 1. Such open acknowledgment of a film's theatrical genesis was sure to draw the ire of those who felt the resurrection of the theatrical was detrimental to the preservation of the cinematic. And the use of sound here (the dialogue, delivery, and symbolic sound—the *Ordoona* is leaving and the characters have no choice but to remain there together) is directly traceable to theatrical use of sound and directions for sound effects in the text of the play. Burch argues that

> these theatrical beginnings are, in fact, the instrumentality of the camera *stripped bare*. Its essential transformational powers (its production of meaning) are thereby *acknowledged*, since even filming the theatre stage as such (i.e. filming the entire proscenium) destroys the representational effect, *causes the image to appear as that of a stage.*
>
> (Burch 1979, p. 75; italics in original)

In other words, he sees no betrayal of the cinematic in this exposure of the theatrical, and certainly in this shot and a similar one at the end of act 2 the text comes very close to revealing the proscenium arch at the top of the frame.[4]

It should also be noted that although the exposure of the theatrical weakens the transparency of the narrative (its diegetic hold or "representational effect"), what might be called the "archaeological effect" grows stronger. We become aware of the age of the film, the archaicism of the acting, the play's "well-made" structure, the hesitant and confused conventions of films of this period. One feels a frisson of loss in the presence of a fragile replica of a moment locked in the past.

Following the first act, three additional scenes develop the visual and acoustic representation of Sadie. Scattered throughout the rest of the film are intriguing shots and parts of scenes that in their "oddness" contribute to the film's idiosyncratic feel: Macphail's oddly singsong delivery of his argument in favor of empiricism and tolerance; a "behind the cans" shot as Sadie reaches for some tamales; Horn rapturously quoting Nietzsche to Ameena; and a sight-gag close-up of a corkscrew, followed by a leering Horn, which is, one hopes, incomprehensible. The scenes I wish to examine in depth include a six-minute tracking shot of O'Hara and Sadie, Sadie's conversion, and the film's climax. It is in these scenes that the woman's voice is revealed *as an issue*, a problem to be contained by the narrative and by the transitional text.

The Veranda Scene

The six-minute tracking shot with Sadie and O'Hara offers an alternative to the camera moves, cuts, and dialogue of the opening scenes, and another possible answer to the question of how to make a sound film. While the shot is certainly a "significant instance of virtuosity," it also exemplifies what Bordwell et al. label "the excesses of early 1930s camera mobility."[5] Taking account also of the complaints of the actors, who criticized Milestone for making them do take after take of these difficultly staged scenes, it is not hard to see why this alternative did not become the norm.

However, the shot seems at first an undeniably egalitarian way of representing Sadie and O'Hara's relationship. The scene with O'Hara and Sadie on the porch employs a moving camera to define the couple and to illustrate their unity. For six minutes without a cut, the camera tracks and dollies and pans to maintain a two-shot of O'Hara and Sadie walking around the veranda of the inn, discussing her future. The dialogue is taken from the play and not significantly changed; it illustrates pursuit without pressure, an offering of common ground. The use of slang and O'Hara's reluctance to directly recommend a course of action as he tries to elicit Sadie's preference both work to gain her trust and consent.

Verbally, O'Hara repeatedly puts himself in Sadie's position, while never overtly telling her what to do. "Looka here! If something should go wrong— that is, about your getting to Apia—what'll you do?" He introduces a series of possibilities in case Davidson causes trouble, always carefully leaving the choice up to her. "Go back to the States, I suppose? . . . You don't want to go to Honolulu either, I suppose?" Eventually he suggests Australia and the set piece of their conversation (and of their courtship and alliance) is the story of Lefty (Biff in the play) and Maggie. This story serves several functions. It preordains the outcome of O'Hara's and Sadie's relationship by relating it through analogy with Lefty and Maggie as if it had already happened. It answers any questions before they can arise and contains the "problem" of her background (O'Hara's stressing of the equivalence of male promiscuity and female prostitution as mutually forgivable failings). It is also the speech whereby he reconciles Sadie to marriage and to men. She says afterward, "I thought I knew most all there was to know about men, until you came along" (Colton and Randolph 1936, p. 141).

O'Hara tells her that there's an "old shipmate of mine has his own place and wants a partner—These three years Lefty's been at me to get my discharge and come in with him. You'd like Lefty. We joined the service same time, sixteen years ago." Sadie says that if she were to meet Lefty and Maggie, Maggie wouldn't approve. He retorts,

> I've an idea what's on your mind, Sadie. But Maggie's not the kind of female you're meaning. She's square from the toes up. Funny thing, how it is those that kick highest seem to settle down hardest. . . . You see, Lefty had been a kind of a hell-raiser. . . . I guess no woman who hadn't been on the rocks herself would have risked Lefty. It isn't likely a guy who didn't know the mill would have risked Maggie, either. Both knew the real thing when they saw it go. And they've never been sorry.

He makes it explicit that Maggie was a prostitute—"It never mattered to either of 'em that they met in Iweili." This cements the identification between Sadie and Maggie and creates the symmetry between the couples that ensures that Lefty and Maggie's "happily ever after" ending will be O'Hara's and Sadie's.

In the silent film *Sadie Thompson*, the equivalent scene is made up entirely of static shots and editing, mostly shot/reverse shot. Sadie and O'Hara sit on a settee in the middle of Horn's inn and chat. The rain, which is omnipresent on the sound track in the sound film's version, is not in any way a factor in the silent version of the scene. The dialogue, which again comes from the play, is drastically reduced.

Here, however, regardless of the dialogue, the camera has already linked Sadie and O'Hara in space and time. They never separate, going everywhere side by side and without a break. Sadie stops, worried about Davidson, and leans against a wall. The camera stops as O'Hara turns to face her. She gets up and begins pacing as the camera dollies back to keep them in a medium shot. For "romantic" dialogue (when O'Hara asks her if perhaps she's going to see someone special at her destination), the camera moves in and reframes them in a closer two-shot, but neither is ever separated for a single close-up. By waiting for the actors to begin or stop, even such extravagant camera movement seems internally motivated.

There are technological, formal, and economic, as well as ideological, reasons for presenting Sadie and O'Hara's courtship in a single long take. In a transitional text—or really in any film—it is necessary to address all of these before we can understand the implications for the speaking woman at their core.

Throughout transitional sound films we find a pressingly felt need to differentiate the new sound film product from silent films. In the many remakes of popular silent films, the underlying (and even overtly expressed) assumption was that the sound film would be "better" because of sound, that sound film could do things silent film could not, and that this would lead to a more effective emotional narrative experience. From a marketing standpoint, the movie *Rain* is able to give the audience more of the hit Broadway show *Rain* than *Sadie Thompson*, where the same scene preserves only a few lines of dialogue from the play. In the scene on the veranda, the film audience is able to hear directly almost all of the dialogue from the play, including great amounts of exposition and character background that had been lost in the silent film, and to hear the oppressive rain while seeing every second of the ebb and flow of conversation between Sadie and O'Hara.

Early critics of sound film (from Eisenstein to Arnheim) argued that synchronized sound, epitomized by synchronized dialogue, was redundant. Here, however, we see that even if the sound (the voice) is meticulously synchronized with the image, what the sound (the dialogue) conveys is unrepresented and unrepresentable visually (short of elaborate flashbacks). The shot presents two people talking; the sound (dialogue and voice) elicits images of dance halls, "friends" male and female, Honolulu, Australia, the island's political structure, and images of women working. Psychological depth and a detailed "back story" for each character are values of drama and literature; they are only partially evoked through image and non-dialogue-bearing sound (the elements of silent film). Sound film increases access to this kind of character construction through use of a greater number of words. Words alone do not, however, account for the full impact of this shot (or any shot like it). The actors' delivery is crucial as well.[6]

Even if the long take had been popular with the public, however, economic considerations made it unlikely that it would be widely adopted. Filming such a long and complicated shot was prohibitively expensive and time-consuming. Lighting was difficult to work out and any mistakes in sound (flubbed line readings, a noise on the set) required doing everything over. Aesthetically, too, this form of realism can be very wearing. The undifferentiated sound effects, the constant drone of the rain, and the unedited take expose the fallacy that total continuity is automatically superior to the *impression* of continuity built by editing conventions. The "realism" achieved by such a shot is technological rather than narrative, and even then the long take is constantly threatening to undermine classical ideals of transparent cinematic expression.

There is only one major section in the veranda scene where the camera moves without an internal (character-instigated) cue. O'Hara and Sadie have stopped walking and sit on the railing of the porch. As O'Hara begins to tell Sadie about Lefty and Maggie, the camera, rather than stopping with them as it has until now, seems to be carried away by its own momentum. It moves off the porch and tracks around O'Hara and Sadie. As it does so, it passes a trellis with vines, which blocks our view of the characters during the crucial (verbal) juncture when O'Hara eliminates what would otherwise be seen as an obstacle to the formation of the couple (her past). The camera continues to move right in a semicircle and eventually returns up the porch steps to reframe them in a standard two-shot. When they stand and begin to walk, the camera dollies back with them as before.

Although this move "breaks up" a long speech by O'Hara, it more than flirts with exposing the enunciation. At the point when O'Hara and Sadie are becoming closest, a moment traditionally filmed in the least obtrusive way possible, the image takes us away from the couple and privileges itself instead. The image in effect denigrates the dialogue (and even the characters) by literally leaving it behind. Bordwell et al. point out that the "omnipresent point of view which cutting had provided during the silent era [and that can be seen in *Sadie Thompson*] was replaced to some extent by a ubiquity yielded by camera movement" (Bordwell, Staiger, and Thompson 1985, p. 308). The absolute power of the transitional-period camera is shown by its flaunting such a bravura move despite the needs of the narrative. With the continued volume of the "rain" sound effects and the loss of synchronization of lip movement and dialogue, the obstruction of our view of Sadie and O'Hara makes the crucial dialogue of this part of the scene hard to follow. Bordwell et al. go on to note that "both techniques"—camera movement and omnipresent montage-based point of view—fulfilled "fundamental functions," such as "narrative continuity, clear definition of space, covert narrational presence, [and] control of rhythm" (ibid.). As we see in this example, the narrational presence is anything but covert, while narrative continuity takes a back seat to technical continuity. The fetishization of the visual/audio continuity threatens to disrupt the seamless flow of the narrative, another reason why this kind of shot and this kind of camera movement did not become standard in classical sound film.

While the tracking shot on the veranda would seem to maintain a strict formal equality between the woman and the man, nevertheless it is O'Hara who urges action on a tormented, but passive, Sadie. And time and again it is Sadie/Crawford who leans into specially lit areas of the set so that the camera can isolate her still, suffering beauty. Even the long take finds a way to single out the woman as visual spectacle.

The woman's voice in this scene has no authority. Although synchronized in exactly the same manner as O'Hara's voice, Sadie's speech is contained by his context. O'Hara's terms are far more flexible than Davidson's, but even so, Sadie is trapped in someone else's discourse. With O'Hara, she is simply allowed more room to play *his* game. The fragmentation that denies her body cohesion in the introductory "Sadie" montage also makes it impossible for Sadie to be "O'Hara's girl." As a prostitute, Sadie belongs to everyone and no one, her body by definition available to many takers. In order for her to be the hero's prize, Sadie has to be put back together again. O'Hara makes her whole—and potentially his—by incorporating her into the fluid, continuous tracking shots that exemplify the marines throughout the text. Synchronous sound in a continuous take makes Sadie available, not equal.

At the very end of the shot, having received a letter from the governor insisting she return to San Francisco and not the idyllic Sydney, Sadie agrees to go and see the governor with O'Hara to appeal. As she and O'Hara exit the frame on the left, the camera executes a swish pan right. This swish pan differs from earlier ones by being slightly slower, so that we can *see* that there are no cuts hidden in it. Through the blurred image we can just make out the back of the wall of the veranda until the camera stops and O'Hara and Sadie run back into the shot from the right. They grab their coats hanging on the wall at the end of the porch and run out left through a door leading into the inn.

Again the importance of the continuous image overwhelms the narrative with its need to announce itself as image, continuity for continuity's sake. The purpose of this slowed swish pan is to maintain the integrity of the six-minute

shot, complete without a cut. Only here the shot is maintained regardless of the *absence* of the couple whose relationship the "wholeness" of the track has been designed to define. The exits and entrances of Sadie and O'Hara before and after the swish pan confuse us spatially. In drawing attention to itself, the shot tempts the audience to reconstruct its production—evidently the actors ran behind the camera as it panned right and reentered the last "shot." Offhand it would seem difficult to problematize space when the continuity of space is so meticulously insisted upon, but this shot does manage it A last reason mitigating against the popularity of the long take is that a particularly long take or sequence shot is hard to get out of without it calling attention to itself.

The end of this scene firmly establishes that sound in no way legitimizes or validates the woman's speech in the absence of visual and narrative support. In the silent film, Sadie's outrage at Davidson after receiving the governor's letter bursts forth in a tirade when she accidentally meets him as she and O'Hara are setting out to see the governor, a scene that takes minutes and is made up of twenty-seven separate shots (not counting titles). In the sound version, the scene takes three shots: Sadie enters the inn and begins to yell at Davidson in a long shot, there is a brief reaction shot of Davidson looking at her, and then we return to the original shot of her yelling until O'Hara drags her out. In effect, it is one long take with a cut-away in the middle.

In the silent version, the editing makes Sadie dynamic—a star—fully constituted by the text in all its systems: composition (she *is* the drama and movement of the scene as she fills the frame with violent gestures), editing (cuts to "keep up" with her as she pursues Davidson from room to room), and titles (presenting highlights of what she says and Davidson's brief, inadequate interjections). Sadie dominates the scene as Davidson stands pinned against the wall, hiding behind furniture.

In the sound version, while Sadie is having the last word, Davidson stands on the stairs high above her, secure in his spatial superiority. Her vocalized tirade becomes less powerful because we see the string of words falling on deaf ears. When O'Hara drags her out the door, undermining her anger, as in every version, it relieves Sadie from occupying a position whose weakness only she does not recognize. Davidson never moves. As with the first close-up of Ameena, sound only allows Sadie to speak her own ineffectualness.

"Radiant, beautiful"—The Voice
That Exceeds Language

Just as visual spectacle competes with narrative, what we might call audio-spectacle constantly invites the auditor to bathe in a wash of sound, music, and voice, all promising pleasure in themselves without need of narrative, psychologically motivated characters, causality in space and time, or closure. As in the theories of visual spectacle of Lea Jacobs et al.,[7] duration, or lingering on a shot, detaches it from the linear progression of the narrative and invites a similarly nonlinear, analogical indulgence on the part of the viewer. Audio-spectacle also guides us away from "content" (language, character psychology, exposition) and toward the quality of the sound, irrespective of whether music, voices, or effects are on the sound track.

Sound's ability to envelop the spectator and abolish the space separating the hearer and the source of the sound has been widely commented upon. Barthes describes the elusive, but overwhelming, pleasure that comes from listening to the voice: "It possesses a special hallucinatory power, [uniting] in one plenitude both meaning and sex" (Barthes 1974, pp. 109–10). Hanns Eisler describes the way music fills the gap between audience and screen—and, arguably, between scenes and between shots in silent films. Mary Ann Doane details how the projection of sound from behind the screen reenforces the bond between spectator and image, minimalizing the threat of sound disrupting viewer/listener identification with the image, and Lucy Fischer adds an analysis of the essentially spatial function of sound effects and early sound film's use of them to add depth, scale, and presence to the image.[8] *Rain* acknowledges this impression of the transcendence of sound, particularly with regard to the voice—a voice separable from dialogue. The last third of the film presents a series of ways of narrativizing that excess so as to *represent* vocal transcendence.

When Sadie speaks to Davidson the night before she is to return to San Francisco and a prison sentence, he is pacing on the veranda. Sadie leans out of a window to say goodnight. In another interesting use of the swish pan, a close-up profile shot of Joan Crawford facing screen right is followed by a swish pan to the right. Instead of seeing what she sees, the pan ends inexplicably on a full-face close-up of Crawford. The effect of the shot, which is spa-

"Radiant. Beautiful."

tially impossible, is as if Sadie has been removed from any real spatial context and instead floats as pure, ethereal spectacle. As she gazes into the great beyond, Sadie quietly restates "her" reasons for going back, couched in Davidson's language of Christian suffering and sacrifice. In this way, the text narrativizes the relationship between the voice and the imaginary. It is Sadie's voice infusing Davidson's words that provokes Davidson's desire. Both her voice and her image—her face on display as an icon of the "star" and of the character's spirituality—are offered as transcendent, promising fulfillment of desire through an appeal to Davidson's imaginary, which is built on religious discourse. To him she has become "radiant, beautiful."

At the same time, Sadie's image and voice are presented to us, the film's spectators. The synchronization of voice and image does not fully recuperate the excess of the voice. As Sadie recites the religious rhetoric on punishment and redemption, her voice filling the dark frame and warming her blank facial expression, the spectator is engulfed in an imaginary unity with the star/image/other. Rather than occupying a spatial position, the lack of ambient sound denies the particularity of the voice in space, allowing it to fill the theater, becoming something inside the hearer rather than "out there." The voice does not so much exceed the symbolic as fulfill it by imbuing it with physical pleasure, the imaginary, and the maternal that complete patriarchal authority with this offering of wholeness to the subject.

The sound of the voice occupies a specific relationship to desire when it is reproduced in film. Every voice one hears reproduced is poised on the edge of poignance, an indicant of loss, a promise of fulfillment that foretells the imminence of its departure. In discussing the relationship between the spectator and the image of an actor, Metz points out that the absence of the physical body of the actor makes one yearn ever more strongly for the star, knowing he or she is already gone and all that is left is a disappearing trace (1982, pp. 62–63). Sitting on the edge of one's seat, listening, the spectator/listener "glimpses" the uncapturable, a voice receding in the emptiness—an emptiness vividly signified in early sound films by the ever-present static and the striking lack of music. Desire is reopened, fulfillment dissolving the moment it is caught. Unlike photography, which freezes time, cinema and phonography replay time in its transience. The voice slipping away is recapturable through repetition, but it is nevertheless always retreating.

In considering sound in film, the voice must be theorized separately from dialogue. The voice is more than dialogue (see Marie 1980). Dialogue existed in silent film as pure language, represented in graphics and linked tenuously to the image through an abstract, logical process of connection through contiguity. But it is the voice in sound film that makes dialogue *matter*, that takes it out of its narrative function and makes it sound, that invokes a psychological, imaginary system of spectacle as opposed to the purely representational association of title and image in silent film.

Dudley Andrew once defined art as "the radical middle between the uncoded and the coded."[9] Although I would demur at the term *art* because it is itself so fully coded in terms of high culture, I agree that what I'm talking about in cinema is precisely the play between the uncoded—the ineffable that beckons the imaginary and is insistently repressed—and that which functions entirely within the symbolic. While dialogue *is* language, is the symbolic, other categories of sound, including voice, can slip out of language and narrative and assume the appearance of the uncoded, ravishing us with seemingly direct sensory experience. While it is asserted that there is nothing that is uncoded, no sensory experience that is experienced directly, I think it can be agreed that portions of the image and the sound track exceed the major code that seeks to contain them, namely, narrative.

Sadie's Conversion

The scene of Sadie's conversion tries to locate the space between voice and dialogue without letting voice escape its function in service to the narrative. In the silent version, Sadie's conversion is a matter of vision. Sadie argues with Davidson and returns to her room, where she paces. / Shot of an open window with rain pouring down. / Sadie, pacing. / The window slams shut and breaks. / Sadie jumps, scared. / Sadie, hiding in a corner, stares into space. / Dissolve to Sadie walking into a jail cell. / She turns as the bars of the cell close in front of her. / Back in her room, Sadie screams for Mr. Davidson. / Upstairs, Davidson and his wife pray. / Sadie screams at the ceiling. / Davidson looks at his wife and goes to the door. / Sadie screams again. / Davidson walks down the stairs to her room. / She opens the door. / In her room he sits, puts her

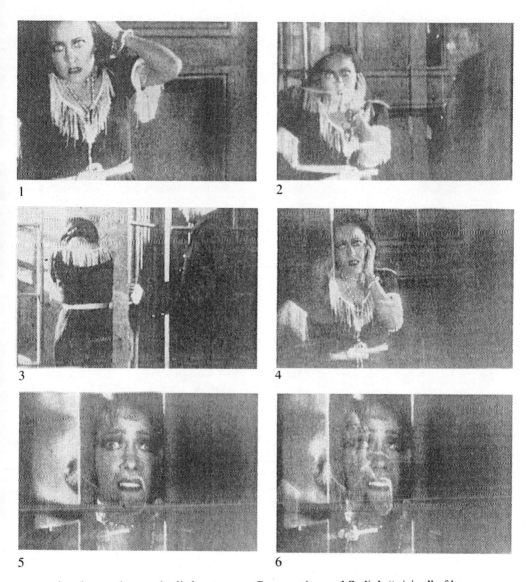

hands together, and tells her to pray. Crosscutting and Sadie's "vision" of herself in prison fuel the scene, which has few titles and establishes its major points through images, pantomime, and editing.

In the sound film, the conversion is not simply a matter of substituting sound or hearing for vision. Instead, a new hierarchy is instituted, one with a complex interaction of camera movement, editing, mise-en-scène (from silent cinema), dialogue, voice (from theater), and voice-recording and sound ef-

fects and their relation in the sound mix from sound technology. The excess of the voice (in this scene Davidson's) is accounted for by relating its power to the process of hypnosis. Twice O'Hara comments that the converted Sadie acts "like she's doped," "like she's hypnotized." The sound film depicts this hypnosis by focusing on the power of Davidson's/Huston's oratorical delivery.

In hypnosis, the voice, as much as the words of the hypnotist, is absorbed by the subject as his/her *own* inner voice and thoughts (see Chapter 1). The conversion scene dramatizes this as Davidson's voice fills the close-up of Sadie, his words becoming hers as if his prayer was her own spontaneous thought.

As Sadie stands at the bottom of the stairs and, looking up at Davidson, begins to tell him off, he begins to pray. Sadie, photographed from a high angle, begins to ascend the stairs toward Davidson, dramatically protesting, "You tell me to go back and suffer. How do you know what I've suffered? You don't know, you don't care, you don't even ask and you call yourself a Christian!" As she moves, the camera pans left to keep her centered and moves in. Davidson, from a low angle, prays out loud, "Our Father, who art in heaven. . . ." Sadie reaches the upper part of the stairs as Davidson's dialogue continues in a sound overlap. Sadie: "Your God and me could never be shipmates, and you can tell Him this for me—Sadie Thompson is on her way to Hell!" Having reached the famous finish of the second act (and at the same time used words all the more potent for being forbidden by the Production Code), Sadie waits for a reaction from Davidson. He continues, uninterrupted, praying on in a droning, monotonous voice: "Forgive our poor lost sister, Our Father who art. . . ." Sadie retreats uncertainly. At the bottom of the stairs, Sadie falls to her knees and slowly begins to repeat occasional words from the prayer. When Davidson, heard in voice-over, finishes the prayer, Sadie is reciting every word. In a close-up, Davidson realizes she is with him and, smiling, raises his voice as they repeat the prayer a third time. The camera moves to a long, high-angle shot of the entire set, then cranes up past the ceiling, panning out into the darkness, where the sound of rain drowns out their voices.

The use of the Lord's Prayer is especially effective because the audience knows it, the culture presumes it to be known, and therefore Davidson speaks not just a vague "religiousness" (in keeping with the Production Code's refusal to let Maugham's "Reverend" Davidson be an actual missionary in the film versions), but a concrete formal expression of religion that exists as a whole and does not need to rest on internal persuasiveness. Because the words of the prayer are so well known, it is not necessary for the audience to listen to *what* Davidson says as much as to how he says it. The predictability of the words guides our attention away from the verbal discourse and toward the rhythmic, hypnotic quality of the reading and Huston's attractive baritone. As Sadie backs unsteadily down the stairs, Davidson's voice imposes on the image of her face, filling all the spaces in the same way the sound of the rain has in other scenes.

Sadie visually enacts the process of absorbing Davidson's voice into herself until it speaks her. There is no invitation to dialogue in this scene, no response she could make. Her blanket rejection of both Davidson and religion a moment before has been met and turned back by the opacity of the thrice-repeated prayer. Davidson does not acknowledge her presence (he looks out over her head or at the ceiling). The only way Sadie can exist within the religious discourse is by accepting the position waiting for her as "our poor lost sister," reembodying herself in submission to the voice.

With offscreen sound, the audience is in a position similar to Sadie's. It is important that, for the most part, Davidson's voice is heard in this scene offscreen, over shots of Sadie. In "The Voice in the Cinema," Doane notes that "two kinds of 'voices without bodies' immediately suggest themselves," one being the electronic/synthetic "voice" of a computer and the other being "the voice of God incarnated in the Word" (1985b, pp. 174–75). The sound, unlocatable in the image except by its pantomimed effect, fills the space of the theater as well. As the words lose shape in their predictability, the voice gains, unchallenged by any other sound on the sound track. Freed from synchronization, which attests to the image as cause, the voice, barely contained, grows in power and volume. *Rain*, through Sadie, shows us the irresistible power of the voice, of unanchored sound, while holding it firmly within narrative bounds.

The climax of the story, the emergence of Sadie after Davidson's death, demonstrates the transitional text's dialogization of its formal heteroglossic hierarchy and the association of the subjected woman with the usually denigrated discourses of sound and the vulgar (in the sense of the vernacular) seen in Sadie's language and dress. The final scenes are missing from the silent version owing to the loss of the last reel. The silent film ends abruptly at the end of reel 8 with Davidson, torn by conflicting desires, finding Sadie alone at night. The camera, in what might be a point-of-view shot, pans suggestively down her body as she sits lost in thought. The reel ends and whatever happens between Sadie and Davidson is, by historical chance, completely unrepresented. However judging from the rest of the film's fidelity to the play, we can assume that the end finds O'Hara and Sadie on their way to Australia, Mrs. Davidson in tears.[10] In the 1932 *Rain*, Davidson's change of heart is portrayed through the interaction of pantomime, sound effects, music, and ellipsis. After Davidson has spoken to Sadie ("radiant, beautiful"), he begins to pound his fist on a barrel in time to the native drums heard in the distance, under the sound of the rain. As Davidson rushes from the veranda, the camera pans to the jungle foliage as the sound of the rain and the drums intensifies.

The partially narrativized drums and the sound of rain physicalize the image, giving it depth and grounding the sounds so as to make them not purely separable as commentary. Although the rain is visible, because of heavy backlighting, the image and the sound of rain cannot be synchronized, only simultaneous. The use of ellipsis in a dissolve from the night to the sunrise leaves the events of the night to be "understood," a cinematic equivalent of the story's enigmatic last line.

The film repeats the traveloguelike montages of natives fishing, with the non-lip-synced sound of native singing superimposed. This third repetition of the montage, until now restricted to serving as a marker at the end of act 1 and act 2, attempts to bring the fishermen into the narrative. As they pull in their nets, one native registers surprise. His hands drop the net. The feet of Davidson become visible as his body floats to shore. The previous montages are thus retroactively designated as foreshadowing this moment.

The sound-plus-montage device shows how nonsynchronous sound in the early transitional period is not necessarily the most dynamic or progressive use of sound. Despite the arguments of Eisenstein and others,[11] this use of sound reenforces the continuation of archaic uses (resembling silent film's use of music and effects) and old ideas ("native" life summed up in a few stereotypical "exotic" shots and snatches of song).

Disturbed "natives" run from their huts in panic. Some of the images are even filmed in fast motion, a holdover from the undercranking of silent film, where it expressed speed and frenzy. There is no sync sound, only an audio montage of indistinct voices *over* the images. The islanders' language is reduced to gibberish, emblematic, exotic, and simply incomprehensible.

Sound speed returns when Horn enters a shot on the beach at the end of the native montage and discovers Macphail already there. It is necessary to go back to sound speed because they will deliver important dialogue, but it is also possible that as "whites" they are presented as "naturally" moving in the heavier "real" time of the sound-laden image.

Changes in image speed are quite tolerable in silent film, but what seems so jarring that it was no longer recuperable by classical film is not the change in image speed but the change in the *sound track*. An image filmed at sound speed with accompanying sound effects has depth, a middle and a background. There is a density to the track, we are aware of the air the voices sound in, of the hollowness and distance surrounding the dialogue and effects. The switch to the silent-style montage approach eliminates any pretension of depth and substitutes an image that is all foreground. The transition from 16 frames per second to 18 to 22 to 24 frames per second is not great. But the transition on the sound track from full sound effects to none is a radical break. The sound is either "on" or "off"; there is no gentle gradation. The shots of the silent-style montage feel particularly empty, whereas the shot of Horn is suddenly "real," even before anyone speaks. The ambient sound presents a *potential* for sound (it is "on") that silent images—at any speed—lack.

Horn and Macphail's dialogue establishes that the body in the water is Davidson and that he has committed suicide by cutting his throat. (This absolves Sadie, just in case anyone thought the ellipsis was broad enough to cover her killing Davidson.) The question is posed, "Why do you think he did it?" Cut to a medium shot of Sadie's door with the beaded curtains. As "The Wabash Blues" bursts onto the sound track, the camera lumbers at great speed toward her door. The image/music combination "answers" the verbal discourse in a bravura demonstration of the new cinematic.

Back at the inn, Horn and O'Hara wonder at great length why Sadie is suddenly playing that music again after putting it away for the length of her conversion. They knock on her door to tell her about Davidson. The door begins to open, the music becomes louder. Close-up of Horn turning his head with wide eyes and a smile. O'Hara in close-up turns and registers surprise. The "Sadie" montage is repeated: one jeweled hand, the other jeweled hand, a right foot, a left foot (the shoes more bedraggled now), then Sadie's face leaning into the shot.

The symmetry of the construction, which visually is supposed to supply us with more clues to the enigma of Davidson's death (though without entirely solving it), takes us back to the introduction of Sadie as well as to the scene (unseen) with Davidson. The scene with Davidson is the climax of the narrative's major conflict. As A. J. Greimas argues, it is there that a logical transformation takes place, where the hero and villain fight it out and the hero emerges (see Barthes 1977, p. 137). After their fight, the end of the story is in a symmetrical relationship to the beginning. What is most notable about Sadie's reemergence is her dress and the accompanying music—she emerges "marked."

Barthes describes this process of "marking" the protagonist in his discussion of Jacob's struggle with the Angel. "A situation of balance [which] . . . is a prerequisite for any marking . . . is disturbed by the unlikely victory of one of the participants; there is an inversion of the mark, a counter-mark" (Barthes 1977, p. 134). In *Rain* it is unlikely from the beginning that a friendless, lower-class, outcast woman should win over a man who has religious, political, and military authority.

> The sequence itself functions to unbalance the opponents in the combat, not only by the unforeseen victory of the one over the other, but above all (let us be fully aware of the formal subtlety of this surprise) by the illogical, *inverted* nature of the victory. In other words . . . the combat, as it is reversed in its unexpected development, *marks* one of the combatants: the weakest defeats the strongest, *in exchange for which* he is marked.
>
> (ibid., pp. 133–34)

The logic of Sadie's victory is perfectly inverted. Davidson loses *because* of his strength, his ability to control Sadie. Sadie wins because of her weakness, her exploitability. She wins by being a victim and she emerges victorious but marked, in fact bearing the marks of her exploitation, her prostitution, in her vulgar clothes and jewels.

The repetition of this scene emphasizes the cyclical nature of her "marking." Every time she "falls" (is exploited), she emerges marked. The text asserts that the only escape from this cycle of exploitation is marriage. Sadie, the fallen woman, falls to Davidson, thus negating her negative condition and emerging as herself, woman, recuperable. Thus the entire story can be seen as the process of bringing Sadie back into the fold—O'Hara's, not Davidson's.

Again the music plays throughout the first half of the scene, standing in for Sadie, here announced as her conscious proclamation of her "brazen hussy" persona. Unfortunately, to achieve the full quality of the music, it has to be turned up so loud that it interferes with the clarity of the dialogue. When

Sadie emerges, she rebuffs O'Hara and Horn when they try to turn off the phonograph. But the level of her words is not high enough to always be distinguishable from the music, for instance when she delivers her famous coruscating line about men and pigs. Sadie turns her back to the camera (which remains in a long shot, framing all three figures), looks over her shoulder at O'Hara and mutters three words: "You men . . . pigs." Needless to say, the lack of clear enunciation and volume mutes its force considerably.

The music seems to be played on disc directly on the set. It is difficult for the actors to time the dialogue to match certain phrases in the music. When O'Hara tells Sadie that Davidson is dead, the "wah wah wahhh" trumpet figure is heard. The volume doesn't change, so it is the silence of the actors that allows it to stand out. However, since both the music and the dialogue readings are "live," recorded simultaneously, the actors step on the music. Its full effect as commentary is lost. The "wah wahh," earlier symbolic of her cockiness, assumes a mocking character as she quietly says, "I thought the joke was all on me." She tells Horn to turn off the music, and it is never heard again as Sadie forfeits her previous character to start anew.

Sadie's outburst—the dramatic end to the story—is muted and passed over in favor of another climax, marrying O'Hara. When the music stops, Sadie approaches O'Hara and apologizes for "that crack." However the intervening dialogue obscures exactly which "crack" she's referring to. In between her insulting remark and this moment, she has been told of Davidson's suicide, expressed what the playwrights and screenwriter Maxwell Anderson feel to be appropriate and heartfelt regret, and accepted O'Hara and Horn's suggestion that the music be turned off. She tells O'Hara she would be happy to try Sydney with him, and they leave arm in arm. Outdoors, as the sun rises and the skies clear, they encounter Mrs. Davidson—who, of course, apologizes to *them*. Mrs. Davidson says, "I'm sorry, Miss Thompson. I'm sorry for him and I'm sorry for you." To which a greatly softened Sadie Thompson replies, "I guess I'm sorry for just about everybody in the whole world." She and

O'Hara walk down the steps and out of the frame as Mrs. Davidson buries her face in her hands and the first overt use of background music since the titles swells for "The End."

Rain's negotiation between silent cinema, the theater, and early and classical sound film conventions demonstrates a particular historical moment, against which we can isolate Sadie's voice as a test case of the place of woman's voice in cinema. Although the conventions of representation are themselves in flux (silent-style montages butting up against theatrical "curtains" and brazen musical fanfares), all the forms of representation are consistently linked to woman-as-problem. In classical cinematic style, the image system contributes not only the display of woman-as-spectacle but cooperates in the deconstruction (*découpage*) that makes her fragmented body a reassuring fetish for the male viewer. While the introduction of a sound track would seem to make the woman's voice undeniably her own, the dominating pressures of narrative and image cancel out any potential gains.

At every step, the woman's speech is reified, sound, image, and narrative joining forces to make her speak her own "weakness" and "passivity"—to make her give voice to her own exclusion. The synchronized long take, at first so equitable, encompasses Sadie within a man's world—one she can struggle against, but with which she must ultimately come to terms.

In *Rain*, the transcendent voice is explicitly male. The "voice of God" effect associated with the voice-over is linked directly to a male spokesman for God and religion, through a standardized prayer (to the Father). Sadie's refusal of Davidson's language is again limited, not only by her later acceptance of it, but by her ultimate acquiescence to O'Hara's language and to marriage. "Her" language of vulgar metaphor and carnivalesque disdain is portrayed as ineffectual and self-defeating. However as Sadie's existence is one with her resistance, when her verbal resistance is taken from her by the text's undermining of her language, any concept of Sadie's true "self" seems helplessly idealistic.

The only area where sound marks out a "female space" not controlled by male figures in the text is in the merging of woman and music, with music serving as a signifier of the disturbing power of female sexuality. This link, however, is more a projection of male desire onto both woman and music than an actual, "essential" connection between woman and a specifically non-linguistic, inarticulate aural medium. (Witness Davidson's distracted, uncomfortable behavior when he first hears "The Wabash Blues.") Sadie's appropriation of the phonograph as a signifier of her "self" becomes an instance of a woman appropriating the markers assigned to her by others in order to express her own limited resistance. But, as in every generation of the character/text "Sadie Thompson," she turns the phonograph off to walk into the sunset with her betrothed.

To be fair, the egalitarian, populist ideals expressed by O'Hara from the 1921 play to *Rain* in 1932 reflect the relatively improved position of American women in the 1920s and 1930s (particularly regarding sexual freedom). In the following decade, however, the position of women in American culture becomes more problematic.

Films produced in the mid 1940s, most notably those imbued with a film noir style, return obsessively to the issue or, more accurately, the *problem* of woman's speech. Sound technology, which prided itself on a scientifically objective, mechanical neutrality, finds itself on trial as its role in the ideological construction of the woman's voice is exposed, conclusively severing any illusion of a "natural" connection between woman and her voice. In the four films I analyze in the following chapter, sound is brought back to its approved role as helpmeet to the image as classical cinema struggles to silence women, to restore them to their passive roles. And it does so with a vengeance.

Barbara Stanwyck in *Sorry, Wrong Number*

The Problem of the Speaking Woman

The Spiral Staircase (1946),
Blackmail (1929), *Notorious* (1946),
Sorry, Wrong Number (1948)

The front parlor of a small hotel. Americana circa nineteen-aught-six. The audience faces the silver screen. A piano player accompanies the quaint melodrama. A young woman watches silently, enrapt. At this point we don't know that she is mute; the situation is one in which silence is natural and socially accepted. However, as the film we are watching proves, this is a primitive period in film, soon to be outgrown, left behind by the demands of progress. As the narrative will prove, the silent character like the silent film is an anomaly in a sound film. Both need to be brought up to snuff or snuffed out.

Upstairs, the camera moving past the chandelier and through the floor, we see a woman with a limp. She is being watched. Through the dresses in the closet we see an eye. It is all-seeing but itself unseen. As the crippled woman reaches her arms up through her dress, her fingers splay and the music strikes a jarring chord. She is murdered somewhere out of sight and out of frame by the possessor of the look.

As the downstairs Sunday picture-show ends, Helen (Dorothy McGuire) prepares to go. We find out that she is mute and that "afflicted" girls are being murdered by someone in town. She walks home, alone. After a few Gothic glimmers (sounds not quite hidden by the wind seem to follow her, a storm is coming), she arrives safely and rushes up the grand staircase to attend to her duties as nurse to the rich invalid woman who owns the great house.

Helen pauses on the landing to look at herself in the mirror. Suddenly we find we are back in the presence of the Eye. It is not "out there," but here, in the house. It stares at Helen with disturbing malevolence. Then we see her as the Eye sees her: a reflection in a mirror, a woman without a mouth. Through

Dorothy McGuire in *The Spiral Staircase*

benign special effects, and in the least disruptive way possible, her mouth has been wiped from her face. All that remains is a blur.

Since Laura Mulvey first identified the privileged relationship between the male spectator and the gaze in her article "Visual Pleasure and Narrative Cinema" (1975) feminists investigating the cinematic representation of women have struggled to find a means or an instance whereby the female spectator could be positioned as subject in classical Hollywood texts. One of the few options left, not accounted for by psychoanalytic approaches that privileged the male eye, was the sound track. And feminists soon began pondering the relationship of the one insignificant signifier to the Other.

The special applicability of feminist film work to the study of sound stems from feminism's situating itself among the structuring absences, amid concepts and processes culture and the film industry have deemed invisible or irrelevant. Annette Kuhn states that "the main focus of interest" in feminist film analysis is "the ways in which woman has been constituted as a set of meanings through processes of cinematic signification" (Kuhn 1982, p. 71). In terms that echo the concerns of sound-film theory, Kuhn argues that feminist film theory has tended to premise itself largely on a notion of representation as mediated, as a social and ideological construct, an autonomous or relatively autonomous process of meaning production which does not necessarily relate immediately to or reflect unproblematically a "real" social world.

> The concern then is . . . that of becoming sensitive to what often goes unnoticed, becomes naturalized, or is taken for granted. . . . The fundamental project of feminist film analysis can be said to centre on making the invisible visible.
>
> (ibid., pp. 71, 73)

Or the silent audible.

In classical film, sound is conflated with the feminine. Sound itself, as a cinematic register, is "feminized," assigned the role of the perpetually supportive "acoustic mirror" [1] that reenforces the primacy of the image and of the male gaze. Sound is made to point away from itself and back to the image and the narrative, while woman is made spectacle for the former and recuperated by the latter. Both sound and woman, in effect, have been made Echo to a vain and self-absorbed Narcissus. As such, they serve the very hegemony that restricts and defines how they can function.

The following films explicitly confront a woman's struggle to speak. In fact, it is the very *difficulty* of speaking that exemplifies women's speech under patriarchy. Despite the entrenchment of classical conventions that so effectively impede the possibility of female subjectivity, what continues to grow in significance is the ever-present *potential* of a break with classical representation within a given text. In all of the films I discuss here, woman's speech sparks a crisis within the texts that mirrors a corresponding breakdown within the dominant ideology. The alleged neutrality of sound technology comes under attack, its role in the patriarchal construction of woman exposed. When admitted to the narrative as a *subject*, sound's hidden status becomes paradoxically powerful as a signifier of the repression of that other potentially disruptive sign, the equally "silent, absent, and marginal" woman (Kaplan 1983, p. 34; see also pp. 36–48).

The term "woman's voice" condenses three issues: (1) the woman's physical voice, (2) her relationship to language or verbal discourse, and (3) her possession of authorial point of view. We have analyzed the voice's relationship to language in *Sadie Thompson* and *Rain* and shall examine the authorial voice in Chapter 6. While it is not possible to entirely separate out the voice from its verbal and visual cinematic context, this chapter will examine how the simple, physical ability to produce a sound is interrupted by specifically patriarchal pressures brought to bear on the women in these texts. In *Blackmail* and *The Spiral Staircase*, the women can't talk; in *Notorious* and *Sorry, Wrong Number*, they talk too much. Secondly, in all of these films to a greater or lesser degree, that natural ability is interrupted, made difficult, or conditioned to a suffocating degree by sound technology itself. *The Spiral Staircase* and *Sorry, Wrong Number* illustrate in different ways the mixed blessing a telephone can be, with its false promises of greater security and its vaunted ability to ease painful isolation—issues of especial interest to women. In *Notorious* the phonograph purports to capture a woman's essential beliefs—but not to her benefit. In *Blackmail* it is the very recording process of sound film that fractures a woman's body and voice into irreconcilable pieces. Lastly, the textual association of man with the image and woman with sound accentuates the way cultural values associated with gender are assigned to cinema's image/ sound hierarchy. These in turn "figure" the woman in sound film.

All four of the films we shall be considering problematize genre identification by combining elements of the woman's film and the suspense thriller. This merger in itself tells us what is at stake when the dominant ideology is disrupted or challenged; in all the films, it is the woman's fate (and her function) that is being held in suspense, while she hangs suspended between recuperation and death. Three of the four films fall within two years of each other (1946–48), at a point that is arguably the peak of the classical sound film period: *The Spiral Staircase* (1946), *Notorious* (1946), and *Sorry, Wrong Number* (1948). *Blackmail*, produced in England in 1929, is an early and illuminating predecessor indicating the subversive potential of sound in film and the critical nexus of woman and voice.

The Spiral Staircase (1946)

Offhand, *The Spiral Staircase* belongs to the Gothic genre, one of the first "women's" genres. Gothics also include elements typical of the suspense thriller. If we take *Jane Eyre* as a model, we find the innocent, plucky heroine who is in some terrible, though undefined, danger. Despite her reduced social status as an orphan, the heroine, educated but poor (literally handicapped in *The Spiral Staircase*), is efficient, reliable, intelligent, and valued by members of the family. The great house in which she lives is not her true home but rather the scene of her work. The house is a character itself, frequently a figure of menace, inasmuch as it shelters the person who threatens the heroine.

In *The Spiral Staircase* it is not only the house that shields the identity of the killer, but, more disturbingly, the cinematic institution. Three scenes in particular develop the complicity between the murderer and the cinematic. The opening scene hides the identity of the killer while endowing him with the authority of the look. When the unknown killer's eye "sees" Helen without a mouth, its point of view is temporarily allowed to subvert the normal codes of realism; these shots are marked, set apart from the "uncoded" shots in the film by being labeled as "subjective" and unreliable.

The unreliable authority given to the "eye" causes an imbalance in the cinematic system, undermining conventions of seeing/seen. The first time we see the killer's eye watching the woman with the limp, the reverse shot that represents his vision is heavily distorted. The top of the image curves, echoing the shadows cast by the brass bed. The woman's body sways unnaturally under pressure of the wide-angle lens. As she raises her arms to put on her dress, the text cuts to a shot that purposely excludes the actor and the act. We see her hands; the murder is below. Her hands, in conjunction with the music, are a heavily coded sign of victimization. They clutch at the air, signaling the violence being visited on their owner, but they are useless for defense. This shot, undistorted and clear, with the authority of an omniscient enunciator, preserves the identity of the killer—even the method of murder—and is merely the first indication that the visual track will be instrumental in obscuring his identity.

In the next and most famous point-of-view shot in the film, we see what the eye sees—the mouthless woman—and are made to share in what is marked as a "perverted" vision. These shots are again an aberration within a classical organization, the use of special effects making possible a frisson of horror and loathing not merely at the sight of a mouthless woman (presented as a monstrous deformity) but at the realization that we are inextricably implicated in the killer's point of view, his "way of looking."

The mixture of horror and recognition is striking. Because the character who sees woman as possessor of the "lack" is a disturbed, psychopathic killer, the film marks his point of view as dangerous and to be resisted. While the text exposes the woman's lack (the killer's "look" shrieks, "Women are castrated!"), it simultaneously enacts and rejects the male character's logical next step: removal of the castrated woman because she is seen as a threat to the male.

The French critic Marc Vernet once said half-seriously, "The most important contribution of psychoanalysis has been to furnish a new alibi for the structure of the American narrative film" (quoted in Altman 1985, p. 526), and *The Spiral Staircase* is very much a post–World War II American Freudian text. The killer's anxiety about his masculinity is the narrative's excuse for his fear of "maimed" women, and of Helen in particular. We first see Professor Albert Warren (George Brent) literally in a closet, surrounded by frilly dresses. His "latent" homosexuality marks him as an emasculated, castrated man, analogous to the women he must kill in order to preserve his precarious grip on his masculine identity. As in many works of this period, the troubled male has an overbearing, overly dependent mother, played here by Ethel Barrymore, Hollywood's grand matriarch throughout the forties. (Seemingly on her deathbed, she states: "Nobody told me. Nobody had to. I always know everything.") Professor Warren's late father could not tolerate signs of weakness. "He always used to say, 'The strong survive, the weak die,'" his brother Steven tells Albert. "Neither of us fitted his concept of what a real man should be—a gun-totin', hard-drinking, tough-living, God-fearing citizen." It was the powerful stepmother, Mrs. Warren, who accompanied Dad hunting. The sons could never compete with her "unfeminine" prowess with a gun.

Although Professor Warren's literal point of view is stylistically isolated, the murderer's Oedipal hysteria seems to be shared to a large extent by the text. Whenever the "eye" presents us with the killer's "distorted" point of view, the filmic organization—the image track, most noticeably—undergoes an equivalent crisis. The power of the Eye is so great, it not only momentarily controls what we see, "its" point of view drowns out the sound track. The preservation of the tinkling piano heard from far away in the room of the first victim fades under the pressure of the Eye's "vision." Non-diegetic strings join the now discordant piano on the sound track. A choir fades up, only the disjointed moans of the victim remaining audible. The film's refusal to confront the implications of seeing "what cannot be seen" (a practice that apparently drives one to psychosis and is only narratively possible when the murderer is present) leads to a breathtaking declaration of disavowal in the next murder.

Brother Steven's fiancée, Blanche, is the only woman in the film who is ostensibly normal. She is neither a servant, a drunk, nor physically or mentally disadvantaged. She is pretty (played by Rhonda Fleming) and works as a confidential secretary, "a suitable job" for a middle-class woman. Her only conceivable flaw (and the one cited by Professor Warren when he explains why he killed her) is that she is an intelligent articulate woman who actively pursues her own sexual desires. When Steven won't marry her, she wastes no time mourning and industriously packs to leave. "I didn't realize you were so strong," Steven responds.

Going down to the cellar to find her trunk, with only a candle for light, Blanche hears a noise and turns. She sees someone she knows but becomes frightened at the person's strange demeanor. The woman's look does not "see," it cannot authorize a reverse shot or point-of-view shot, particularly in situations of stress such as this (Williams 1984, Doane 1984). The woman stares "madly" at what she fears, yet her look is merely the symbol of her impotence with regard to the cinematic system. We cut to a single eye, circled by light. This cannot be Blanche's point of view because it matches the shots we've seen before with the special use of light and shadow to separate the eye from the face. The killer's look can authorize a point-of-view shot, and, as before, the choir fades in on the sound track, the camera dollies in on his eye, and we now cut to what he sees: a visually distorted, subjective shot of Blanche, staring wildly at the camera as she backs away in fear. The shot is a superimposition—she is literally surrounded by an image of an eye. Behind her, the world seems to melt and flow downward. Again, the text cuts to a non-subjective shot: a gloved hand in the foreground, ready to strike; Blanche, much smaller in the background, cowers against a wall. She does not scream.

The hand smashes the candle, and the frame is slashed by shadow. On the left and the right, we can see Blanche's hands, gripping the wall. Her body is swallowed in the darkness. We hear her gasp and moan as her hands slide down the wall. By now we know the manner of death is strangulation, a point especially chilling in relation to Helen (already rendered mute) and to the speaking woman in general.

But where is the killer? The shot is a long shot. Logically there is no way we could be watching from this angle if it were seen by the killer and no way we could fail to see his back in an "objective" shot—except that the entire central section of the frame has been blotted out. The diegesis makes no effort to supply an internal justification for the shadow cutting across the center of the frame; the only source of light, the candle, has been extinguished.

The sexual connotations of the murder, the attack as rape, as literal extinction of the woman, might account for the impression of censorship associated with masking parts of the frame. But by hiding Blanche's body and what is happening to her, the shot accentuates the degree of violence, calling attention to it as censorship tends to do. Another possible explanation is that this is the killer's view of the murder, with his own presence torn away, his authority so strong that it momentarily exceeds the narrative and disrupts the camera's ability to see. But the killer doesn't need to exceed the narrative. The visual system has obscured his identity from the beginning.

In this single shot, the cinematic signifier forfeits its ability to claim authorial distance from the killer's point of view. In a brazen revelation of the enunciation, the center of the frame is ripped away, the woman reduced to nothingness, the camera obliterating her as fiercely as it shields him.

Early in the film, Helen accepts a buggy ride from a handsome young doctor (Kent Smith). In a scene that verges on parody, the doctor is forced to carry the entire conversation himself, awkwardly providing expository dialogue about Helen's past (on the order of "I know seeing your parents burned alive must have been traumatic and your inability to scream then has lead to this silence"). By her silence, Helen allows the doctor to position her in ways that appeal to him.

However, as long as her true feelings about the doctor and the past are held in reserve, and as long as she refuses to obey those who insist she speak, the danger looms that this seemingly pathetic silence might be a cover for rebellion. Her silence is what makes her inscrutable and a source of obsession for the other characters and the audience. The problem of woman's insistent silence is that it acts as a goad to, an overt expression of, even an accusation against patriarchal society's deafness to women's discourse.

In the male/eye, female/mouth dichotomy, a woman's voice, her ability to speak, is figured as the corollary of his eyes. Helen's mutism is a lack she can overcome, but she can only do so within the narrative by assuming her approved social role as "woman"—helpless, grateful, and dependent. The engine driving the narrative and providing the suspense is whether or not Helen will recover her ability to speak in time to save herself from the unseen killer who stalks her. Vocally, this is represented in the text by screaming. In classical texts, women are supposed to scream; it can signify sexual arousal, victimization, helplessness, death, or act as the hero's cue. In fact, it is as unusual for women *not* to scream as it is for men to resort to vocal expressions of fear.[2] (Perhaps this is because women recognize their position in culture with horror, while men seldom see "the horror"—or else, as in this case, they *are* the horror.)

And in fact she does recover the ability to speak when she screams. As the professor (another kind of doctor) explains his revulsion and his intention to kill Helen too, she cowers, but cannot speak. Just then his invalid, masculine mother, assuming the power of the father, aborts her abnormal, effeminate stepson by shooting him. This unexpected display of female power (a *coupe de mère*) evidently so shocks Helen that she forgets she can't speak and does what "comes naturally"; she screams. Helen rushes to the telephone and finally assumes her proper place—on her knees, calling the doctor for help.

E. Ann Kaplan summarizes the feminist debate on the political implications of women's silence. Using Lacanian concepts of language, "it follows that if language is by definition 'male,' women who speak it are alienated from themselves" (Kaplan 1983, p. 93). Silence, then, seems the only alternative. However, "a real contradiction faces women: as long as they remain silent . . . 'they will be outside of the historical process'" (ibid., quoting Xaviere Gauthier). Because of this, "it is dangerous" to adopt silence as a response and so "accept women's exclusion from the symbolic realm," Kaplan observes. "Silence seems at best a temporary, and desperate, strategy, a defense against domination, a holding operation, rather than a politics that looks toward women's finding a viable place for themselves in culture" (ibid., pp. 102, 103).

How women are to confront language, to speak in their own voices, is not addressed in the fundamentally conservative *Spiral Staircase*. The mother is left having negated her motherhood, so exhausted by the effort as to be on the verge of death. Helen learns to scream, accedes to language, and is thus recuperated into her role as dependent, helpless, soon-to-be wife.

Blackmail (1929)

In the even more interesting *Blackmail*, patriarchal culture is indicted with the exposure of its intentional suppression of the woman's voice. Although it was made seventeen years before the other films discussed in this chapter, *Blackmail* provides an illuminating second "take" on the traumatized, silent woman. The dis-synchronization of the female character's image and voice and her problematic relation to language are the central issues of nearly every scene in Hitchcock's first sound film.

The most striking manifestation of the heroine's visual/aural fragmentation lies in the dubbing of the lead character, Alice White, marking the material conditions of post-sync sound in the transitional period as crucial to the issue of the representation of the woman. The decision to dub the central female character was made by Hitchcock and the British producers. Anny Ondra, a silent film star in England, had a heavy Czech accent. Dubbing was a common solution in the earliest days of sound for studios and producers whose success in the years prior to sound had depended to a great extent on foreign actors. Although audiences knew these players were foreign (a great deal of publicity having established this as part of their "other-worldly" personas), in silent films an actress like Ondra was free to play either a foreign princess or the girl next door. In sound films, accents locked such stars into "exotic" roles at a time when vamps and sheiks were distinctly out of fashion. The desire to hear everyday speech, slang, and the vernacular created new stars in America and was felt in England as well. "Hear our Mother Tongue as it should be Spoken," a British poster for *Blackmail* proclaims (Barr 1983). Consequently a "woman," in effect, was constructed according to the production team's idea of what a woman should be—half agreeable appearance, half acceptable accent. The desire to dub Ondra was therefore in response to a cultural/realist demand ("local English girls don't talk like that") and the subsequent economic demand (the public wouldn't "buy" a Czech "posing" as a Chelsea shopgirl).

The technical limitations of the day made accurate lip-syncing virtually impossible. While Ondra mouthed the words, a second actress, Joan Barrie, spoke the dialogue offscreen. The failure of synchronization between lips and words makes a present-day audience constantly aware of the process of synchronization, taken for granted in every other sound film and ostensibly the "talkie's" reason for being.

The dubbing of Alice is a literal example of what Rick Altman calls sound cinema's ventriloquism. In arguing against the alleged "redundancy" of sound and image, Altman states that the two have a "complementary relationship whereby sound uses the image to mask its own actions" and vice versa. "Far from undermining each other, . . . each track serves as mirror for the other. . . . the two are locked in a dialectic where each is alternately master and slave to the other." Through this illusion of wholeness, untainted by the "scandal" of a mechanical source, the "myth of cinema's unity—and thus that of the spectator" is perpetuated (Altman 1980b, p. 79).

The failure of synchronization fragments the unified subject created by successful synchronization by revealing the material heterogeneity underlying the sound film. It exposes "Alice," the character with whom the audience would usually identify, as a (re)production, a composite made up from several

Alfred Hitchcock with Anny Ondra on the set of *Blackmail*

sources. Because the convention of synchronization is designed to make lip-syncing seem "natural" and easy, the actress's painfully apparent exertions to say one word "right," in perfect sync, break down illusions of smoothness, as well as interfering with spectator identification. The spectator is denied the specular and auditory pleasure realized in simply watching an image appear to "speak." In being dubbed—and badly at that—Alice becomes a voiceless Echo, betraying the inadequacy of the image, its nature as shadow, and the vague threat of a voice that is not fixed, not fully secured to the narrativized image.

It is difficult to say whether audiences in 1929 were as intolerant of lapses in synchronization as contemporary audiences. Accepting that "meanings are not fixed and limited for all time within a text," and that "it is likely that they will be read in different ways at different times and places" (Kuhn 1982, p. 94), and rather than try to recapture whatever phenomenological impact *Blackmail* might have had upon its audience in 1929, the following analysis is an attempt to read the film according to contemporary issues: the ways in which woman is positioned by cinematic processes of signification, and the function of the sound track in this process.

Although 1929 was rather late for a "first" sound film, the delay enabled Hitchcock to produce an advanced meditation on the possible uses of sound. The text incorporates silent footage (lifted whole from the original silent version, made immediately prior to the sound version), which allows for a series of comparisons/contrasts between sound and silents/silence. The conceit of this early sound film is an attempt to keep a man silent (paying off a blackmailer). The heroine spends over a third of the film virtually speechless. When she finally speaks, her boyfriend urges her to keep quiet. The dialogue is laughably banal, yet the right word can cut like a knife. The opening scene, an exciting silent chase, is immediately contrasted with a poorly dubbed, confusingly cut dialogue scene that seems as if it will never end. But before we glibly assume silents were "better" movies, sound becomes a moral force, while silence is linked with corruption and moral lassitude.

The text's position on "sound plus image" versus "image alone" is carefully paralleled with the depiction of Alice. Thematically, she veers from one extreme to the other. She is introduced as a chatterbox. After a violent assault, she becomes almost catatonic. Finally, she accepts speech as a moral imperative, achieving maturity and the audience's respect before slipping back under patriarchal control and enforced silence. Alice White becomes Hitchcock's personification of the course the sound film must take.

After the opening scene, detailing an arrest, Frank, a Scotland Yard detective, meets his girlfriend, Alice, back at the station. Totally caught up in his work, Frank explains why he's late by telling Alice that the great (male) machinery of the Yard cannot be rushed for a woman. As they walk outside, Alice begins to giggle. Frank asks what she is thinking about, but she keeps it to herself. In another context, Mary Ann Doane describes the result of such a construction: "The voice displays what is inaccessible to the image, what exceeds the visible: the 'inner life' of the character" (in Weis and Belton 1985, p. 168). Already the sound marks Alice's voice as the signifier of an inner woman inaccessible to Frank.

At dinner, Alice is again dissatisfied with Frank. His idea of a good time is to see a movie about Scotland Yard, called *Fingerprints*. (Fingerprints, incidentally, like the silent film image, are visually perceptible physical imprints, whose alleged ability to indicate guilt or innocence would prove totally inadequate in the case we are about to see.) An artist, on the other hand, has sent her a note saying that *he* is waiting to see *her*. While Frank is clearly the force of order (safe, secure, predictable), the artist attracts Alice with a bohemian quality that suggests he is outside Victorian expectations and constraints. Yet Alice has trouble deciding. Verbally, all she does is equivocate. Frank, exasperated, walks out (making her choice for her), and she leaves with the artist.

In his apartment, the artist seems unhurried, kind, and enjoys Alice's company. However, this scene is gradually revealed as a series of subtly graded attempts by the male character to control both the female's image and her speech. Alice draws a face that could be either male or female. The artist, controlling her hand, adds a sexy female body. Alice toys with the idea of putting on a fancy dress and asks if it will fit. She may sound a little silly, but she clearly feels free to try new things. He urges her to try on the dress while he plays the piano. Hitchcock indulges/accuses his/our voyeurism as she undresses behind a black screen but remains visible to the camera. This creates a split-screen effect. Alice looks like an idea in the artist's mind, a projection of white on black, a silent image to his "all-singing, all-talking" one. He sings a song about the twenties' "wild youth" ("There's no harm in you, Miss of Today") and when Alice steps out, he informs her, "That's you," defining her in the lyrics of the song. While Alice takes dressing up as part of her adventure, one of the possibilities opening up to her, the artist uses it as an excuse to kiss her, implying that her willingness to experiment with her image shows that she has in fact agreed to accept the image he has given her. The kiss upsets Alice, and she wants to leave, but the artist dominates her further by witholding her dress. Finally, he physically drags her out of the frame despite her reluctance. He terms her objections "silly."

The series of uninterrupted, static long takes in the scene leading up to the rape give Alice's exchanges with the artist an unstructured quality noticeably absent from the stilted restaurant scene with Frank. The limited camera movement in contrast to the acoustic "opening up" (the use of music and verbal wit) allows the characters constantly to experiment with their positions, increasing the sense of freedom. Alice's being forced by modesty to retreat behind a screen to change her dress underscores the psychological progression of the scene by indicating to us that she isn't as free as she thinks she is and that the open apartment could become a trap.

Charles Barr compares this scene with its counterpart in the silent version of *Blackmail* (apparently released only in Britain). The silent version of the scene in the artist's studio has eight shots and two titles, both of the artist addressing Alice: "Alice" and "I've got it" (when she is looking for her dress). As Barr describes it, "The silent sequence, then, is based on montage, reverse-field cutting and mobility of the camera and viewpoint; the sound sequence has none of these." He disagrees with "Rotha's 1929 verdict that the silent version was infinitely better by virtue of 'the action having its proper freedom.'" Barr argues that as "post-Bazin era" spectators, "we have more 'freedom' watching the sound sequence" (Barr 1983, p. 124). While the spectator/auditor's "freedom" is, of course, constrained in both versions, the sound version offers a greater potential ambiguity in attributing psychological motivation to the two characters.

The series of shot / reverse shot alternations reproduced in the stills accompanying Barr's article resemble classic melodrama, intimating an impending "fate worse than death." This construction is so much a part of the "damsel in distress" silent film that the next shot could well reveal Frank and the Mounties riding to the rescue. The use of the long take in the sound version, with Alice unwittingly trapped in a large empty set that invites her to feel free, and where any choice she makes is ultimately revealed as having been the wrong choice, is finally more claustrophobic and threatening than the looming close-ups of a sinister Cyril Ritchard as the artist cut opposite high angle shots of a cowering Alice. The sound version is a more subtle achievement, with the bright and inviting apartment of the easy-going artist changing imperceptibly into a suffocating enclosure.

Up to this point, Alice's words have had little individual impact. Her dialogue has consisted of clichés, slang phrases, and expressions of indecisiveness indicating that she doesn't know her own mind. Ironically, when she definitely says "No," it is discounted. The futility of her discourse, her attempt to establish an independent identity in the face of male domination is now forcefully introduced. By cutting to a static long shot of a draped bed, Hitchcock eliminates the image's ability to tell us simple facts of plot or action. The only movement is Alice's hand, fingers flexing against the air, literally unable to come to grips with the assault taking place.

With the visual obstruction of the action, the spectator must rely on the sound track for information. Alice screams, "No! Let me go!" over and over, her voice the only instrument that keeps her from being absorbed into the oblivion represented by her invisibility. However, her words are ignored; her attacker doesn't listen; the policeman outside is oblivious; Hitchcock doesn't spare her. Alice is forced either to allow herself to be victimized or else resort to violence. The music is suddenly brought in at full volume as Hitchcock returns action to the image with a cut to a close-up of Alice's hand finding the knife that will free her.

The trauma that occurs in this scene and that must be worked through for the rest of the film is the separation of image-track and sound track. Alice is stratified; she becomes a silent image or (as in the rape scene) a disembodied voice. The question the film raises is whether or not it is possible to reunite image and voice, the very question film itself was facing in the early sound era. As long as Alice occupies the two irreconcilable extremes—silence and screaming—she remains powerless. The question dramatically posed by the rest of the narrative ("When will she speak?") implies the text's resolution of her verbal impotence/catatonia: mature speech unified with her image. However, as we shall see, the wholeness and potency associated with the synchronization of image and voice are ultimately denied to Alice, who cannot bring herself to speak at the right time and whose voice is (literally) never her own.

The power of words, when wielded by others, is imposed on Alice at breakfast the next morning, when she is presumably in the bosom of her family. As Alice sits down, a local gossip relates in gory detail the horrible "murder" that has occurred. The near-monologue fades to a murmur while the word "knife" is amplified, sharpened. The blurring/accenting functions as audio "point of view," a famous use of subjective sound.

The manipulation of the sound track is augmented by the use of standard point-of-view construction in an alternation of shots of Alice staring avidly before her and close-ups of a breadknife. The combination of image and sound track develops a clear, even overemphasized, depiction of Alice's psychological state and of the relationship between knives and her efforts at control. She used the first knife to regain control of her environment and stop the attack; here, she unconsciously tries to deny she ever had control of the original knife by suddenly flinging the breadknife to the floor. Sound functions here as the representation of moral consciousness, reflecting on and deepening the meaning of the earlier action/image.

At this point in a classical Hollywood film, the hero would enter and take over—speaking for the heroine, protecting her, explaining situations, devising scenarios, and verbally controlling the world for both of them. However, Hitchcock insists on Alice's discourse. Although she is often speechless, instead of turning to the detective to relate the "truth" and take charge, Hitchcock makes us wait for Alice. Frank has been assigned to investigate the "murder" of the artist. He finds Alice's glove at the scene and goes to ask her what it means. As Frank impatiently waits, Alice (center of the frame) plays with her sweater, looks away and shakes her head. No music fills the space. We are left with a silence that is consequently all the more uncomfortable for character and audience.

Thus the dramatic structure of the film has been transformed. The suspense now rests entirely on Alice's asserting her version of events, her discourse, the truth. This is the need established in the audience, which must now be satisfied. Instead of wondering, "Who done it?" we ask, "When will she speak?"

But Alice finds it extremely difficult to speak except in the near-nonsensical utterances of a young lady at tea. A blackmailer who had seen Alice and the artist together outside the artist's apartment arrives and tries to blackmail Alice and Frank. Attracting the attention of Alice's parents, he brazenly invites himself to breakfast. With all eyes on her, all Alice can manage to blurt out after the fact is "Would you stay for breakfast?"—clearly inadequate to the tense situation, but for the moment all she can handle.

Kaplan points out the inadequacy of language to express crises common to the lives of women. The character Norah in Fritz Lang's *The Blue Gardenia* is in a situation similar to Alice's: an attempted date-rape resulting in the woman's seemingly killing the man in self-defense.

> Norah's inability to "remember" or *to say* what actually happened represents the common experience of women in patriarchy—that of feeling unable to reason well because the terms in which the culture thinks are male and alien.

Women in patriarchy do not function competently at the level of external public articulation and thus may appear "stupid" and "uncertain."

(Kaplan 1978b, p. 85; italics added)

This encapsulates Alice's position as well, and might account for some of the hostile reactions to her character in writing on *Blackmail*.[3]

Just as the artist would not concede Alice control of her image or validity to her speech, Frank also tries to suppress her. Far from helping Alice overcome her fear of speech, when she succeeds in getting out a word, Frank snaps, "Don't interfere." It's her life, but it's his job, which from the beginning has taken precedence over Alice. Visually, Frank and the blackmailer work together, surrounding Alice or forcing her to the edges of the frame. Dramatically, the men are engaged in an effort to keep Alice's actions secret.

Where the standard film detective's goal is to find and thus establish for us the "truth," here Frank knows the truth. His job has become to suppress it in deference to a greater goal—the Victorian patriarchal control of women's sexuality. In this case, it is preserving the illusion of control while ushering Alice back into the fold that counts. After all, what Frank is protecting Alice (and society) from is the public admission that she chose her own male companion and assumed the authority to say whether or not she would have sex.

Formally, the respective moral sensitivities of Frank and Alice are linked to cinema. Codes of silent and sound film are made to interrogate each other, each representing the two characters who are at odds with each other, Frank and Alice. While it might seem that Frank, earlier so dedicated to the Yard and police procedure, would have scruples about hiding evidence, Hitchcock (never a fan of the police) reveals that he has surprisingly few hesitations. To keep things quiet, Frank considers paying blackmail. He finds it more appealing to frame an innocent man than to seek justice. Frank's job is redefined; he is not supposed to find the truly guilty but to maintain law and order, the status quo, appearances. Caught in his failure to control Alice, Frank simplifies the situation. He accuses the ex-convict blackmailer of the "murder." Forced to run, the man dies in the chase.

Police procedure is characterized throughout the film as a silent film chase. The pursuit of the wrongly accused man refers us back to the opening scene, which used the same set of silent film conventions. Through the comparison we can now recognize the lack of moral thoroughness that results when action (visual only) proceeds without verbal (moral) qualifiers; the power of force is celebrated over the power of reflection, appearances over truth. In the opening scene, the police push their way into the room of a man who looks typically "criminal" (unshaven, surly). Suspenseful music reminiscent of that in silent film melodramas is laid over the visuals, while ambient sounds and speech are removed. When the man is arrested, however, his neighbors object and crowd around the police. Who is this man? What is the charge? What do we the audience know about him except the stereotype of the silent film thug? The image shows us the surface, but we never do find out the purpose or justness of the arrest. The haste to judge on the basis of appearances foreshadows the end of the film's second chase. The wrong man dies in a mindless, impurely motivated chase, persecuted by the police because it is convenient for the police. They pursue the matter no further. Once the action has been carried out, they wash up and go home (as in the first scene).

The framing of the blackmailer is the dilemma that forces Alice to break her silence. The chase is intercut with Alice sitting at a table, troubled by her conscience. She writes a note, refusing to participate through her silence in what amounts to a lynching. She writes that she must "speak up" to save "this poor man." However the crosscutting reveals that her efforts are too little and too late. As the blackmailer is about to shout the true identity of the killer, he falls to his death.

Alice arrives at the police station ready to speak. The station is a male cloister, where a woman must apply to the doorman in writing (!) for admission. The sergeant, who recognizes Alice as Frank's girl, laughs at the thought of a young lady knowing anything about a "murder." Alice is led to the chief inspector's office. Frank arrives to "rescue" her by preventing her from carrying out her plan. As she struggles to choose the right words, Frank interrupts to tell the chief that what she has to say can't be important. The chief interrupts her by taking a call in the middle of her statement.

The dialogue warns us that Alice is doomed to fail. She is still unable to finish a sentence. She stutters, repeats herself, announces that she is about to say something and generally prevaricates. The space between sound and image remains a chasm. She has not been able to unite image and voice. On the contrary, if Alice wants to keep her "good" image, she has to keep silent and let Frank usher her out of the room. Where Frank, the chief, and the sergeant take it for granted that speaking moves straightforwardly along pre-set male-controlled channels of meaning, Alice is completely incapable of making the words serve or even accord with her intentions when she is called to account for herself to the male head of the law. Her attempt to speak has failed and she is hustled away.

Out in the hall, Alice breaks down and tells Frank her actions were in self-defense, but what she says clearly does not matter. Out of convenience, the forces of law and order have blamed a dead man. Frank has returned Alice to her constrained place within patriarchy. She has been forced to submit herself to the judgment of the police, to "confess" her "crime," and her confession has been totally contained by the system. Alice's story is dismissed (the *real* truth) and she is turned over, in effect, to Frank's custody.

Standing between Frank and the sergeant, Alice is literally surrounded by the police. "Next they'll be having lady inspectors," the sergeant jokes. Alice joins in the laughter. She is back in line and won't step out again. Another policeman takes the artist's painting of a clown to be filed away. The leering, pointing clown reminds Alice to look at herself. She stops laughing.

In *Blackmail*, maturity comes at the cost of innocence. Alice resumes her place in patriarchy, but has to acknowledge that she is neither innocent nor free. Frank succeeds in containing Alice, but is forced to compromise his duty and any idealism in favor of maintaining appearances. Frank and Alice are painfully aware of the price of socialization. The recognition of the workings of patriarchy and language precludes a romantically happy ending. Alice and Frank are fragmented and must confront that what society holds they should be is actually very far from what they are. The end only increases their disintegration. Their images are false and they are struck dumb.[4]

Notorious (1946)

In many ways the relationship between sound and the woman in Hitchcock's *Notorious* is the exact opposite of that found in *Blackmail*, produced seventeen years earlier. The sound design flawlessly adheres to classical conventions governing sound. Far from being dubbed, the film's sound track devotes special attention to the synchronization of the image and voice of leading lady Ingrid Bergman. Despite a certain wariness regarding issues of feminine specificity in connection with the voice, the function of the woman's voice, even when contained by classical sound conventions, is far from simplistic. In fact, in this film, the woman's voice is presented with such fervor, approaching reverence, that it becomes almost an audio-fetish, the voice of the star as a new source of cinematic spectacle. And in a scene that serves as the turning point of the narrative, the woman's control of her voice is radically undermined when the technology of sound recording is exposed as a male prerogative.

The voice is an integral part of the star system, and Ingrid Bergman's accent was an important part of her persona. Doane notes that "the voice serves as a support for the spectator's recognition and his/her identification of, as well as with, the star" (Weis and Belton 1985, p. 164). Bergman's lilting Swedish accent was publicized and frequently accounted for in the roles she played. In her first English-speaking role in the remake of *Intermezzo* (1939), Bergman's accent, combined with her wholesome, well-fed looks, lent her a "farmer's daughter" quality of openness that contrasted favorably with the wan upperclass angst of the British Leslie Howard and Edna Best. (It would be interesting to compare the English language version of *Intermezzo* with the original, in which everyone spoke Swedish and where Bergman would have been more "the girl next door" and less the "innocent abroad.") Bergman's shining persona was very popular and, packaged as innocence, was worked into *Casablanca* (1942), *The Bells of St. Mary's* (1945), and *Joan of Arc* (1948).[5] *Notorious* invokes Bergman's accent more complexly and the question of whether her accent *is* good becomes a central concern of the film.

Michael Renov (1980, p. 30) suggests that the central issue of the film turns on the labeling of Alicia Huberman as "notorious"—"the key term" in the narrative's "enunciation of sexual difference." In addition to the dubious moral accuracy of Alicia's "notoriety," there is the question of her "virtue" as defined by the war. Can she be trusted politically as well as sexually? Or, put another way, will she harness her sexuality in service to the government and ultimately to male-dominated monogamy? This question is constantly posed subliminally by Bergman's accent as the film's narrative works to uncover the persistent presence of the "enemy" in the immediate postwar period. The carefully enunciated "Huberman" (rhymes with *über Mann*) sounds suspiciously Teutonic. The film's only explanation of Alicia's accent occurs at the precise moment when the question of who she is—a Nazi or a "real" American—hangs in the balance. While the answer is being worked out at the narrative level, her accent continually marks her as "other."

The dialogue, combined with several striking close-ups, repeatedly directs our attention to the star's voice as well as her accent. In the opening scenes, Alicia is drunk and slurring her words. She hesitates before choosing a word, then rushes on. The resulting slightly unpredictable rhythm, the alternation of blurry, then precise, enunciation, exacts an extra attentiveness toward Alicia's dialogue. In comic scenes, her use of everyday slang becomes an amusing surprise considering the source is a suspected foreign spy. At one point Alicia dismisses a love song by saying, "It's a lot of—hooey." Her unsteady negotiations around English parallel her unsteady walk in the drunk scenes, as well as signifying the character's psychological confusion.

The use of internal rhymes, alliteration, and repetition in the dialogue emphasizes the musicality of Bergman's voice, stressed particularly in the romantic scenes.

> "I'm happy. Why won't you let me be happy?"
> "Why won't you believe in me, Dev. Just a little. Why won't you?"
>
> "Oh darling, tell me what you didn't tell them."

In these scenes the sound is sculpted, intimate tones amplified, private, but clearly available to the audience. Bergman's voice is brought forward in the mix, placed in strong relief to the background sounds so that there is literally nothing else to hear.

In *Notorious*, what is out of place, a scandal to patriarchal control, is the speaking sexual woman. Alicia's control of her voice represents control of her sexuality. In the opening scene, the government agent Devlin's (Cary Grant) point of view is undermined by Alicia's cynical, sarcastic wisecracks. Despite her occasionally uncertain enunciation, Alicia's constant talk and movement dominate the scene. In marked contrast, the male romantic lead is introduced with the back of his head to the camera, a mere spectator at Alicia's wild party. The apparent undercutting of the male's point of view is part of Hitchcock's "continuous manipulation of the most disruptive elements of classical cinema," Renov asserts (1980, p. 30), but through a "complex system of projection and fragmentation" (supported by a classically "gendered system of spectatorship"), the patriarchal (negative) characterization of the woman as that dangerous object of desire (rather than desiring subject) is consolidated and reenforced.[6]

Janet Bergstrom argues that in Hitchcock's films "the woman's desire is the central *problem* or challenge for the male protagonist." The narrative reduces the threat posed by the woman through the process of fetishization, "the pleasure of seeing the woman's body in pieces," which becomes "a guarantee of the safety (coherence, totality) of the man's" (1979, p. 53). In *Notorious*, Alicia is deconstructed as a speaking woman and re-presented as an object of visual and auditory pleasure.

After spending an evening with a bitter and drunken Alicia, Devlin proposes that she volunteer to assist the government—the "cops" she "detests." She leaves the room, uninterested. He takes a phonograph record he has brought with him and plays it. It is a recording of a conversation between Alicia and her father, a convicted Nazi spy now in prison. While we hear Mr. Huberman urging Alicia to help the Nazis, we see a shot of the doorway to Alicia's room. Slowly she steps into the doorway in the center of the frame. Distractedly brushing her hair, she listens to her own voice proclaiming her patriotism. Devlin enters the shot, joining her in the doorway. They stand facing forward and listen to the diegetic voice-over.

Watching Alicia listen, the audience is presented with a fragmented woman, stratified evidence that in its very construction invites reevaluation of the character of Alicia. "If the ideology of the visible demands that the spectator understand the image as a truthful representation of reality, the ideology of the audible demands that there exist simultaneously a different truth and another order of reality for the subject to grasp," Doane observes (Weis and Belton 1985, p. 55). Alicia's asynchronous voice, captured on a hidden phonograph, is narrativized as revealing her "true" feelings. The voice-over effect as Alicia and Devlin listen ideologically positions the dialogue as representing a deeper, previously hidden level of truth. "The voice displays what is inaccessible to the image, what exceeds the visible: the 'inner life' of the character. The voice here is the privileged mark of interiority" (ibid., p. 168).

Devlin positions Alicia as a patriotic woman. When she objects in person, he whips out the "real Alicia," a recording he has had in his possession all along. Because the introduction of the audible brings with it a new level of interiority and a concomitant greater "truth" value, Alicia's protests cannot

Cary Grant and Ingrid Bergman in *Notorious*

bear any weight. Her synchronized "spoken" dialogue is discounted as surface, a pose, while the asynchronous dialogue is the deeper, unmediated truth.

In a reversal of the ideology of the camera obscura, Devlin has in his possession the essence, the inner truth of Alicia's enigma—what she *sounds* like.
Furthermore, this "audible essence," like the visual essence of the world provided by the camera obscura, is ownable, portable, and available for exhibition. Compared to this powerful combination, the physical Alicia and her
voice (the real Alicia) are markedly reduced in value. "In dominant cinema,

women do not tell their own stories or control their own images [or voices], but are ideologically positioned in patriarchal terms," Kuhn says, paraphrasing Claire Johnston (Kuhn 1982, p. 88).

Jean-Louis Comolli identifies the extreme care taken to preserve synchronization as the sign of ideology at work. Synchronization carries with it "the concept of the 'individual as master of speech' [and] indicates a desire to preserve the status of speech as an individual property right—subject only to a manipulation which is not discernable" (quoted in Doane 1985a, in Weis and Belton 1985, p. 58). The dis-synchronization of Alicia's voice from her body and from her control is a radical manipulation of sync, obvious and discernable, and denies to her as a woman the "individual property right" scrupulously maintained in the film for the male characters. Because he operates the technology, Devlin can orchestrate a conversation with Alicia when she is out of the room, dictating when "she" will speak, turning her dialogue on or off as it suits him. By disregarding the woman's right to be the "master" of her speech, the male is able to re-position her in patriarchal terms. Through control of her voice, she is recuperated.

After the recording ends, Devlin asks Alicia for her decision, but she is mute. Her voice has been taken from her. A yachtsman, her friend, arrives and suggests she hurry, because they are about to sail. Alicia, conceding that Devlin has the power to speak for her, turns to him and says, "You had better tell him."

Devlin exits the two-shot he shared with Alicia and she is left alone, watching him go. The next shot is the reverse angle showing Devlin's back as he disappears out the door. There is a cut to Alicia watching. This classically constructed point-of-view shot briefly presents us with Alicia as the one who looks and Devlin as the one who runs. But coming at this point in the narrative, when she has just lost control of her image and her voice and submitted to Devlin's authority, the woman's ability to authorize the look is fleeting and of no consequence.

Once Devlin has attained control of Alicia's speech, and thereby resolved the issue of her political notoriety, it is a brief step to resolve the question of her sexual promiscuity. In "Spectacle and Narrative Theory," Lea Jacobs and Richard de Cordova discuss how alternating close-ups in *The Scarlet Empress* at a certain point begin to lose their function of advancing the narrative and assume the function of spectacle (1982). In key shots in *Notorious,* Hitchcock presents Bergman in shimmering close-ups for the male gaze. When she makes declarations of love and dependence to Devlin after forfeiting all control of her actions to him, her face glows with "star" lighting and soft focus, completely at odds with the hard-edged long-shots used in the opening party scene. The romantic transformation is supported by the manipulation of the sound track. Alicia's voice is mixed forward and amplified. There is a slight echo-chamber effect that softens the tone, giving it a richness verging on excess. Alicia is no longer presented on the sound track the way Devlin is, as a functioning character in the narrative, but as a visual and aural object of pleasure.

The handling of Bergman's voice exceeds what could be called the "narrative volume," the recording and mixing practices allotted Devlin and the other male figures, and even Alicia prior to her romantic submission. Even in those earlier scenes, with her promiscuity and outspoken criticism of the system, Alicia is playing by their rules. She is aware that she is trapped, that others (the press, the FBI) have defined her, and in a rage perversely tries to live "down" to their image of her. She drinks too much, drives too fast, and in effect tries to kill herself rather than conform to society's rules. But Alicia is only marginally freer in her rebellion than in her submission. There is no place for her that is not already inscribed within the poles of "womanhood," as either whore or wife.

Instead, the dangerous sexual, speaking woman slides out of the narrative into shimmering light, murmuring promises of pleasure to male spectators as she steps into the realm of audio/visual spectacle.

The conclusion of *Notorious* illustrates Alicia's positioning as a fetishized object available to the audience and the men in the narrative (Devlin, his boss, and the Nazi sympathizer Devlin's agency wants her to marry, Alex Sebastian). Following the loss of her voice, Alicia becomes an object of possession and exchange, passing through the roles prescribed for women by patriarchy— employee, prostitute, wife—finally becoming the ultimate object, the helpless female waiting to be rescued by the active, heroic, coherent male.

Sorry, Wrong Number (1948)

In films such as *Notorious* and *Sorry, Wrong Number* where women initially seem to have the power of speech, they talk too much and must be silenced. Furthermore, their words are meaningless, characterized as babble (fitting term for those trying to speak an incomprehensible language imperfectly heard from a far-off country).

Sorry, Wrong Number was adapted from a very successful radio drama.[7] As such, it is one of the few cinematic texts that has a free-standing auditory text to which it can be compared, the appeal of radio competing, as it were, with film's cinematic pleasures. The central figure of the woman, controlling the narrative through the telephone and her voice, becomes the focal point of a tense negotiation between sound-based narrative and the power of the image, the dangers of an overweaning sound track merged with the figure of an overbearing woman.

After a brief prologue illustrating the labor of telephone operators, the film introduces us to Leona Stevenson (Barbara Stanwyck), a woman trying to call her husband at the office. The bedridden Leona accidentally overhears two men on a party line plotting to kill a woman that night. Torn between trying to alert the indifferent police and contacting her husband Henry (Burt Lancaster), Leona grows more and more distraught. In addition, she receives a

series of disturbing calls from strangers, informing her of Henry's recent il-
legal activities. She finally realizes that *because* of her husband, she is the
woman the men are planning to kill, and, as she finally reaches him on
the phone, they do. Though confined to her bed, Leona in effect organizes
the narrative through what she hears. She is the one who makes sense of the
narrative, and as such becomes our surrogate, an auditing spectator within
the text.

It is interesting to compare the character of Leona as a spectator-surrogate
(especially a female one) with L. B. Jeffries in Hitchcock's *Rear Window*
(1954). The films illustrate differing male/female relations to knowledge,
marriage, work, and voyeurism, as well as differences between sound and image and their related technologies. In place of the man who actively looks/
sees/knows, *Sorry, Wrong Number* presents a woman who accidentally overhears, against her will learns, and, because she knows, dies.

The characters are similar, as are their circumstances. Both are invalids,
Jeff confined to a wheelchair, Leona to bed. Her illness is a (the) feminine
condition of invalidism and smacks of nineteenth-century antecedents like
Henry James's sister Alice, strong women who could not openly exercise
power and who masked their extraordinary will by an extravagant show of
physical weakness.[8] Dr. Alexander, praising the miracle of twentieth-century
psychiatry, insists that Leona's illness is all in her mind. ("Oh, the pain's real
enough," he says to Henry, who smashes the nearest phone.) Jeff has become
incapacitated in a more masculine way, through a violent collision in the
course of his work. Each is a busybody and a meddler. Jeff uses his camera to
shut out the woman in his life, to avoid marriage and fix the world as it is.
Leona, on the other hand, is very much married and uses the telephone to
obsessively track Henry down.

From the central base of a single room, both characters are isolated and
free to use their instruments. His is the camera; hers is the telephone. However, while Jeff is able to make a living off of his visual drive, what Leona can
get from the telephone is transitory compared to Jeff's captured (and saleable)
moments. What Leona hears comes and goes like the train rattling her window at night, and when it is gone there is no proof that it ever passed. When
Leona tries to tell the police she overheard a conversation, the problem remains that she can't prove it and they can't trace it. While Jeff can prove em-
pirically that something is buried in the garden by comparing an old slide with
a new image, Leona's "voices" remain unidentified throughout the course of
the film. Jeff and Leona also have differing relations to voyeurism. Jeff looks
for pleasure; Leona listens for information. *Sorry, Wrong Number* is not so
much *sound*-based as dialogue-based. There is little audio-voyeurism or pleasure in hearing for the *character,* however the original radio audience would
have enjoyed the double thrill of eavesdropping on a woman talking on the
telephone *and* on the people on the other end. Although both films end with
the main character being overwhelmed when the necessary voyeuristic dis-

tance is violated, Leona's listening is a sign of her dependence rather than her will to pursue her own pleasure.

In *Sorry, Wrong Number*, the telephone becomes the woman's instrument, calling to mind the cultural canard about women "talking too much," "all the time," or compulsively on the phone.[9] Like the radio and other sound apparatuses, the telephone is also strictly linked to the home, the woman's sphere under patriarchy.

Several notable texts present the telephone as literally a woman's lifeline. In Jean Cocteau's *La Voix humane* (first filmed in 1948 by Rossellini) and the film *The Slender Thread* (1965) the telephone is our means of access to the "star" and the purpose of the narrative is to ensure that she keeps talking— that is, stays alive. In both cases the women are suicidal, alienated, and isolated, and the telephone is their only means of making tenuous contact. Versions of Cocteau's drama strive to be faithful to their source by maintaining the single set and restricted point of view of this one-woman monologue as we watch the woman talk without our hearing the voice on the other end, but this is essentially theatrical and has nothing to do with the specific character of the voice on the radio or the telephone. By keeping voice and image synchronized, they lose the peculiar quality of the voice as disembodied, as alienated from the body, wandering, lost in the symbolic. Such a quality is preserved in *The Slender Thread,* where a woman calls a suicide prevention hotline. Her only chance of contact is through language and a machine. Each inadequate, together they form an illustration of what is killing her.[10]

Culturally, the telephone has long been offered as a palliative to women. In a study of assumptions about women and telephones, Lana Rakow notes that "early commentar[ies] . . . extolled the virtue of the telephone in reducing women's loneliness." One author, she notes, "claims that by the end of the 1880's, 'telephones were beginning to save the sanity of remote farm wives by lessening their sense of isolation'" (Kramarae 1988, p. 207, quoting John Brooks).

In keeping with the exaggerated claims made for the telephone and aimed at women, a 1938 advertisement for Bell Telephone pictures a Lilliputian woman sitting on a giant telephone over the words, "Few things give you so much convenience, happiness and security—all rolled into one." The title crawl at the beginning of *Sorry, Wrong Number* modifies this optimism with the ubiquitous contemporary fear of crime:

> In the tangled networks of a great city, the telephone is the unseen link between a million lives . . . It is the servant of our common needs—the confidante of our innermost secrets . . . life and happiness wait upon its ring . . . and horror . . . and loneliness . . . and . . . *death!!!*

To some extent the telephone empowers women, enabling them to combine their piecemeal knowledge and find out what is going on in the separate world

Big *in* Value

...Little *in* Cost

of men. In *Sorry, Wrong Number*, we see what amounts to a network of women using the telephone to talk behind men's backs: the secretary talks about her boss, and Sally about her husband, not to mention the rows of telephone operators making these connections possible.

Talking behind her husband's back becomes literal in the case of Sally Lord, an old friend of Leona's and ex-girlfriend of Henry's. She reads in the newspaper that her husband is investigating Henry, but when she asks him about it, he tells her to mind her own business (presumably his isn't hers). She sneaks into the other room to call Leona, then creates an excuse for leaving the house so that she can call Leona back from a pay phone. But no matter how much or little women know, they can only subvert (Sally's husband's plans) or disrupt (Leona interrupts Dr. Alexander's evening out and her father's philandering with her incessant calls). The women talk, but they can't *do* anything. Sally cannot stop her husband's investigation, and Leona cannot make Henry call her back.

Ultimately, the telephone is a sign of Leona's impotence. When she calls for a nurse because she is all alone in the house and frightened, no one will

come. When she calls the number left her by a man who knows something about Henry, she finds she is talking to the morgue. At the same time she is bombarded with incomprehensible information. Henry reassures her that she is safe because there is a telephone right by the bed; she says, "I've been prey to every kind of horrible call." By the time she understands what all the pieces mean, she is incapable of saving herself. As in *The Lonely Villa* (1909), the telephone is revealed to be an instrument that underscores helplessness instead of alleviating it.[11]

The clash of genres, everything frilly and domestic in Leona's sphere compared to the heavy angles and foreboding shadows in Henry's, puts further pressure on the text. As in *Mildred Pierce, Sorry, Wrong Number* illustrates the necessary imbalance that results from trying to combine two antithetical genres, film noir and the woman's film. The strongest dissonance comes when women try, if only momentarily, to control visual point of view and the film's narration. As we have already seen in the earlier films, that very distortion forms the value of these tortured texts. "If female sexuality and female discourse are regarded as together posing the threat of disruption to the linear process of the classic narrative, then that threat must be recuperated or repressed if the story is to have any kind of 'satisfactory' resolution," Annette

Kuhn argues. "Repression of the discourse of the woman," she says, is achieved "by means of a cutting-off," limiting "female control over the film's enunciation" (Kuhn 1982, p. 104).

Doane argues that in the "paranoid gothic . . . there is a concerted effort to locate [the woman] as the subject of knowledge"—in direct contradiction of classical codes. This branch of the woman's film insists "on situating the woman as agent of the gaze, as investigator in charge of the epistemological trajectory of the text" (Doane 1987, p. 134). Although she is quite explicitly barred from control of the gaze because of *Sorry, Wrong Number*'s dependence on hearing and consequent virtual elimination of standard shot/reverse shot, Leona *is* able to control much of the narrative, the cuts determined by what she hears and not what she sees. It is this adherence to radio's different forms of address and different means of constituting the listener/subject that comprises the threat Leona poses toward classical cinema.

Radio dramas are based either on the listener overhearing (a position similar to that of the film viewer, who sees without being seen, or the playgoer, who watches the characters through an invisible "fourth wall") or on direct address (by announcers, narrators, and even characters). Orson Welles's radio broadcast "War of the Worlds" (1938) incorporates both forms, particularly direct address, whereas the original *Sorry, Wrong Number* sticks exclusively to a series of overheard conversations. The third-person form is less potentially disruptive when translated to film than direct address, and is in practice quite compatible with existing classical film structures. As used here, however, the dependence on overhearing, both by the viewer/auditor and characters within the narrative undermines the authority of the visual, resulting in a potentially subversive text.

Occupying the German expressionist/film noir crossroads favored by many European émigrés, such as the film's director, Anatole Litvak, *Sorry, Wrong Number* tells its story through an increasingly complicated flashback structure held together by voice-overs and the central organizing presence of the woman to whom the flashbacks are being narrated. The voices we hear and the stories they tell come to Leona (and us) over the telephone. The telephone conversations are presented by crosscutting between Leona and the caller on the other end. These in turn lead to flashbacks, signaled by a slow dissolve and a marked increase in the volume of the music, as either Leona or the speaker remembers or narrates previous events.

The use of voice-over narration with flashbacks is not in itself enough to distinguish the film from other films of the time. In fact, it is rather common in film noir, where it signals the fragmentation of the narrative. In the 1946 film *The Killers*, a film in many ways similar to *Sorry, Wrong Number*, the flashbacks *are* the story. However, in *The Killers*, directed by Litvak's fellow émigré Robert Siodmak (who also directed *The Spiral Staircase*),[12] the flashbacks assume the authority of an omniscient point of view. Although each major segment is initiated by a particular character, who verbally covers the transitions from present to flashback, nothing within the flashbacks themselves marks them as being to any extent subjective or controlled in any way by the character. In *Sorry, Wrong Number,* as Leona grows more hysterical, the flashbacks and even the cuts to the caller become increasingly expressionistic, both visually and on the sound track. As the film progresses, there is a growing dissolution of any sense of reliable, objective visual information.

Of the six major flashbacks, Leona herself directly authorizes one. She calls Sally Hunt, whom we have seen Henry meet for lunch that day. Sally warns Leona that Henry might be in trouble, but she cannot say what kind of trouble and has to hang up. Leona, speaking to herself, repeats the name "Sally Hunt." This leads in standard form to a flashback (with minimal narration) showing how the rich and glamorous Leona Cotterill stole Sally's hardworking, poor but ambitious boyfriend, Henry. The flashback ends where it began, with Leona in bed, thinking. This is the only flashback that does not make extended use of voice-over, because it is not presented as a story Leona hears, but as something she remembers.

When Sally calls back, she tells Leona that her husband, who is with the district attorney's office, is investigating Henry. As we cut to Sally on the phone, we see a flashback detailing how Sally found out about her husband's work. Sally's story is presented in a strongly expressionistic way, oddly reminiscent of Susannah York's "dream" in *Freud* (1960). In voice-over, Sally says: "It was one of the weirdest days I've ever spent. . . . Parts [of Staten Island] seem to exist in a kind of dream, like the lonely beach we went to that day. It was quite a desolate place, Leona. Far out on the island."

They're on a beach, empty and cold, near a dilapidated, boarded-up house. Sally ducks behind a broken boat, watching her husband and his men. They hide in a nearby shack and watch the house. Nothing happens. After time drags on, she sees a signal from the house. A boat appears. A man with a briefcase steps out and walks into the deserted house. The men follow. Sally runs to a net-strewn stair to get a closer look. Her husband and his men leave, carrying the briefcase.

What is notably different about Sally's story are the strongly disturbing visuals, with their emphasis on diagonals and extreme angles, and the disjointed and incomplete nature of the information. Sally doesn't know a lot and is in constant danger of being discovered by her husband. Her fear seems to infest her perception: "I didn't know what I expected to see. As a matter of fact, there wasn't much I *could* see at first." As she is unaware of what anything means, it all becomes heavy with portent, resulting in the exaggerated images typical of classical "subjective" scenes such as dreams. Leona, our listener-surrogate, repeatedly asks what it can mean. As the central organizing "ear" for whom the story is being told, she knows as little of the significance of this striking scene as we or Sally do.

The third and most complicated structure occurs when Leona's doctor, treating her progressively worsening heart condition, tells her of a meeting he had with Henry where the doctor revealed that Leona's condition was psycho-somatic. As Dr. Alexander (Wendell Corey) narrates his flashback, set in his office, Henry begins to tell him how Leona's heart condition first began as a result of a conflict of wills between them. This triggers Henry's flashback within the doctor's flashback. Inside Henry's flashback, Henry comes across as a well-meaning and tender husband. The question, however, is whether or not this is Henry's view of himself, represented subjectively in his memory, or the doctor's view of Henry. The question of who is "authorizing" Henry's flashback leads to a third possibility—that we are seeing Leona's images. (She listens to the doctor and supplies images to both his story and his version of Henry's story.)

The accelerating expressionism of the visual design and in the foreboding music begins to put not only the control of the flashbacks in doubt, but the crosscutting as well. The reason crosscuts to the speaker work so well is because they fill the slot usually served by conventional shot/reverse shot, with the cut being signaled by the dialogue and not the look. When Leona receives the strangest call of the night from Waldo Evans—a man she does not know—the "reverse shot," the cut to identify the voice on the other end of the line, reveals nothing. As he speaks, we see a silhouette shot from a very low angle. Behind him is a dark room lit only by light coming through the tran-som. The only time we "see" Waldo Evans is in his heavily noir-ish account of his and Henry's black market drug dealings.

The (non)representation of Waldo Evans reenforces the possibility that we have never left Leona's room at all. Each cut to other characters is put in doubt retroactively, submitted to Leona's subjective, but authorial, auditory point of view. As the organizing subject, Leona supplies the faces that go with the voices she hears, the rooms they occupy, the clothes they're wearing (Sally's "poor but honest" milieu, Dr. Alexander's tuxedo and impatient wife, as well as the unidentifiable Mr. Evans). Some voices are never given faces at all (the operators or the hospital receptionist Leona asks to send a nurse). Their func-tion is all we and Leona need to know. This is not to say that Leona imagines the entire movie. The voices are "real," the phone calls real (i.e., not under Leona's control). It is merely the images accompanying them that are called into question as objective visual representations of the voices we hear.

Listening to the radio or talking on the telephone thus become acts of read-ing, even more than watching films. Leona occupies and demonstrates the position of the radio listener, sitting in his or her home, overhearing others speaking yet unable to intervene or make herself heard. Unlike film viewers, the original radio audience would be doing the work Leona does here (through her control of the cinematic signifier), providing faces for the voices and fill-ing in the image of the caller.

No one's images in the radio audience would be more correct that any one else's. In a film, though, the images tend to carry authorial weight. And at first, the crosscutting seems to present equally objective worlds outside

Leona's bedroom, balancing her growing hysteria. It is the authority of these cuts and of the flashbacks within them that are put into doubt by the obsessive return to Leona listening, asking what it means, and the breakdown of "objective" style as Leona struggles to make sense out of the words and voices pouring into her ear.

Depending on flashbacks and crosscutting to open out the original radio play results in a precarious instability of space and time that increases our dependence on Leona as the center of the narrative, the subject constituted as "the one who hears." Classical cinema's rules of spatial, temporal, and narrative continuity strive to ensure a text that seems transparent and unmediated, the story telling itself. Here, the narrative threatens to fly apart and requires an entire system of compensations to hold it together. In order to contain the potential spatial and temporal incoherence, the film constructs a "present" set in a coherent space: Leona in her bedroom from 9:30 to 11:15. Everything else is firmly tied to this, constantly referring back to it in order to preserve a sense of unity.

In radio drama, space and time are far more fluid by nature, program, advertising, and bracketing material all blending into each other, interruption and flow being characteristics of the medium. ("War of the Worlds" is the model textual restatement of the way the form functions.) The construction of space and time therefore requires less regulation than in the classical cinema text. In the original "Sorry, Wrong Number," the "present" is the half hour the program covers, as the narrative observes the dramatic unities, taking place entirely in the present as we listen in on Leona's telephone conversations. Spatially, to radio listeners eavesdropping with the help of radio/telephone technology, we are not so much in Leona's room as on the same line. The "where" is simply where we can hear her. When we no longer hear her, she ceases to exist.

The film maintains a sense of temporal continuity by (1) using voice-overs to make constant reference to the present and having characters address Leona ("Have you ever been to Staten Island, Leona?" Sally asks, over shots of a ferry approaching a dock); (2) employing deadlines in the present tense to give pressure to the scenes outside Leona's bedroom, which are themselves under time constraints (Sally's "five minutes are up" as she tries to speak to Leona, Henry stands in the train station with a clock saying 11:10 prominent behind him); and (3) quickly answering enigmas posed in the present in the flashbacks ("Sally . . . Hunt," Leona says, and we dissolve to a ballroom where Henry is dancing with a blonde, while Leona repeats "Sally Hunt" in voice-over).

Space is inevitably even more fragmented, hence the insistence on the technology of the phone system that links the scattered locations. The protocol of placing and receiving calls is stressed again and again. Operators ask standard questions, speakers repeat the numbers they want, callers ask first whether or not they have the right party. There are pay calls and person-to-person long distance calls and over-the-phone telegram deliveries, and of course a wrong number which is in fact an inadvertently correct connection. In addition, voices are frequently "filtered" so that we hear them as if over a telephone, attesting to the literal connection of the far away with the speaker whom we see before us. Filtering usually occurs near the beginning or end of a conversation as a way of bringing our attention back to the technology.[13]

Verbal transitions are also used. When Leona is talking to Henry's secretary, the secretary asks if Leona got the flowers. "I thought camellias might be nice this time." As she says "camellias," there is a dissolve to a close-up of an arrangement of blossoms and her voice switches to a filter, each marking the transition back to Leona's room. Cutting between speakers in the middle of a sentence eases the transition between physical spaces, while creating the sense of intimacy of a personal conversation, much like shot/reverse shot. Further, *Sorry, Wrong Number* literally softens the movement from space to space (and from time to time) with a heavy use of dissolves, implying the connection between spaces rather than the distance that separates them.

The more disjointed the spatial and temporal systems of the film become, and the more difficult it becomes to determine who "authorizes" the image as the scenes become progressively more subjective, the more heavily we depend on Leona as the subject, the point where all the pieces will be organized into meaning.

The challenge Leona poses to classical cinema is the elimination of "seeing/seen" and the substitution of "hearing/heard." Leona understands everything eventually strictly through what she's heard. If she makes seeing irrelevant, it becomes the job of the camera to render her hearing ineffectual—to place the ear at the mercy of the eye.

When Leona realizes what she has been hearing, it is presented in terms of an audio-montage. The killers have said that "the woman's" bedroom has a window overlooking the river. The servants are gone and her husband will be out. They will kill her when the train goes by because it will drown out her screams. After trying desperately to reach Henry and receiving calls from Sally and Waldo Evans implying Henry is in imminent danger of being arrested, Leona receives a call from Western Union. It is a telegram from Henry saying he won't be coming home because of business. As the train begins to rumble past her window, Leona clutches her forehead. Bits of conversations she has had during the evening echo on the sound track: the train, the location, her husband Henry's trouble with the law. She is at the center of it, the subject of all she has heard, the only place where all the pieces come together.

What Leona recognizes with such horror is the degree of hostility the world (and specifically Henry) holds toward her. The fact that she "accidentally" discovers this is significant: women are not supposed to know their exact place in the scheme of things—that is, that they are not subjects, but objects. Leona's "crime" lies in thinking she is a subject and in struggling to exert a degree of control over her own life. When she meets Henry, she is the sexual exploiter, taking advantage of the well-built young man's poverty. Their marriage montage is dominated by Leona repeating in voice-over, "I, Leona, take thee, Henry." (The poster advertising the film reads, "Heiress to millions . . . who bought everything she wanted . . . including this man!") [14] However, after they're married, Henry wants to decide where they will live and to support them on his salary. Leona, who had fought her father for the right to marry, to control her own money, and to decide where she will live, realizes that she is trapped, this time as Henry's wife (as opposed to Daddy's girl), and has a heart attack. She does not intentionally fake her illness according to the narrative ("the pain's real enough"), and from this point on her will to control her own life (and Henry's) is masked by an increasing physical deterioration.

As far as Henry is concerned, Leona's crime is turning out to have been strong all along. To Henry, Leona is a signifier of her father's wealth, a status symbol (the "Cough Drop Queen") with jewels and furs, a house, a job, and, finally, an insurance policy. Although Henry's flashback presents him as a considerate husband, he is nonetheless willing to bet that she'll be dead within the month, anticipating that her insurance will cover his debt to the mob. When Dr. Alexander tells him her heart is sound, Henry discovers that all the time he thought he was being strong for his fading clinging vine, he was actually performing in *her* scenario. Her strength is figured as being necessarily emasculating, making his superfluous, and interfering with his ability to function as a subject.

By pretending to a power intolerable to her husband, and furthermore by occupying the center of the narrative, through which all information must pass, Leona threatens to disrupt (if not supplant) the male hierarchy, especially that of the film noir world the male characters inhabit. This is why, like other strong women in the genre, she must be eliminated. (It is also possible that Leona has been using her illness to avoid maternity, the reluctance to become a mother a sign of the noir woman's refusal to take her rightful place in the family.) [15]

In the radio play, Leona's "guilt" is moot. As a matter of fact, we can never really be certain that her husband was involved at all. We don't know him. In the original, "Mrs. Albert Stevenson" (she has no first name) gets a busy signal when trying to call her husband. She asks the operator to redial. The phone rings on the other end. A man answers. Mrs. Stevenson begins to speak, but simultaneously we hear another man speaking. One of the men seems to have a foreign (most probably German) accent, perhaps reflecting the drama's World War II provenance. The other sounds as though he's from Brooklyn. After trying to interrupt, Mrs. Stevenson is silent for the remainder of the conversation, until the men, about to specify the address, are abruptly cut off.

She calls the operator back, explaining the missed connection and demands that the operator reconnect her with that wrong number. The operator tells her that is impossible, and Mrs. Stevenson tries the police. Again she tells about the wrong connection. This time, *she* is the one who mentions the similarity of her location and that described by the conspirators. "The coincidence is so horrible . . . I'd feel a lot better if you sent around a radio car." The policeman demurs that it is not likely that they were discussing her house, "unless you thought somebody was planning to kill you." She proclaims everyone's devotion to her "since I took sick twelve years ago." Hanging up, she begins to talk petulantly to herself: "Why doesn't Albert come home?" and "Oh, if I could only get out of this bed."

The phone rings. She answers. No one is on the line. She hangs up and it rings again. Again there is no one there. Getting more and more uneasy, she calls the operator, whom she accuses of being "spiteful." "I haven't had one bit of satisfaction out of one phone call this evening," she rages, and threatens to report the woman to her supervisor. The phone rings but she refuses to answer. "It's a trick," she says to herself. "I won't answer." When it stops ringing, she becomes frightened and demands that the operator get her the police. Their line is busy.

The phone rings and she grabs it, yelling. A man identifies himself as calling from Western Union. Her husband will be out of town. He had tried calling her, but her phone has been busy for the last half hour. In despair, Mrs. Stevenson calls the hospital and requests that a nurse be sent to spend the evening with her. They refuse because of a wartime shortage of nurses. Her clock has stopped, and she asks the time. It is 11:15.

The radio play is famous as an example of suspense. The anthology program that originally featured the drama was called "Suspense," and its weekly opening identification stated that the hope was "to offer you a precarious situation and then withhold the solution until the last possible moment." The narrator continues, "And so it is with 'Sorry, Wrong Number,' and the performance of Agnes Moorehead. We again hope to keep you in . . . Suspense!"

However, the film's narrative is actually better constructed and more suspenseful than the original. Because the radio play depends on the dialogue, there is less emphasis on time, and consequently that device is not used. In the film, the camera frequently singles out a clock in Leona's bedroom at the beginning of a shot in order to keep us aware of time passing. Henry's impending arrest, though not specified to the minute as is Leona's impending murder, becomes an additional, interwoven time-constrained plot, increasing the suspense.

By "opening up" the story and defining the character of Leona's husband, the film provides a motivation for the murder that is missing in the original. In the radio version, we can never be sure whether or not Mrs. Stevenson's husband is involved. We do not know whether he is suffering business difficulties or merely resents her; moreover, despite the length of her invalidism, there is no indication that it is in any way ungenuine.

When a psychological background is provided for Henry, with his desire for financial independence and an explanation of Leona's illness added, the motivation for the murder becomes stronger, making it seem all the more inevitable. In the film, Leona becomes Oedipus, pursuing a mystery whose answer lies in her character and her past actions. Her blindness to the consequences of her obsession with controlling those around her leads inexorably to her fate. Henry's arrest in the last shot of the film smacks of Production Code retribution; in the original, all indications are that the cipheric Mr. Stevenson has gotten away with murder. On the other hand, the film's conclusion perfectly ties up the two lines of suspense, bringing all actions and their consequences full circle.

Leona's "will to power" extends beyond the psychology of the character within the narrative. As the "organizing ear," she poses a challenge to cinema's image-based construction, redefining the subject as the one who listens. In *Mildred Pierce,* another woman who has succeeded in asserting her independence, thus putting her "rightful" husband to shame, is silenced by the text's validation of the noir discourse, embodied by an omniscient policeman.[16] At the end of the film, Mildred is (re)placed in her husband's custody. Leona cannot be handed over to her husband, as he has failed to control her to begin with and is being stripped of his power by the other males. Throughout the course of the film, Leona proves her prowess. She is able to decode the complicated series of events that make sense of an errant phone call merely by using the phone—by listening and speaking. In order to recuperate or destroy the speaking woman, the system must reassert the power of the image.

The scenes in Leona's bedroom are the center of the film. In the first scene in the film, Leona waits for her call to be answered. The camera follows her movements. She reaches for a cigarette, and the camera pans right, revealing a clock that says 9:30 and Leona and Henry's wedding portrait. She reaches for a tissue, and the camera pans left showing a table filled with medicines near a wheelchair. ("I'm an invalid, you know," she says to the operator.) However, after Leona hears the killers' conversation and calls the operator back, the camera begins to establish a certain distance from her point of view. As she begins to relate the story so far to a second operator, the filtered voice of the woman on the other end fades out, so that all we hear is Leona. The repetition of the plot makes it less important for us to attend to what she is saying, and the camera begins to investigate Leona's room. The camera pans toward the open window as the sound of a train gets louder, threatening to drown out Leona's voice. As the camera continues to pan around the room, our attention to what she is saying fades in and out, depending on occasional congruencies with what we see. When she says, "I'm all alone tonight," we see a nurse's coat and a hospital bed through the doorway. Dissolving to a shot outside on the landing, the camera cranes down the staircase and into the kitchen, leaving the sound of Leona's voice farther behind. As it moves in for a medium shot of a servant's jacket hanging next to the downstairs phone extension, we hear Leona say, "There isn't a *sound* downstairs, not a sound." When we cut back to her, her eyes are cast down and she is concentrating on the telephone. No part of the shot was from her point of view.

Such salient camera movement does several things. First, it functions like a small descriptive paragraph, showing us the set in detail before handing over control of the narrative to Leona. (There is a similar examination of Jeff's apartment at the beginning of the equally set-bound *Rear Window.*) Second, the set establishes that we are, for the moment, in woman's film territory, with that genre's attention to domestic decor and a central female figure. Most important, though, as in *Rear Window,* the foregrounding of the enunciation with this early camera movement makes clear that there is a narrative presence separate from Leona, and further, that it is a strictly *visual* presence, unknown to her. The camera exposes the limits of Leona's strictly aural point of view, countering with a potentially dangerous visual point of view—dangerous because it is out of her (and our) control. Camera movement not motivated by Leona's look or her gestures continues throughout the scenes in the bedroom and shifts the position of the spectator/auditor from one of listening to/with Leona to one of *watching* her listen. The sense of threat posed by the untethered camera is borne out in the climax of the film, when the camera lets the killer in

There are three major sequences not controlled by Leona's auditory point of view: the opening prologue, the entrance of the killer, and the end. Each of these sections is distinctly marked as narrated. Single long takes characterized by elaborate camera movement (tracks, dollies, crane shots) call attention to themselves and to the fact that they are not authorized by anyone in the text (i.e., Leona).

The prologue sports a long title roll delineating the wonders and potential horrors of AT&T. We see a cityscape at night. Dissolve to a shadow-filled office somewhere in the city. In the distance we hear a dial tone. To foreboding music, the camera pans to an office door, dollying dramatically up to the name "Henry Stevenson" written on the glass. With a dissolve, the camera passes *through* the door and up to a close-up of a telephone with the receiver off the hook. Dissolve to Leona in bed listening to a busy signal. She demands that the operator connect her with the number, not knowing what we know. It is this unanswered telephone that will set the entire plot in motion. The camera has already given us privileged information that sets us apart from Leona.

Later, knowing Henry is about to be arrested, Leona calls for a nurse to come stay with her. In the middle of her hysterical pleas for help, the camera indulges in a slow retreat, pulling back from the bed, dollying out the bedroom window, sinking two storeys past a tree to reveal a man's shadow against the house. A hand reaches in and opens the kitchen window the killers had said would be left unlocked. The extravagance of this gravity-defying move is pointed: it is, in fact, the return of the repressed. After an hour and some minutes, the camera forcibly reestablishes the preeminence of the visual discourse over the heretofore verbally dominated narrative structure.

As we follow the killer moving through the kitchen toward the telephone extension, we cut to Leona, literally cut off in mid-speech.

LEONA: What was that? . . . As if someone had lifted the receiver off the hook of the extension downstairs.

OPERATOR (filtered):   I didn't hear it, ma'am.

LEONA: Well, I did. There's someone in this house. In the kitchen downstairs. And they're listening to me now—

She clasps her hand over her mouth and hangs up. Leona's technical knowledge and telephonic expertise (understanding the meaning of the quiet click and instantly making the correct deduction) do her no good at all. Her voice, the exclusive sign of her presence in the radio version and her sole connection to others, is denied her now and puts her in danger. When the phone rings immediately, she is afraid to pick it up, but must. It is Henry.

The competing discourses, the auditory identification with Leona versus the identification with the camera (linked to the killer), put the viewer in a bind. If we identify with Leona, our listener/surrogate, we identify with the victim. The establishment of an alternative identification with the camera allows us to escape at the cost of rejecting Leona and auditory identification in favor of classical cinema and the primacy of the image. Radio is put in its place, cinema triumphant.

By the time Henry calls, Leona's death is defined as a "mistake." The mobsters have been arrested, so they won't need to be paid off with Leona's insurance money. Henry does not want her killed, because it will send him to the chair. However, Leona's death serves a greater purpose—the reestablishment of the priority of the image.

Leona hears footsteps coming up the stairs. Henry tells her to walk to the window and scream, but she cannot pull herself out of bed. "He's here!" she tells Henry, staring at something beyond the camera. As noted earlier, the woman's look is insufficiently empowered to control the narrative in the "paranoid" woman's film, of which Sorry, Wrong Number could be a raucous prototype (see Doane 1987, pp. 123–54). As we have shown, Leona has been able to control much of the narrative through the acoustic. However, the woman's inability to "see" is powerfully reinstated at the film's climax.

In the last shot of the film, as the killer approaches her bed, there is no reverse shot as Leona screams. We see her staring wildly, but there is no reverse shot that would legitimate her fear. The horror of the unseen is a carryover from the radio play. However, a more compelling reason why we do not see the killer here is because what kills Leona in the *film* is not only invisible but unvisualizable. It is the system itself—language, patriarchy, cinema—that needs to destroy her. As she pleads for her life, the camera pans to the window where the train passes, drowning out her screams as planned.

In the radio play, Leona is stabbed to death. We hear screams, coughing and hacking—shocking and violent effects that verge on the pornographic.[17] In the film, Leona is more fittingly silenced. Her hands, gripping the edge of the nightstand, loosen and fall out of the frame. Music and sound effects (which are not inimical, merely subordinate, to the classical image-based system) overwhelm her ability to hear or make a significant sound. In a phone booth, Henry begs her to scream. When we return to her bed, she is gone, literally wiped out. (A character falling out of frame like this is called a "natural" wipe, as opposed to optical wipes, where the hand of the enunciator is present.)

To reiterate: "If female sexuality and female discourse are regarded as together posing the threat of disruption to the linear process of the classic narrative, then that threat must be recuperated or repressed if the story is to have any kind of 'satisfactory' resolution [or] closure" (Kuhn 1982, p. 104). Never a role model, Leona accepts the guilt for her actions and begs Henry's forgiveness, but it is too late for her to be recuperated. Having exposed the potential power of the woman's voice, the ability to gain knowledge despite both isolation and a culturally imposed passivity approaching paralysis, Leona has to be fully repressed for a "satisfactory" resolution.

In the silence of her room, the phone rings. The killer's gloved hand reaches in and gruffly answers, "Sorry. Wrong number." He hangs up, ending the conversation and the film.

In the films discussed above, the woman's voice does not free her; she is either reduced to silence (Alice and Leona) or gives up and echoes the words provided for her (Alicia and Helen). In each of the texts (except perhaps *Blackmail*), there is no doubt that putting sound and the woman "in their place" is presented as a good thing, perpetuating cinematic and patriarchal hegemony. Nevertheless, for moments in each of these texts, Echo is presented as someone *rendered* mute. Helen can't speak; Alice does not know how to find the right words; Alicia's words are used against her, her active speech discounted and dismissed; Leona *lives* on the telephone—and dies. In *Notorious*, control of the technology is wielded within the text by the male character (and so, too, at the very end of *Sorry, Wrong Number*). In *Blackmail*, Alice's silence is a function of language and film sound, both loaded and used against her. In *The Spiral Staircase* and *Sorry, Wrong Number* the image itself moves to aid the violent repression of the active woman who would speak. The challenge the woman's voice poses to the cinematic hierarchy and its representation of woman as object is met with the reassertion of the power of the image. Sound and the woman are contained, suppressed, in the revenge of classical cinema.

Rita Hayworth in *Miss Sadie Thompson*

Recuperating Women's Speech

5

Miss Sadie Thompson (1953),
Sunset Boulevard (1950)

In *Miss Sadie Thompson* (1953) the visual and aural representation of "woman" is central to the narrative, yet the woman's relation to each always (already) exceeds her control. In the third adaptation of Maugham's story, the repressive ideology of the 1950s is reaffirmed, woman and her voice back in their old familiar places as the favored objects of spectacle.

Abetted by Technicolor, Hawaiian locations, several musical numbers, and the new process of 3-D, *Miss Sadie Thompson* provides a star vehicle for "sex goddess" Rita Hayworth. Music sweeps over the opening images of exotic tropical landscapes as spectacle expands from the woman's body across the cinematic itself. Hayworth's Sadie arrives special delivery on a speedboat. Dressed in red against a stunning blue-green background, she is propped up on boxes of "goods" being delivered to the sex-starved armed services. Sergeant O'Hara (Aldo Ray) and the other men stare in disbelief. "What kind of gear did you say was comin' in?" "Now that's a piece of equipment that's really equipped." They agree to "share and share alike"—"We'll rotate every fifteen minutes."

The marines invite her to a nightclub. Hayworth's exoticism is underscored when the Reverend Alfred Davidson warns her, "You'll be the only white woman there." At the after hours club, Sadie (the only *woman* there) jitterbugs with man after man as the camera closes in for tight shots of her shimmering red dress. Even when seen "flat," it is not hard to imagine what was being thrust into the laps of spectators.

This relationship as privileged object of spectacle is pointedly reserved for Sadie, the film's "white woman." Before her arrival, O'Hara stares longingly at a parody pinup of a large Hawaiian woman in a muumuu. An officer tells him, "When she starts looking good, that's when you've had it." And in fact in both *Sadie Thompson* and *Rain*, Horn's native wife, Ameena, is a visually androgynous figure, smoking and wearing shapeless clothes. In the Raoul Walsh film, her hide is so tough her husband literally strikes a match on her behind. In the 1953 film, Ameena is clearly a woman (and "quite a woman," as Sadie says when she sees Ameena's eight or nine children). The difference between Ameena and the "packaged" sexuality of Hayworth in her tight-fitting designer clothes and 3-D musical numbers is one of function over spectacle. While Ameena's actual sex is never in doubt, she is not "feminine." That highly codified, constantly changing set of characteristics falls to Sadie, who (besides being Rita Hayworth) bears multiple signifiers of Western femininity: her clothes, her smile, her suggestive dancing, cascading hair, and sensuous voice. The sexuality of the white woman is translated into a matter of visual—and vocal—display.

Doane argues that "when the female body is represented . . . as spectacle, as the object of an erotic gaze, signification is spread out over a surface—a surface which refers only to itself and does not simultaneously conceal and reveal an interior." In the process of being reduced to spectacle for the male gaze, "the female body exhausts its signification entirely in its status as an object of male vision" (Doane 1987, p. 39). However, when the voice is separated from the body by conventions of sync typical of the musical and, as I shall argue, applied with particular effect to the voices of women, the voice, too, can become a matter of pure surface.

When she sings, Sadie's voice enters the realm of the spectacular. As Sadie begins to sing the ironic "See No Evil, Hear No Evil," she starts to slide out of the diegesis into a specialized realm. In her room, talking to the children, Sadie's synchronized voice exists in the same aural space as the voices of those around her. Music enters on the sound track, providing a transitional moment, an aural cushion for a new object. The prerecorded singing voice we now hear does not belong to the acoustic environment occupied by Sadie's speaking voice. Instead, it seems to float outside of the image with the orchestral accompaniment, which is by convention assumed to be unreal, outside the diegesis.

Kaja Silverman argues that the conventions governing sound and image in classical Hollywood cinema function to keep woman voiceless, a guarantor of male cohesion and fluency. Classical cinema provides "a textual model which holds the female voice and body insistently to the interior of the diegesis, while relegating the male subject to a position of apparent discursive exteriority by identifying him with mastering speech, vision, or hearing" (Silverman 1988, p. ix). She identifies three "textual operations" by which women are positioned in relation to their voices: (1) by presenting the woman in "a recessed area of the diegesis," most commonly in performance (both visual and acoustic); (2) by "obliging [her] to speak a particular psychic 'reality' upon command"—for instance, presenting conscious or unconscious "confessions" elicited by male characters who are doctors, psychiatrists, or detectives; or (3) by emphasizing the very texture of the woman's voice as pure sound (as opposed to meaning). In each of these ways, Silverman argues, "Hollywood places woman definitively 'on stage,' at a dramatic remove from the cinematic apparatus" (ibid., p. 63). In this chapter I examine how these operations function in *Miss Sadie Thompson*, especially where they overlap, contradict or reenforce each other, and their ideological effect in a particular genre (the musical) in a specific period of American history (the ideologically reactionary fifties).

The big performance numbers ("The Heat Is On" and "Blue Pacific Blues") demonstrate the simplest way to restrict the woman "inside" the diegesis as sign rather than as signifying subject, by placing the "female voice in a recessed area of the diegesis," a show within a show, a story within the story. "The Heat Is On" (strongly reminiscent of Hayworth's "Put the Blame on Mame" in 1946's *Gilda*) attributes catastrophe and mayhem to a mousy girl who has learned the sizzling power of female sexuality: "I might have formerly been cold as ice but I'm a forest fire now . . . spontaneous combustion in a satin gown." And even more threatening, considering the Cold War climate: "I've got an awful lot of oats that haven't been sown, they might start a chain reaction and I might explode." During the number, Hayworth grinds past sweaty, overheated marines, and lusciously straddles a chair.

More subtly, as in "See No Evil," the switch from dialogue to song, the use of prerecording, and the consequent alteration in ambient sounds, strongly draw our attention to the texture of the voice. This does two things. First, this acoustic cradling points to the voice as "a voice" (the way a singer has "a voice"). As Silverman notes, emphasizing the "grain" of the *woman's* voice, its physicality and material source, enables the classical text to "impart to [the voice] the texture of the female body" (ibid.). In other words, rather than the woman *using* her voice to communicate, the voice communicates the body as *object*, bypassing any attempts at female subjectivity or female control of signification.

When a man's voice is highlighted, the effect is often very different. When Walter Huston speaks in *Rain*, for instance, the "grain" of his voice gives him not a body but authority, a physical integrity that backs up what he has to say. Men with notably low voices are frequently not cast in romantic roles but in roles associated with power. Huston, for instance, played Lincoln (*Abraham Lincoln*); President of the United States (*Gabriel over the White House*); an industrialist (*Dodsworth*); an ambassador (*Mission to Moscow*); George M. Cohan's father striding across the stage as Uncle Sam (*Yankee Doodle Dandy*); the devil in *The Devil and Daniel Webster*; and in the *Why We Fight* series during World War II, he was the voice of the United States Government. The "voice of God" (a facetious term for voice-over narrators in documentary) cannot be far behind, and many actors noted for deep, gravelly voices can be found working as narrators. (John Huston in *The Bible* combines God *and* narrator.) The ideal of "masculinity" becomes the voice, extending its jurisdiction beyond the body by pointing instead toward a "presence" that is pure language, God the Father as the Word. When Orson Welles (another actor who went in big for narration) hides himself behind (or *as*) a microphone for the trailer and the credits of *Citizen Kane*, his voice *substitutes* for the body. The voice in *Miss Sadie Thompson* signifies it. When a woman is represented, her voice is one of the promises her body has to offer.

Secondly, "Sadie's" voice is only tenuously connected to the body we see by an approximate synchronization. Prerecording is a subtle form of non-sync sound. If it is not visibly at odds with the image (because of lip-syncing), the differences are still distinctly *audible*. (They are usually meant to be read as "aesthetically superior.") At the same time that numbers like "See No Evil" and "Blue Pacific Blues" make a *show* of the process of sync, they present the impossibility of a woman joining such a body with such a voice in a realistic space. For instance, in "Blue Pacific Blues," Sadie lies on a bed, stretched horizontally across the width of the screen. The lip-sync is bad, but irrelevant; no one in the real world could produce such sounds. The marines, eyes closed, sway to the music. She *is* this voice, an all-encompassing aural embrace evocative of the maternal voice, an image of the musical muse. With Hayworth, too, there is the question of dubbing and whether the voice is even hers. Her actual voice has been taken away from her in pursuit of an aesthetic ideal presumably only technicians are capable of. "What is demanded from woman . . . [is] sound that escapes her own understanding, testifying only to the artistry of a superior force" (Silverman 1988, p. 77).

Dis-synchronization has potentially radical effects, and has been employed for that purpose in feminist and avant garde films. But as used here, this subtler, institutionalized way of separating the voice from the body deprives the woman of control of her voice by putting both voice and body on display—simultaneously, but separately—as spectacle.

The separate recording of voice and image is true of all musicals, but in *Miss Sadie Thompson* it is unique to Sadie and thus bears considerable ideological weight. For instance, when the children reprise "See No Evil" later for company, their voices were recorded on the set, in the same acoustic space as the subsequent dialogue. What was a convention of musicals is commandeered here for a specific effect in regard to the woman. There are no men who share this impossible double space.[1]

Women are frequently held to standards of perfection they cannot meet, while a male actor's physical integrity is preserved whether he can sing or not—for example, Marlon Brando performing several numbers as the lead in *Guys and Dolls* to Frank Sinatra's one, and Lee Marvin and Clint Eastwood warbling in *Paint Your Wagon*. There are only two major films I can think of offhand where the actor's image was irreconcilable with "his" voice: Larry Parks in *The Jolson Story* (1946) and Sidney Poitier in *Porgy and Bess* (1959). What gives Parks any degree of authenticity in the role is what is always outside his grasp—the voice dubbed in by the real Al Jolson. The voice in *The Jolson Story* resists being read as a sign of interiority precisely because its source is so insistently external to the image. And in *Porgy and Bess*, Poitier, dubbed by opera singer Robert McFerrin, lip-syncs to a voice that is clearly not his, as the film struggles to reconcile featuring *the* black star of its day while satisfying issues of "class" with a voice acceptable to opera fans.[2] When an actor has no control regarding her/his voice, with the face, body, and voice all equally on display, spectacular, without depth, and without the ability to vouch for their own authenticity, I would argue that by definition that space is a feminine space.

The musical scenes in *Miss Sadie Thompson* are only the most noticeable indications of Sadie's isolation from discourse. To consolidate her exclusion, the film uses more naturalized forms of suppressing the woman's voice. It is, for instance, not surprising that when Sadie tries to speak, words exceed her control: "the discursive potency of the male voice is established by stripping the female voice of all claim to verbal authority" (Silverman 1988, p. 77). When Sadie sings, she is the object of visual and audio spectacle. When she speaks, her claim to verbal authority is undercut by male characters in the text. In the scene below, the double standard, conspicuously rejected by all the earlier versions, is reintroduced with a vengeance. The issue, significantly, is her singing.

After failing to persuade the governor not to deport her, Sadie tells O'Hara what she thinks is the worst news—that she has to go to jail. He doesn't care. "But that other stuff," he says, "Working in the Emerald Club. That can never wash off." As she tries to state her case, O'Hara disbelievingly repeats her words, reducing and negating them.

SADIE: I sang there.

O'HARA: Sang! I *know* the Emerald!

SADIE: I had a straight job.

O'HARA: Straight job! How come you picked that joint to work, of all the clip joints in Honolulu.

SADIE: It paid best.

O'HARA: Paid best for what?

In this exchange, singing becomes a euphemism for promiscuity and prostitution. In earlier versions of Maugham's story, such as *Rain* in 1932 and *Sadie Thompson* in 1928, Sadie's assertion that she had a singing job is an evasion, a lie she tells Davidson when he's pressuring her about her past. Iron-ically, this is the only film where it is not only possible that she was a singer, but likely, and it doesn't matter—or more accurately, the meaning has changed. Sadie's display of her voice is given the moral weight of displaying her sex.

Literally in a corner, Sadie turns on O'Hara and exaggeratedly confirms his greatest fears.

> Alright, you wanta know the truth, I'll tell you. Sure I worked at the Emerald. Took the men over for all they had. They filled the place, millions of 'em. They lined up in the streets and all of them came just to see me. Does that make you happy?

As it does in visual spectacle, the verb "to see" collapses several different meanings, all converging on a pattern of "female object" and "male desire." Here, when Sadie says "all of them came just to see" her, "see" refers to audio spectacle in the witnessing of a (vocal) performance; to the gaze, the men seeing Sadie as the signifier of their own desire; and "seeing" someone, as in making an appointment for services. In this system, being visible, audi-ble, and sexually available (being "seen," "heard," and "had") are finally the same thing.

When, broken and in shock after her breakup with O'Hara, Sadie suc-cumbs to Davidson's calming recital of the Twenty-third Psalm, we see how "by aligning woman with diegetic interiority, and so . . . isolating her defini-tively from the site of textual production," the male character—and the male voice especially—can be presented as being at one with the apparatus, privi-leged as speaker of the ideology of the text. As the camera closes in for a frame-filling close-up of Sadie, Davidson's voice is freed from his body to float asynchronously over the image. Delicate strings play on the sound track adding a "spiritual" feel. A tear drops, perfectly, onto Sadie's cheek on the last word of the psalm as the image fades to black.

With the dolly-in toward Sadie, Davidson becomes the offscreen voice of the enunciator, almost literally the voice of God. If "the voice is privileged to the degree that it *transcends* the body," Sadie's voice does not transcend her body so much as "sell" it (Silverman 1988, p. 49). However, when Davidson speaks in this scene, his body becomes irrelevant and unvisualized, Jose Ferrer's sonorous voice conveying a hallowed, spiritual message. In this con-text, the asynchronous male voice has healing powers and Sadie loses herself inside it.

Just the opposite occurs when Sadie's voice is deprived of a visual source. In two scenes where Sadie becomes enraged, she inexplicably charges off to her room, slams the door, and *then* begins speaking, literally talking to her-self. "How do you like that double-talking, no good louse! Handing me a line like that! If he starts that guff again, I'll really tell him off!" The camera remains outside as the other characters stand around befuddled. Rather than endowing herself with the "voice of God" effect typical of offscreen narration, Sadie's unvisualized tirade suggests verbal incompetence and Old Testament babble.

Despite the fact that Davidson is here presented at his worst in any of the film versions of the story, with a graphic depiction of his raping Sadie, his "spiritual message" remains unchallenged. From the 1921 theatrical adaptation of Maugham's story through both previous films, Davidson is a figure of religious intolerance, and Sadie after her conversion is presented as a zombie, reciting by rote the religious rhetoric pounded into her by Davidson's psychological pressure. Here, Sadie quietly and with dignity relates how she came to reassess her life. "When O'Hara walked out on me," she says, "and I had nobody to turn to, Mr. Davidson helped me. I didn't feel lost anymore. I'm back to myself again. Like I was, long ago."[3] Seeing an open Bible on her dresser, Dr. Macphail, the text's representative of "objective" modern science, nods contentedly, as if to imply, "She can't go far wrong with the Good Book."

After being raped by the minister (who, since a Hays Code ruling in 1928, still cannot be identified on film as a minister), Sadie's newfound "faith" waivers. However, in the 1950s text, the tolerance Dr. Macphail urges is not of Sadie as victim but of Davidson. "You mustn't confuse what he did with what he believed in," he tells her. Macphail's unprecedented defense of the lapsed theocrat is part of the text's desperate attempt to preserve the religion already shielded by Davidson's unofficial status. By reconstructing Davidson as an example of "abnormal" psychology (he explicitly disparages "Freud, Adler, and Jung," the decade's other gods), the conservative religious ideology can be upheld as being essentially correct; only individuals occasionally go wrong. As Macphail says of Davidson after the rape, "He just couldn't practice what he preached." Sadie closes the circle uniting the men in the text verbally as well as vocally (and politically and sexually) when she says to the doctor, "You talk just like him." And Macphail says disingenuously, "Do I? I didn't realize."

As a reward for her final capitulation, the forfeiture of her anger, O'Hara miraculously returns, suddenly willing to forget Sadie's past. He belatedly explains that there should be no double standard for B-girls and marines, putting it in acoustic terms: "Counting up all I've done . . . I had no right to sound off." Reunited and reengaged, Sadie rides off, propped up on her speedboat, happily restored to spectacle status, awaiting a rosy future with O'Hara.

The most reactionary and conservative version of Maugham's story, *Miss Sadie Thompson* locks the woman into spectacle on all sides. Sadie's happiness for the first hour rests on being the prized object, prime spectacle, "the only white woman" there. In the musical numbers, she cannot capture her own voice, and when she does speak her own experience, she is either barred access (presented as "hysterically" talking to herself offscreen) or unconsciously repeats the dominant ideology, presented at every point as inevitable. According to this classical text, the woman's submission to spectacle status in both image and voice is, finally, the only possible course.

The convulsive repressiveness we saw in response to women's efforts to speak in the films of the forties went underground in the fifties, camouflaged by spectacle on the one hand or transmuted into hysteria and melodrama—as in *Sunset Boulevard*.

Sunset Boulevard (1950)

"We didn't need dialogue. We had faces!" (she says).

As the fifties put Sadie Thompson resoundingly in her place, the original Sadie reappeared as the decade's definitive manifestation of the monstrous, transgressive woman. As Norma Desmond, Gloria Swanson made an indelible mark in sound film as the last word in silent-film excess. *Sunset Boulevard* foregrounds the issue of cinema's representation of women, calling attention to the history of that representation as it evokes the history of the medium. The transition to sound film is most frequently alluded to as the alleged cause of Norma Desmond's maddening estrangement/exclusion from cinema. The true cause is the nature of the industry, specifically the forms of sexual exploitation that lie at the heart of the dream machine. Although both men and women are destroyed in the film by their desire to be embraced by the industry, *Sunset Boulevard* shows that the criteria by which people are discarded differ according to gender, position in the work force, and history.

Sunset Boulevard can also be seen as another version of the Echo and Narcissus myth restated in cinematic terms. But here Echo and Narcissus trade places: the disembodied voice is now the ghostly echo of a dead man, while the image holds out an unattainable, yet infinite, promise to a female Narcissus. As before, Echo cannot break Narcissus's absorption in her own image and, as Echo dies, Narcissus is engulfed in madness. But when the woman occupies the position of Narcissus (not an unfamiliar position historically) there is a subtle shift in power. Sound is now dominant. Echo becomes a cynical hack with a story to tell—and this time, it's *his* story. While it is certainly not surprising that a film written by two of Hollywood's best dialogue men, Billy Wilder and Charles Brackett, would privilege the spoken word by making its anti-hero a screenwriter, what I would like to look at is the way *Sunset Boulevard* establishes a hierarchy not only of sound over image but of sound over sound, an audio hierarchy noticeably gendered with the voice-over narration male and the synchronized voice a woman's.

The film opens in the gutter, the title written in white on asphalt. A chatty

Gloria Swanson in *Sunset Boulevard*

male voice-over draws our attention to a body in the pool—Joe Gillis (William Holden), recently deceased screenwriter. Over the extended flashback that comprises the body of the film, he tells us how, on the run from creditors, he met the aging silent film star Norma Desmond. She mistakes him for a mortician. Finding that he is a down-on-his-luck screenwriter, Desmond hires him to rewrite the script of her "comeback" film. ("I hate that word," she snaps, "It's *return*.") Thinking he's found a gravy train, Joe moves in. After suitable displays of reluctance, he accepts progressively larger gifts and eventually becomes Norma's lover while she awaits word from Cecil B. De Mille on her return to the screen. "The whole business culminates, inevitably, in a head-on collision between illusion and reality and between the old Hollywood and the new; and in staring madness and violent death" (Agee 1958, pp. 412–13).

As with any myth, *Sunset Boulevard* has a strong sense of perfection about it, one that exceeds mere narrative closure or classical transparency. The film was hailed as an instant classic by contemporary critics. In his review in *Sight and Sound*, James Agee called it "one of those rare movies which are so full of exactness, cleverness, mastery, pleasure, and arguable and unarguable choice and judgment, that they can be talked about, almost shot for shot and line for line for hours on end" (ibid., p. 413). Part of what makes the film seem so self-contained is the way it builds itself by balancing contradictions. Joe and Norma present us with the new Hollywood and the old, younger man /

older woman, the snappy dialogue writer and the star who can say anything with her eyes. He begins the story, she ends it. If he seems unfeeling, she is a monster of feeling. As narrator, he is in a position of control, and yet before he begins to speak, he has already lost everything.

Norma Desmond herself balances a wide span of contradictions. She has been described as "a human vampire," a "gargoyle of vanity and manipulation," and a "spider woman" embodying "the perverse, decaying side of film noir sexuality."[4] (As well as being called an "egotistical relic," "hopeless egomaniac," and "psychopathic star.")[5] Norma is "half mad, suicidal, with the obsessed narcissistic arrogance of the once adored and long forgotten," Agee says; and yet she and her past "are given splendor, recklessness, [and] an aura of awe" compared to the more mundane people of present-day Hollywood (Agee 1958, pp. 412–14). When thinking of *Sunset Boulevard* "one always thinks first and mostly" of Norma Desmond,[6] of the "barbarous grandeur and intensity" of her excess (Agee 1958, p. 414).

Sunset Boulevard for many people *is* Norma Desmond, but as with Ovid's myth, the stories of Echo and Narcissus are intertwined and interdependent. This Narcissus is defined by her relationship with Echo, just as, in a reversal for classical cinema, the image is defined by sound. In *Sunset Boulevard*, the woman's relation to sound is historicized and made to stand for woman's vulnerable position in cinema overall. I shall focus on three aspects of the film that highlight the historical position of woman in sound film: Norma's attitude toward sound and the image, her true standing in relation to the cinema industry, and the implications of Joe's voice-over narration.

Norma Desmond is a woman who has been discarded by the cinema industry, displaced, she implies, by the coming of sound. Norma is the film's spokeswoman for silent films. She equates sound with death. Of course, death invades every aspect of *Sunset Boulevard*, from the title to the decaying mansion, the eerie midnight funeral for the dead chimpanzee, and Norma Desmond's planned comeback role as Salome. (John the Baptist "rejects her," she tells Joe with relish, "so she demands his head on a golden tray, kissing his cold dead lips.") And, of course, death supplies the climax of Norma and Joe's love affair. But death is also central to the film's sound/image debate.[7] Norma insists films are lost: "They're dead! They're finished!" The reason for their demise is sound: "There was a time when [Hollywood] had the eyes of the whole world. But that wasn't good enough for them, oh no. So they opened their big mouths and out came talk talk talk." On learning that Joe is a writer, Norma moves toward him, hissing: "Writing words, words, more words. You've made a rope of words to strangle this business, but there's a microphone right there to catch the last gurgles and Technicolor to photograph the red swollen tongue."

Norma depends on the power of the image and the star system, at its peak in her heyday, to protect her from the death induced by sound. What Norma posits as the source of *her* power is distinctly visual—her eyes and the ability to see. When we first see Norma, she is partially hidden behind bamboo blinds, wearing dark glasses that make her eyes glow strangely. Throughout the film, these dark glasses return, simultaneously shielding and announcing the power of her gaze. Joe remarks on the sound track, "I could sense her eyes on me from behind those dark glasses." When he questions her judgment about making her dead chimpanzee's coffin "bright, flaming red—let's make it gay!" she whips off the glasses and fixes him with a piercing stare.

Norma identifies her eyes as the equivalent of her stardom. When Joe, who has agreed to be her "ghostwriter," suggests her screenplay needs more dialogue, she retorts, "What for? I can say anything I want with my eyes." Later, when Joe has moved into the mansion on Sunset Boulevard, he and Norma watch private screenings of Norma's old silent films. "Still wonderful, isn't it? And *no* dialogue. We didn't need dialogue. We had faces!" She jumps up suddenly, raging at "those idiot producers" who have ceased to employ her. "Those imbeciles! Haven't they got eyes? Have they forgotten what a star looks like?!"

The promise of stardom, as Norma perceives it, is invulnerability and immortality. As she slips into psychosis before shooting her gigolo lover, she hisses, "I'm a star! I'm the greatest star of them all." He walks out, leaving her staring fixedly in front of her, whispering to herself, "No one ever leaves a star. That's what makes one a star!" Having killed Joe and gone completely mad, Norma leans against a stone pillar, whispering, "Stars are ageless, aren't they?"

But neither the star system nor the silent image does better by Norma, even at their most magical. Early in the film, Joe takes a moment out from rewriting Norma's "hodgepodge of silly melodramatic plots" to look at her living room. The camera tracks past row after row of photographs of Norma/Swanson from the twenties, the image twice dissolving, like time, as Joe muses, "How could she breathe in that house crowded with Norma Desmonds, more Norma Desmonds, and still more Norma Desmonds?" The images are magic, but they are stills, stilled, frozen, life in death just like "that grim Sunset castle," "the whole place . . . stricken with a kind of creeping paralysis." Even moving images such as the luminous excerpt from *Queen Kelly* that Joe and Norma watch as an example of her former glory are presented *within the film* as unreal and ghostly. The silent film image is inserted into a broader text that holds the power to define and comment on it.

Norma is the embodiment of what Doane identifies as woman's "overinvestment" in the image. In *The Desire to Desire*, she describes a shot of Mia Farrow in *The Purple Rose of Cairo* (1985) gazing at the screen "in spectatorial ecstasy, enraptured by the image, her face glowing (both figuratively and literally through its reflection of light from the movie screen). . . . What the shot signifies, in part, is the peculiar susceptibility to the image . . . attributed to the woman in our culture. Her pleasure in viewing is somehow more intense," her spectatorship "yet another clearly delineated mark of her excess" (Doane 1987, p. 1). This description applies equally well to Norma watching *Queen Kelly*, "forgetting she was [Joe's] employer—just becoming a fan, excited about that actress up there on the screen." But here, "the actress up there on the screen" is Norma herself. Being "outside" the silent image makes Norma feel estranged from "her celluloid self." The reason she watches her own films so avidly is because she is searching for a way back in.

Norma believes that she will have power if she can *become* the image, but as Janey Place demonstrates, even when Norma does succeed by "visually dominat[ing]" the frame in *Sunset Boulevard*,

> she is presented as caught by the same false value system. The huge house in which she controls camera movement and is constantly centre frame is also a hideous trap which requires from her the maintenance of the myth of her stardom: the contradiction between the reality and the myth pull her apart and finally drive her mad.
>
> (Kaplan 1978a, p. 43)

What Norma cannot admit is that the cinematic *image* excludes her in its function as part of a commercial system. As Brandon French points out, the Hollywood film industry is founded on the selling of "glamour" (a euphemism for sexually attractive young people, often women). This is a system young silent film goddesses like Norma Desmond / Gloria Swanson made possible and for which they no longer qualify. Norma's "value to the movie industry is almost entirely a function of her youth; consequently she has never grown up and is obsessed with her appearance" (French 1978, p. 6). When Norma believes her screenplay is about to be produced, she submits herself to a "merciless series" of beauty treatments, "in her effort to turn fifty years into a camera-proof twenty-five" (Agee 1958, p. 412). It isn't sound that truly excludes Norma, but age—and it is the camera that has become the real enemy. Corroborating Norma's legitimate anxiety about her looks is the story the aspiring screenwriter Betty Shaeffer tells Joe about having had her nose "fixed" so that she could be a film actress. By topping Norma in terms of self-sacrifice, Betty establishes the intensity of Norma's desire as a culturally shared willingness to endure almost anything in order to be chosen for cinematic exploitation. Betty's story redefines what up until now may have passed as personal excess on Norma's part by reinserting Norma's desire into history.[8]

The silent images are at least kind to Norma Desmond; *Sunset Boulevard*'s images betray her cruelly. Visually, Norma is associated with wild animals. She wears leopard-skin turbans and trim, and her Isotta-Fraschini is upholstered in leopard skin. When she matter-of-factly informs Joe that all of his debts have been paid and he will now be living with her, coils of fabric are draped around her neck. As Salome descending the grand staircase, a snake bracelet entwines her upper arm. Throughout the film Norma hisses and jibes at Joe, her hands working the air like a snake charmer's or a witch's, grasping and clutching, revolting and hypnotic at the same time.

Every shot of Norma accentuates her grotesque image. She throws her head back and stares, her lips painted a harsh dark shade, set off against her overpowdered skin. Her hair falls into a shapeless mess of curls that she pushes and tears at with her clawlike hands. In *Sunset Boulevard*, Norma Desmond is Medusa. Her power is in her eyes, the snakes in her hair.

In presenting Norma Desmond as monster, image and sound are completely in sync. Norma seldom speaks—she whispers or declaims. Sometimes she uses a wheedling, sickly, singsong voice that calls to mind Margaret Hamilton in *The Wizard of Oz* (1939). Even when she pleads for sympathy, the image works against her. While under her tortuous beauty regimen, Norma won't let Joe see her even when she begs for attention. "All I ask is for you to be a little patient, a little kind." Her face taped to hold back the crow's-feet, white gloves on her hands, a chin support absurdly wrapped around her face, the grotesqueness of her image undercuts the sincerity of her plea. When Joe finally becomes her lover following her suicide attempt on New Year's Eve, Swanson plays most of the scene with her face covered, her bandaged forearms often all that is visible of her in the shot. It is as if Norma can only be approached (like Medusa) if her eyes are closed. When Joe takes her arms down from her eyes and says, "Happy New Year, Norma," the mad stare returns as she clutches him to her with her clawlike hands.[9]

Although her voice and image seem to be used against her, Norma is not entirely at the mercy of words. Ironically, Norma has all the best lines (though only when she is speaking an "impossible" position, arguing against the sound that makes her words possible). Most of the time, though, her relationship to speech is as filled with pitfalls as the problematic relationship of her image and voice. As in *Sorry, Wrong Number*, when Norma tries to control the narrative by using the telephone, it backfires. She is reduced vocally and verbally to a malicious gossip, whispering insinuating tales to the clean-cut All-American Betty. Joe walks in, unseen by Norma, and overhears her. He rips the phone out of her hand and reasserts his right to control the narrative by telling Betty to come over and see the truth for herself. Norma's antagonism toward voices and dialogue is partially justified by the diegesis—as we can see, when *she* uses them they're no use at all.

The most salient factor about the sound/image hierarchy of *Sunset Boulevard* is the subordination of Norma Desmond's voice, image, speech, and story to the male voice-over. Joe's voice-over narration begins the narrative, defines the characters, relentlessly sets the tone. J. P. Telotte sees the voice-over narration of *Sunset Boulevard* in terms of "the self's impelling desire for a voice even in death, for a say in and about the truth of the world, despite a prevalent, even deadly power for silence or for submission to a popular discourse and its given truth." [10] Although Telotte posits a universal urge to speak, he does not acknowledge the gender implications when the voice, as it is here, is male. In the above quotation, the "self" is male and the "deadly power for silence [and] submission to a popular discourse" is Norma Desmond. Even though we've seen that silents/silence and submission to the popular discourse of stardom has in no way empowered Norma Desmond, she is held responsible for death and the false consciousness of Hollywood, while Joe becomes the voice of "truth." As I shall argue later, Joe and Norma share more values than this reading would suggest: both possess the urge to speak, and both are victimized by the industry they equally desire.

Initially, the voice-over makes Norma's story part of Joe's (just as Medusa's story is supplanted by Perseus's). Norma becomes the monster who has brought Joe to the fatal context of his narration. She is the one who has displaced him from *his* story—his life. It is only with the assistance of the cinematic—and at the level of the cinematic (as voice-over)—that Joe can finally establish the upper hand as narrator that he lacks within the diegesis. Joe's narration provides the frame that surrounds Norma Desmond, seeking to contain her story within his.

But the male voice-over in *Sunset Boulevard* is not the "voice of God," just as Joe is not the Reverend Davidson. Silverman differentiates between the totally disembodied male voice-over (where the narrator is never visually identified) and "the embodied or diegetically anchored male voiceover" (Silverman 1988, p. 52). According to this reading, the latter is typical of films of the late 1940s and 1950s (particularly in film noir, but also in noir-inflected films such as *Pride of the Marines*), which frequently present a narrator who is limited both as filmic enunciator and as a man (ibid.). Silverman argues that when the narrator is visualized, he becomes physically limited (unlike the limitless voice of God) and thus vulnerable to death. (Her examples, from films such as *D.O.A.* [1949], *Double Indemnity* [1949], and *Laura* [1944], are all of men who are dead, dying, or fatally impaired). The closer the narrator is to being "inside" the diegesis, the less likely he is to be in a position of control (ibid., pp. 53–54). Being inside the film's visual and narrative system as a character, Joe becomes subject to death *and* to Norma (for Telotte, same difference).

The embodied male narrator thus occupies what is in effect a feminine space. Silverman suggests that "diegetic interiority is equated with discursive impotence and lack of control, thereby rendering that situation culturally unacceptable for the 'normal' male subject" (ibid., p. 54). Throughout *Sunset Boulevard*, Joe is troubled by occupying a feminine space. The reason he flees his apartment in the first place is to keep his car from being repossessed. Begging his agent for a loan to repay his creditors, he says, "If I lose my car it's like having my legs cut off." Joe is frequently passive, often yielding his ground and taking orders. When Norma invites him to read her script, he begins to make an excuse until she lowers her voice and lays down the law—"I said sit down." He backs away obediently, as his voice on the sound track returns to qualify his surrender as strategy. When Norma has bought Joe a new wardrobe in preparation for their private New Year's Eve party, she pooh-poohs the shirt studs the men's store has provided and says she wants to see him in pearls. He jokes, "Well, I'm not going to wear earrings." His eventual acceptance of the position of gigolo is presented in the film as the ultimate humiliation because (we can assume) prostitution is usually defined as woman's work.

Much of the time Joe is also in a feminine position vocally. When his speech is synchronized with his image, he is subject to *Norma's* offscreen voice. If her synchronized voice is ultimately ineffectual, her offscreen voice possesses as much power as her gaze. When Joe first turns in to the driveway of Norma Desmond's mansion on Sunset Boulevard, he strolls around the grounds of the house. Suddenly a voice interrupts. "You there! Why are you so late! Why have you kept me waiting so long?" Joe struggles to make out who is speaking, but all he can see is a strange figure hidden behind blinds, looking down on him. When he hurries to leave her house, having incurred wrath by suggesting she "used to be big," his escape is cut off by her brusque, "Just a minute, you." Later, Joe vigorously objects to her butler's having moved Joe's belongings into the room over the garage. As Max continues playing the organ, unperturbed, Joe demands, "Who said you could?" Norma's offscreen "I did" cuts off his impotent tantrum. It is only when Joe is leaving her that her offscreen commands are disobeyed (although the final gunshots may be the ultimate demonstration of offscreen sound's power over the image).

The sound hierarchy in *Sunset Boulevard* places synchronized speech at the weakest, most "feminine" pole, with offscreen and embodied voice-overs in ascending order of narrative authority. If a truly disembodied voice-over exists in *Sunset Boulevard*, it is during the first few minutes of the film, when we do not yet know that the narrator is dead. In these first few moments, the narration is privileged as the site of objective truth: "Before you hear it all distorted and blown out of proportion, before those Hollywood columnists get their hands on it, maybe you'd like to hear the facts, the whole truth. If so, you've come to the right party."

Although audiences surely recognize William Holden floating in the pool, the narrator does not acknowledge the relationship, referring to the corpse as "he" until the flashback begins: "Let's go back about six months and find the day when it all started. Things were tough at the moment. *I* hadn't worked in a studio for a long time."

Joe's "introduction" marks the first time voice, image, and "person" (first rather than third) are synchronized and this moment also draws the first parallel between Joe and Norma. Both have been rejected by the industry, neither one of them has "worked in a studio for a long time," and both are desperate to get back in. They have each tied their identities to their careers, Joe as a writer, Norma as a star. Joe talks about that ambition: "All us writers, itching with ambition, panicked to get your names up there—'Screenplay by,' 'Original Story by.'"

Joe is as vulnerable as Norma to the whims of studio heads. His epic "about Oakies in the dust bowl" is rewritten as a wartime saga on a battleship; his producer friend at Paramount wants to remake his baseball story as a Betty Hutton musical ("It Happened in the Bullpen: The Story of a Woman").

It is clear at the narrative level that Joe is up for sale like everyone else. Even Betty Shaeffer started as an actress and now aspires to be a writer—both roles equally susceptible to scorn and rejection. *Sunset Boulevard* consciously situates Norma Desmond and Joe Gillis's crises within the history of Hollywood production, and in doing so presents a critique of that system. Names of actual actors and producers, from the old Hollywood and the new, are frequently invoked (Valentino, Garbo, Rod LaRoque, Alan Ladd, "Ty" Power, Betty Hutton). Part of this is for verisimilitude, as are the uses of location photography outside Schwab's drugstore and the Paramount gate. But the list of names also underlines that men as well as women are discarded by the industry, as actors and, as we've seen, as writers. Everyone in Hollywood is not only vulnerable to exploitation for his or her labor but subject to sexual exploitation as well. *Sunset Boulevard*, after all, indulges in its bit of "beefcake" when it presents William Holden dripping wet.[11]

Cecil B. De Mille is probably the most famous "real" person mentioned in the film and the contradictions that surround his appearance "as himself" are indicative of the film's conflicting attitudes toward Hollywood. Norma sends the polished version of her screenplay to her old friend De Mille. ("We made a lot of pictures together," she tells Joe.) When word comes down to the soundstage where De Mille is shooting that Norma Desmond is on her way in, an assistant suggests they "give her the brush." De Mille sadly retorts, "Thirty million fans have given her the brush. Isn't that enough?" The assistant mentions that Norma was a legendary terror to work with, but De Mille generously puts her behavior in context. "You didn't know her when she was a lovely little girl of seventeen with more courage and wit and heart than ever came together in one youngster. . . . A dozen press agents working overtime can do terrible things to the human spirit." By calling attention to the star-making apparatus, this speech recasts Norma, not as a monster, but as a character who has been formed by the industry in which she worked.

French points out that the film goes to some lengths to preserve De Mille as a kindly father figure. He calls Norma "little fellow" and she calls him "chief" or "Mr. De Mille"—terms of endearment borrowed from Swanson and De Mille's actual relationship. (Many of De Mille's big successes in the silent period were, of course, Swanson pictures: *Don't Change Your Husband* (1919), *Male and Female* (1919), *Why Change Your Wife?* (1920), and *The Affairs of Anatol* (1921); see Swanson 1980, pp. 480–89.) However, as French argues (1978, pp. 6–7), it is possible to see De Mille as representative of the casual cruelty of Hollywood. When Norma visits the set and is left alone in the director's chair, an offscreen voice softly calls to her—"Hey! Miss Desmond!" A gaffer who has recognized her from the old days turns one of the big spotlights on her. Norma is literally back in the limelight, and for a moment we find out what it means to be a star, the heart-stopping magic, as if time had never passed. People all over the set recognize her and crowd around. "Hey, it's Norma Desmond!" "Norma Desmond!" The only fly in the ointment is when an errant microphone brushes Norma's hat; she bats it away. And appropriately, it is through a microphone that Norma's moment is taken away. De Mille eyes the crowd. An assistant hands him a microphone. We hear his artificially amplified voice, cold and mechanical, order the lighting man to "turn that light back where it belongs." Darkness returns and the fans wander away. It is De Mille, and through him the powerful men of Hollywood, the producers, directors, and studio heads, who have the power to determine where the light "belongs." [12]

Norma shares Joe's "impelling desire for a voice," the urge to define the world (and herself) as she sees it. Both assume roles to express themselves. Joe speaks the hardboiled cynicism of a former newspaperman. Norma envisions herself through the plots others have given her—as seductress, as a woman who needs a man, as Salome, Salome whose glitter Norma wears in her hair as she descends the stairs. Norma's "crime" parallels Salome's, preferring to "keep" a dead man rather than be rejected. Norma, like Salome, refuses to subordinate her story to a man's. Janey Place sees this egotism as Norma's ultimate transgression—her interest in herself, her sexuality, her career (Kaplan 1978a, pp. 46–47). In film noir terms, both Norma and Salome are femmes fatales.

But Norma's identification with Salome also draws attention to the cinema *industry*, past and present. *Salome* not only evokes silent film and Nazimova's definitive 1923 version of the Wilde play, it invites a direct comparison with the film De Mille is directing, *Samson and Delilah*. This, too, is included for verisimilitude; it was De Mille's next release, starring Victor Mature and Hedy Lamarr. However, the continuing economic viability of De Mille's overblown biblical melodramas makes *Norma's* "hodgepodge of silly melodramatic plots" instantly more plausible. If De Mille can still churn 'em out, why can't she? Of course, Wilder and Brackett probably thought the De Mille–style epic *was* ridiculous compared to their sophisticated swipes at popular culture. (Only Wilder's *Ace in the Hole* [1951] matches *Sunset Boulevard*'s bite on the subject of American taste.) But that's show biz, that's what gets the bucks circa 1950. Implicitly, though, *Sunset Boulevard* presents the argument for

Wilder/Brackett's kind of films over De Mille's because unlike De Mille who turns the light away, Wilder and Brackett *can* make room for the Norma Desmonds Hollywood has left behind. After all, who else would understand Norma Desmond's mad, monstrous, "barbarous grandeur"?

Although everything in the film seems to work against sympathy for Norma Desmond—the image, the sound track, the narrative and the narrator—feeling for her survives and not simply because of the charisma of the actress. Agee found the film "cold," saying, "if it falls short of greatness—and in my opinion it does—I suspect that coldness, again is mainly responsible." He accused Brackett and Wilder of failing "to make much of the powerful tragic possibilities . . . inherent in their story," and of not exploring "the deep anguish and pathos" which Norma's decline would seem to warrant (Agee 1958, pp. 412, 415). If there is sympathy for Norma Desmond in *Sunset Boulevard*, one place to locate it is in the voice-over narration.

Joe, caught in a feminine/masculine space, is a site of ambivalence, something reflected in his narration. He is cynical about women, age, youth, Hollywood—in other words, all the things he loves and wants deeply. For instance, Joe follows up his meditation on the desire to write with the crack, "Audiences don't know somebody sits down and writes a picture—they think the actors make it up as they go along." Deep feelings are hidden in *Sunset Boulevard* and not surprisingly; when they spill over, as Norma's frequently do, they are frightening and ridiculous, the stuff of camp.[13] About his own ambitions, Gillis is curt. Over his own corpse, floating in the pool in the first scene, he says, "The poor dope. He always wanted a pool."

On the other hand, Joe shows a keen understanding of Norma's emotional state. Reading her manuscript as she watches him, "coiled like a watchspring," he muses, "I could sense her eyes on me . . . defying me not to like what I read, or maybe begging me in her own proud way to like it—it meant so much to her." When Norma orders Joe to restore a scene he's cut from her script, he remarks, "I didn't argue with her. You don't yell at a sleepwalker. He may fall and break his neck." Looking at her bedroom later in the film, he considers it "the perfect setting for a silent movie queen. Poor devil. Still waving proudly to a parade which had long since passed her by." And when reporters swarm around the mansion the morning after Joe has been killed, "with as much hoop-de-doo as we get in Los Angeles when they open a supermarket," Joe adds bitterly, "Here was an item everybody could have some fun with—the heartless so-and-so's."

The *absence* of Joe's narration can also mask powerful emotion—especially in the film's central scene, when Joe gives himself to Norma after her suicide attempt. The emotions that trigger his rush back to Norma and whatever he may feel when he kisses her are left not only uncommented upon, but visually unrepresented—Joe's back is turned to us when he approaches Norma's bed and receives her embrace. The softness of his voice when he takes her arms away from her face and says, "Happy New Year, Norma" can be read equally as tenderness or resignation. Either way, at this moment Joe voluntarily forfeits his superior position as narrator to join Norma in her fantasy.

Joe would not be the first man to relinquish the world for Norma. The only other character in the film who loves Norma and can appreciate her "barbarous grandeur" is Max von Mayerling (Erich von Stroheim), her first husband and first director. On the one hand, Max is Norma's first victim, sacrificing his career to become her butler and see her through a succession of lovers, husbands, and periods of suicidal despair. However, at the same time he controls Norma's life and illusions; it is Max who sends the fan letters, massages "madame's" ego, and keeps the creaking machinery of stardom (the house, the car, the organ) well-oiled. Max can be linked with the other powerful men who cast Norma in their fantasies. "I discovered her," he tells Joe. "I made her a star. And I cannot let her be destroyed." He directly aligns himself with De Mille when he recounts his early fame. "There were three young directors who showed promise in those days —D. W. Griffith, Cecil B. De Mille, and Max von Mayerling." And it is Max who "directs" her last scene. But I think it is more accurate to describe Max and Norma as being equally in thrall to the fantasy of Hollywood. To escape Hollywood, a prison made up of his and Max's and Norma's own desires, Joe must assail what they love most in order to escape.

Nevertheless, Joe's sympathy for Norma continues after death. In the film's final scene, it isn't his own murder that concerns Joe, but rather "What would they do to Norma?" Hedda Hopper takes up the narration for a moment, describing Norma's condition to her editor over the telephone: "A curtain of silence seems to have fallen around her." Like Echo, Gillis watches from somewhere incorporeal, speaking his final words as Narcissus is fatally entranced.

> Life, which can be strangely merciful, had taken pity on Norma Desmond. The dream she had clung to so desperately had enfolded her.

But it is Norma who has the last word in the film, even if it is filtered through madness. As Norma slowly descends the stairs, "the princess" on the steps of the palace, everyone seems to be frozen. She stops and breaks the spell. "I can't go on with the scene, I'm too happy. Mr. De Mille, do you mind if I say a few words?" Blurring fantasy and reality, breaking the fantasy/film to speak directly to the real/fictional crew, Echo silenced, Narcissus speaks:

> You see, this is my life. It always will be. There's nothing else, just us, and the cameras, and all those wonderful people out there in the dark.

Striking a pose, she tilts her head back and stares directly into the camera: "All right, Mr. De Mille. I'm ready for my close up." Gliding directly into the camera as the light grows too bright and the image blurs, Norma moves into a truly transgressive space, trespassing beyond where the lens can see, trying to merge herself with the woman on the screen and all those "wonderful people out there in the dark."

Neither Joe nor Norma actually possesses authorial control. Though Norma is more firmly contained within the diegesis than Joe, she vividly asserts the value of herself, even if doing so necessitates ignoring the truth about the industry that both gave her her dreams and took them away. *Sunset Boulevard* delineates the effect of the film industry's "business as usual" on its employees, especially the women who let themselves be defined by the industry's images, its stories and its commercial needs.

In *Sunset Boulevard* we've seen that men's and women's voices can occupy the "feminine" position of synchronization "inside" the diegesis, just as women and men can each assume the temporary authority of the offscreen voice. Is it possible for a woman to speak from "outside" the diegesis, as the enunciator, claiming the cinematic apparatus as *hers*, her tool of expression, her language? Is there any way a woman can assume for herself, not only the voice-over, embued with authority by Hollywood convention, but the authorial voice?

Gregory Peck and Mary Badham in *To Kill a Mockingbird*

Disembodied Desire

To Kill a Mockingbird (1962)
*Miss Lee considers the novel to be
a simple love story.*
Contemporary Authors

I yearn for the Law.
Julia Kristeva

The question of whether a woman's voice can assume authority *as* the voice of a woman turns on all the issues of women's speech we've examined so far: the way women's voices are positioned within narratives that require their submission to patriarchal roles, how female characters are made to use language that silences them, how the cinematic conventions of visual and audio representation convert woman to spectacle, precluding her status as subject, and the placement of women on the weak end of sound/image hierarchies. The authorial voice is rarely heard as a *woman's* voice in classical cinema, but when it is, it can illustrate some key points about the differences between women's and men's voices in film. While the male disembodied narrator has historically been positioned as the authoritative "enunciator" of his cinematic text, the ability to assume a position of bodiless invulnerability (the voice of God) is tested when the disembodied narrator is a woman. The *value* of sacrificing the body in order to embrace this illusion of mastery is also subjected to serious questioning.

To Kill a Mockingbird is a major work in American popular culture both as a novel and as a film, although it has not been seriously addressed in either film or literary studies.[1] In this essay I would like to propose a reading of *To Kill a Mockingbird* (1962) that challenges traditional accounts of the film as a liberal statement on race relations and focus instead on the film's construction

---

Contemporary Authors: First Revision, vols. 13–16, ed. Clare D. Kinsman (Detroit: Gale Research Company, 1975), p. 481; Julia Kristeva, "Stabat Mater," in *The Kristeva Reader*, ed. Toril Moi (New York: Columbia University Press, 1986), p. 175.

of a female authorial presence. First, by looking at the construction of the author, Harper Lee, in the press around the time of the novel's publication and the film's release two years later, I propose to examine the various ways Lee's image could be appropriated to bolster readings of the film as a story "authored" by a woman. "Authorship" in this case encompasses the common literary definition ("the occupation or career of writing books")[2] as well as a cinematically constructed "authorial presence" made vivid by the film's incorporation of a voice-over narrator speaking in the first person. How do the film's narrative and narrator develop the relationship of novelist Lee with the main character, Scout? How is Scout's relationship to language confounded with desire; what does this desire enable and what does it foreclose? What are the implications of giving the woman-author a cinematic presence through the use of voice-over? And, more important, what is it about not only the story but *her telling of it*—the fact that it is presented as being "authored" by a woman—that ultimately makes the film compatible with patriarchal ideology? And, lastly, is there any way a feminist rereading of the film can open it up and allow us—if briefly—to hear the female voice?

The film's credits pose the first of a series of disjunctions that will figure throughout the film. A little girl hums on the sound track as we see a series of objects that will assume significance in the course of the film. We see only her hands as she makes her first attempts at creation, drawing pictures around the objects of her life. The splits between sound and image, language and voice, character and authorial consciousness that will be central throughout the film are immediately reformulated with the introduction of a woman narrator, herself a figure in crisis as a disembodied voice exiled from the image. Over the film's opening shots, a woman's voice introduces us to Maycomb, "a tired old town," and to herself: "That summer I was six years old."[3] The camera sweeps down langorously as a child in overalls swings into the frame on a rope.

The woman we hear, whom we shall never see, is the adult the child will become.[4] It has been argued that when there is a temporal disjunction between the offscreen self of the narrator and the figure we see, it is caused by trauma.[5] The narrative of *To Kill a Mockingbird* relates the trauma that divorced the voice from the image, the adult woman from the physical, unselfconscious child. Through her voice, the narrator assumes the place of author as literally (and only) a *speaking* female subject. As we shall see, what she authorizes— the sacrifice demanded of the female who would speak—is the writing out of her own body.

To Kill a Mockingbird concerns two children, Scout (Mary Badham), a six-year-old tomboy, and her ten-year-old brother Jem (Philip Alford). They live with their widowed father, Atticus Finch (Gregory Peck), in the small town of Maycomb, Alabama, in the early 1930s. While exploring their world over the course of two summers, Scout and Jem seek to discover the secret of the mysterious Boo Radley, a recluse living in a dilapidated house down the street, and witness their father's controversial defense of a black man accused of rape.

When the film was released, it was the liberal civil rights stance of the rape trial that was seen as the "point" of the film and of the book before it. Critics hailed or dismissed the film according to their perception of its presentation of the racial issue. John Russell Taylor's review in *Sight and Sound* labeled the film an "Oscar trap with a bait of high-toned liberal sentiment."[6] No small part of the film's appeal as "respectable," "progressive" entertainment was its status as an adaptation of an award-winning best-seller. The novel, published in 1960, won the Pulitzer Prize and within a year had sold 500,000 copies and been translated into ten languages.[7] Harper Lee was transformed into an instant celebrity, interviewed in *Life, Newsweek,* and the *Christian Science Monitor.*[8] The formation of Lee's public image was strongly influenced by the perception of the novel as a thinly veiled autobiography. As the consciousness of the "author" inflected contemporary readings of both the novel and the film (and as the concept of author-as-woman will be central to my reading), a short biography of Harper Lee is in order.

Harper Lee, a patrilineal descendant of Robert E. Lee, modeled the character of Atticus Finch on her father, Amasa Lee. Finch was her mother's maiden name. A biography of the author states that, "Her decision to attend law school is attributed to the strong influence of her lawyer-father."[9] However, for reasons unstated, Lee left law school at the University of Alabama shortly before she was to complete her degree and turned to writing fiction. Although she left the law, her turning to literature only brought her home. In an interview, Lee exults in contradicting Thomas Wolfe: "I can go home again."[10] "Home" is her father. She wrote *To Kill a Mockingbird* in "her father's law office."[11] A photograph states their symbiotic relationship visually: an aged Amasa Lee sits in a rocker on a front porch, facing left. Harper Lee reclines on a chaise opposite, facing him. Like a pair of inward-facing bookends, they form two sides of a single figure. We must see her through him.

The Lawyer/Father

As the description "lawyer-father" indicates, the role of the father is everywhere inflected by Atticus's function as upholder/performer of the Law. At one point, when asked why he defends a black man, Atticus identifies his integrity as a lawyer as the basis for whatever moral (prohibitive) authority he may have as a parent. He says that if he didn't do his best, "I couldn't hold my head up in town, I couldn't even tell [Scout] or Jem not to do something again."

With their mother dead, Atticus softens the strict precepts of the Law with a maternal compassion. He councils Scout not to torment the eccentric, unseen Boo Radley or to ridicule a young backwoods guest, or to embarrass a poor man who pays his legal fees with hickory nuts. Although he is a crack shot, he admonishes the children never to kill a mockingbird because mockingbirds only exist to give pleasure. At all times, the father teaches fairness, compromise, and balance. At one point, Scout is dead set against ever returning to school because of a fight with her teacher. "[She] said you were teachin' me to read all wrong and to stop it. . . . If I keep goin' to school we can't ever read anymore." He asks her if she knows what a compromise is. "Bending the law?" "Uh . . . no," he explains, "It's an agreement reached by mutual consent. . . . You concede the necessity of goin' to school, [and] we'll keep right on readin' the same every night, just as we always have." In this case "lawyer talk" substitutes for and demonstrates the best brand of "father talk."

The subject of this altercation shows not only Atticus's paternal/legal technique but *what* Atticus teaches that Scout values most. He teaches her to read. In the first and most striking "writing out" of the mother (which I shall address in more depth later), Lee echoes a tendency identified across the work of literary women, the "massive disavowal of the tutelary role the mother classically assumes with respect to the child's linguistic education, of her function as language teacher, commentator, storyteller" (Silverman 1988, p. 105, discussing Julia Kristeva's work). In *To Kill a Mockingbird*, the mother has been dead since before Scout, our storyteller, can remember and, significantly, since before she learned to speak. Atticus is all, and Scout's happiest moments are when she and Atticus read together at night. Literature becomes the focus of a privileged, private time.

Early in the film, Atticus sits at the foot of Scout's bed as she reads *Huckleberry Finn* aloud. At first it seems as if Scout has escaped socialization into her gender role. Looking like a female Huck Finn, she has short straight brown hair that is always falling in her eyes, an accent you could cut with a knife, and wears overalls most all the time. However, in teaching language, Atticus teaches gender difference. After Scout puts down her book and gets ready for bed, she asks to see Atticus's pocket watch. She snatches it as he dangles it hypnotically in front of her. "Atticus? Jem says this watch is gonna belong to him some day." "That's right." "Why-y-y?" she asks. He answers, "It's customary for the boy to have his father's watch." Scout asks: "What are you gonna give me?" and he replies, "I don't know that I have much else of value that belongs to *me*." He mentions her mother's jewelry. Scout stretches and purrs with pleasure as her femininity is inscribed for her by a commanding masculine figure.[12] While his age desexualizes him (he is early on identified as "old"), Scout's calling Atticus by his first name obscures his position as father, making him ripe as a focus for infatuation. As "her father," he is abstract, like the Law. As "Atticus," the incest taboo is obscured, and a mythical equality allows Scout to play at feminine wiles while her father paternally seduces her into femininity.

Just as Atticus's role as father is always measured and balanced by his position as a lawyer, his standing as a lawyer is affected by his fatherhood. Atticus is appointed to defend Tom Robinson, a black man accused of raping Mayella Ewell, a poor white woman. *Time* accused Peck of playing "Abe Lincoln of Alabama,"[13] and when a lynch mob gathers outside the local jail the night before the trial, the scene is shot in a way strikingly reminiscent of a similar scene in *Young Mr. Lincoln*. As Marsha Kinder points out, Lincoln, political patriarch and upholder of the law, *becomes* the phallus, unwinding to intimidating height, and possessing a solidity that (1) cannot be moved and (2) assumes not only the authority but the raw power to symbolically castrate lesser men who seek to act outside the Law.[14]

Atticus/Peck is found sitting casually in a tipped-back chair on the porch of the jailhouse, reading a massive law book. Cars pull up and the lynch mob assembles. Peck uses his friendly, but masculine and authoritative, voice to encourage the men to go home. He invokes the Law. Like Lincoln, "he throws back on the crowd the threat of its own violence,"[15] saying that the local sheriff is nearby, presumably with a gun. This is a bluff. As the editors of *Cahiers du cinéma* point out in their analysis of *Young Mr. Lincoln,* "in the ideological discourse, Law must have power insofar as it is legitimised by its own statement, not through physical strength [or violence], which is used as a last resort and often [as here] simply as a verbal threat "[16] The members of the lynch mob tell Atticus the sheriff has been lured away on a phoney emergency. Just then, the children, who have been watching from nearby, break through the crowd and jump onto the jailhouse steps. Atticus, frightened for the children, orders Jem to take Scout and their friend Dill home. Jem, being a brave boy (and knowing his gender role), refuses. He will stand and fight. It is Scout who ingenuously disarms the crowd by saying, "Hey!" to one of the men. Shamefaced at her innocent kindness (shades of Shirley Temple), the men withdraw. It is Scout who completes, but at the same time subtly undermines, the Lincolnesque stature of her father. In the 1939 film, it is Lincoln who "defuses the crowd's anger" by "shifting" to a strategy of "complicity/familiarity with the crowd" and by "addressing one individual amongst the lynchers."[17] Through Scout, a "feminine" and childlike compassion enables the phallus to remain standing and rescues the Father/Law from suffering a direct assault.

The centerpiece of the film and the book is Tom Robinson's trial. Our first introduction to the major participants in the case occurs when the children rush down to the courthouse and, standing on each other's shoulders so they can see in, relate to us the arraignment going on inside. Everything about the trial has resonances of a "primal scene"—in its confusion of sexuality and violence (a misperception typical of children witnessing sexual activity), in the scandalized adults, and particularly in the fact that children are barred from the proceedings. Jem and Scout are present at the trial because of the kindness of an elderly black minister who lets them sit with him in the balcony reserved for blacks.[18]

Although it is acknowledged that the black defendant cannot win in a case that depends on his word against a white woman's, Atticus is able through cross-examination to establish that Mayella was beaten by someone who was left-handed, that her father Bob Ewell is left-handed, and that, as both principals testify, Tom Robinson was in her house when her father found them together. In traditional rape defense, she says he attacked her, he says she attacked him.

Atticus's summation to the jury establishes his position not only on civil rights, but primarily on the law:

> Now gentlemen, in this country our courts are the great levelers, and in our courts all men are created equal. I'm no idealist to believe firmly in the integrity of our courts and of the jury system—that's no ideal to me, that is a living, working reality.

In Atticus's system, the law is not an oppressive, castrating law (John Ford's Lincoln) nor is his humanity dependent on a maternal weakness (Griffith's presentation of Lincoln as the "Great Heart," for instance).[19] Rather than envisioning the law as ubiquitous and oppressive, in this vision, the law wielded by the father is a tool for accomplishing justice. This is what makes Atticus fundamentally a *liberal* lawyer. If the justice that can be accomplished through the law lies only somewhere in an undefined future, so be it. Atticus is not a radical or a revolutionary. Knowing its flaws, he still maintains the law first and foremost as a safeguard against impulse, darkness, and sexuality.

Woman is made to stand as the negative term against which the Law defines itself. In Atticus's summation, it is explicitly the woman who is guilty, and what she is guilty of is desire. According to Atticus, Mayella committed perjury "in an effort to get rid of her own guilt":

> She has committed no crime, she has merely broken a rigid and time-honored code of our society. . . .
>
>   What did she do? She tempted a Negro. She was white, and she tempted a Negro. She did something that in our society is unspeakable: she kissed a black man. Not an old Uncle, but a strong young Negro man. No code mattered to her before she broke it, but it came crashing down on her afterwards.

In standing on the "time-honored code" Atticus redirects the trajectory of the legal/moral process of guilt-finding. "The defendant is not guilty, but somebody in this courtroom is."

During the trial scene, Scout and the voice of the narrator are shunted aside as the male characters work to expose Mayella's transgressive desire. Yet vi-

sual, verbal, and structural parallels abound that connect the women in and around the text. Mayella has two feminine first names, as does Jean Louise Finch, who is labeled with this double dose of femininity when she's being socialized for school and can no longer use the androgynous "Scout" (much as Nellie Lee assumed the pseudonym "Harper"). The character of Scout and Harper Lee, writer, were explicitly compared in the press. According to *Newsweek*, Miss Lee "strongly calls to mind the impish tomboy who narrates her novel," both in her "Italian boy haircut" and "the heavy touch of Alabama in her accent."[20] In *Life*, Lee is pictured without makeup, wearing a short-sleeved sports shirt, pants, and tennis shoes—what the magazine labels "hometown getup."[21] Collin Wilcox, as Mayella, in turn looks like an ungainly, adolescent Scout. Her hair is straight and unkempt, a hair ribbon pathetically failing to keep scraggly bangs out of her eyes. She also wears no makeup. The nondescript print dress Mayella wears at the trial is strongly reminiscent of Scout's dress on her first day of school. ("I *still* don't see why I hafta wear a darn ole *dress*," Scout declares.) Both child and adolescent wriggle inside their clothes as if trapped by shapeless tributes to an ideal of femininity that just doesn't seem to fit. Mayella, the discredited and exposed "white trash 'victim,'"[22] is the link between the child we see and the woman on the sound track, and the cause of their division.

When Mayella is being cross-examined by Atticus, she quickly reverts to childlike behavior. She perches on the edge of her chair, clutching the seat with her hands. When Atticus asks if the evening of the attack was the first time she ever invited Tom Robinson inside her yard, she nods and barks an emphatic "Yes!" When he asks her if she hadn't asked him in on previous occasions, she shrugs, bites her lip, and puts her arms behind her. "I mighta . . ." The camera lingers on Mayella so that we can see the rapid transitions from childlike confusion to rehearsed certainty. When Atticus asks her about the details of the attack, she squints up at him through her bangs with a quizzical look. Atticus fixes her in a stern authoritative stare, the judgment he passes upon her as a lawyer replicates his disapproval of her from the position of the father.

The film makes it abundantly clear that Mayella is lying and Tom Robinson is surely innocent. It is part of the liberal grounding of the film, however, that in order for Robinson not to be the racist specter of the black rapist, he must be figuratively castrated. Long before we see Robinson, we hear him as a ghostly offscreen voice asking Atticus, "They gone?" after the mob outside the jail has gone. The first time we see Robinson speak is at the trial, when he is made to stand and declare his impotence; he can't have beaten Mayella with his left hand because it was mangled in a shredder when he was young. His entire arm is "useless." Atticus calls him "not an old Uncle but a strong young Negro *man,*" but the Robinson we see is defined as physically incapable. He only speaks when prompted and cued by Atticus.

John Ellis finds a similar process at work in another film of the period, John Ford's 1960 *Sergeant Rutledge.* Pam Cook summarizes his argument: "The film produces a commentary on racism by taking the myth of black super-sexuality as its central problem, displacing the myth in favour of the proposition that blacks are a-sexual; Rutledge [a black cavalry officer accused of rape] becomes a human being only insofar as he foreswears his sexuality" (quoted in Pam Cook, ed., *The Cinema Book* [London: BFI 1985], p. 188). This is why ultimately *To Kill a Mockingbird* is next to useless on the issue of race, except as an artifact of early 1960s liberal sentiment. Cook also points out how "the trial device enables commentary to be carried out at all points of ambiguity. . . . Thus multiple meanings are limited and controlled"—potentially militating against feminist, progressive, or resistant readings (ibid.). However, I would like to propose a feminist reading that resists the film's smooth liberal surface by examining how women are distorted and fragmented (both in their relationships with each other and in relation to their own desires) by the racist and patriarchal system delineated in the film.

When Mayella begins her scathing assault on the system in which she is becoming ensnared, the camera zooms in.

> I got somethin' to say and then I ain't gonna say no more. He took advantage of me. And if you fine, fancy gennelmen ain't gonna do nothin' about it, then you're just a bunch of lousy, yella, stinkin' cowards. The whole bunch of ya. And your fancy airs don't come to *nothin'.* Your "Miss Mayella," it don't come to nothin', Mr. Finch. No—no—

Diving out of the bottom of the frame, she runs off the witness stand and plunges into the crowd.

As regards the case, everything Mayella says is identified as false. Everything about the way she speaks, the hesitancies, the fact that what she says does not bear on the case, and especially her accent, brands her as "incoherent" and "inarticulate." In a point I shall take exception to later, Silverman argues that for women in Hollywood sound films "every corporeal encroachment, from a regional accent or idiosyncratic 'grain' to definitive localization in the image," causes the voice to "lose [its] power and authority" and become, like the body, subject to aging and death. . . . Synchronization marks the final moment in any such localization, the point of full and complete 'embodiment'" (Silverman 1988, p. 49). One could say that Mayella's outburst is obsessively synchronized, her accent and the zoom in to a close-up calling attention to every word as she forms it. The Southern Californian Gregory Peck as Atticus, on the other hand, supplies barely a nod in the direction of an accent. As the embodiment of all-are-created-equal sentiment, his nondescript middle American is appropriate.

Yet I would argue that it is precisely the *way* Mayella speaks that supplies much of the power of her tirade and is the source of a particular power for all of the women in the film. Scout doesn't hide her accent, saying "Hey!" to everyone. Nor does Harper Lee. Scout's language is as unsocialized as her hair and clothes. For instance, at one point she says that another character "won't take nothin' from nobody." While I shall argue the perverse embodying power of the regional, feminine voice in relation to the narrator, for now, Mayella's accent traps her in her gender and her class, and the fine fancy airs of Atticus, and the court's careful show of concern for her as "victim," "don't mean nothin'."

The effect of the trial on Scout is another matter. In the novel, the trial is seen through the eyes of the children. Scout is sleepy, and it is Jem, a budding lawyer, who appreciates the formality and abstractness of the law, the rules of evidence and the ritual nature of the cross-examination, which, incidentally, humiliates his father's client. In the film, Jem eagerly watches the first two witnesses. When Mayella testifies, Scout is lost in the background of a long shot that favors Jem. As the trial proceeds through the testimony of the police chief, Bob Ewell, Mayella, and Tom Robinson, there are ten reaction shots either isolating or favoring Jem. When the testimony is over and the jury is considering its verdict (and Mayella, for our purposes, has been "convicted"), there is a shot of Scout. She is sitting on the floor looking through the slats of the balcony railing, visually behind bars. The jury returns with a guilty verdict against Robinson, and Jem cries. Scout remains impassive. As the courtroom clears, the black minister who has let them sit with him in the balcony murmurs, "Miss Jean Louise?" Scout looks up from her figurative cage. As Atticus slowly leaves the courtroom, the black population of Maycomb rise in silent tribute. The minister tells her, "Miss Jean Louise, stand up. Your father's passing." It is the first time Scout has to be instructed to pay respect to Atticus.

What comes between Scout and Atticus is the law. Scout does not rebel in

any way against her father, but they are kept apart from this point until the film's climax. (In the scene immediately after the trial, when Atticus is informed that Tom Robinson has been shot down "trying to escape," we forget Scout is even present as Atticus leaves with Jem to inform Robinson's family.) At the trial, Scout confronts the problem of her future. Her desire—a conflation of desire for the father with desire for language—is even more forbidden than Mayella's. Jane Gallop writes that a woman's "desire for the father's desire (for his penis) causes her to submit to the father's law, which denies his desire/penis, [and] operates in its place."[23] I would like to suggest *To Kill a Mockingbird* as an illustration of the process whereby a young woman learns that to love language as epitomized by the Law, literalized here as her father, is to sanction the terms of her own exclusion. To speak, on these terms, demands such a complete identification with the Father/Law that it obliterates any chance of a woman speaking in her own voice. And yet Scout, as both child-character and adult author, strives to maintain the father as some kind of ideal. The question, then, is how to become a woman—an adult, a wielder of language, a subject—and not be rejected by the father. What is at stake in this process of extricating language from the Law is not just the girl's preservation of an idealized father, but the possibility of creating a position for herself as subject and author—of constructing a voice. However, we eventually have to ask to what extent this voice is ultimately coopted *for* the Law when the father is held immune from criticism and the mother is radically excluded.

The Bad Father

Although the trial might introduce ambivalence to Scout's idealization of her father, true antipathy is precluded with Bob Ewell around. The polar opposite of Atticus throughout the film, Ewell is the dark side of paternal authority that Atticus's liberal, maternal goodness conceals. The Methodist teetotaler confronts the alcoholic when Ewell staggers up to the car to glare menacingly at Jem as Jem waits outside the Robinson house for his father.

Atticus always wears a suit and a tie (at home a sweater and a tie), while Ewell throws a jacket over his overalls and scrunches a hat on his head as he sways in the street yelling "nigger-lover" after the Finch's departing car. In place of Atticus's measured, thoughtful reasoning, Ewell asserts the "time-honored" wisdom of racist slurs. More important, where Atticus uses stern disapproval to browbeat Mayella, the testimony at the trial draws a vivid picture of Ewell's style of fatherhood—physically beating his daughter to repress her sexuality. Both fathers are repressive; it comes down to a matter of degree. Ewell and Atticus's deeper relationship as the dual sides of the role of the father is revealed in their complementary actions. Ewell's abuse of the law prompts Atticus's exposure of Ewell's daughter, Mayella. Atticus's actions as the enforcer of the law looses Ewell on Atticus's children.

Some time after the trial, when Jem and Scout are returning from an agricultural pageant, Scout finds out what it can mean to be a woman. She has been transformed by costume into a representative of one of the state's prime agricultural products, a ham. In the dark, threatening woods between school and home, the instinctual violence her father's law means to control is unleashed. The good father, whose actions have provoked the attack, is nowhere to be found.

The scene is presented through the severely restricted vision of Scout. A man grabs Jem and breaks his arm, but before he can hurt Scout, immobilized by her costume, another figure appears. As a close-up of Scout's eyes shows her desperately trying to see what is happening, we hear the heavy breathing of a struggle. Scout, choosing between the confinement of respectability and near-nakedness, wriggles out of her costume and runs home. In the distance, she sees a man carrying Jem up the front steps. Atticus runs out of the house and Scout jumps into his arms. As the police chief and Atticus grill Scout to find out who was fighting with Ewell, Scout points to a shadowy figure behind the bedroom door. "Why, there he is. He can tell you his name. Hey, Boo!" And Boo Radley, never before seen, emerges from the shadows.

Although they had never seen him, Boo has played a major role in the fantasy lives of Scout and Jem. The children dare each other to go near his house. He leaves them trinkets in the hollow of a tree, which they save and keep secret from Atticus. Boo lives in the kind of old dark house Annette Kuhn calls "the classic 'other scene,' the site precisely of enigma and mystery." [24] The "Radley place," like the house Kuhn describes from *The Big Sleep,* is the object of the children's "obsessive return," and the subject of major set pieces in the film's first half (Scout's precarious inner-tube ride that crashes her into the front porch, Jem's brave venturing to touch the front door, the nighttime raid, etc.). The children's secret project of "making Boo come out," of making the house divulge its mysterious tenant, is interrupted by the trial and its consequences. But the house returns in the film's penultimate scenes, with Boo himself as the answer to the final enigma.

Boo stands as the test case that proves the superiority of literature *over* the law. When it becomes apparent that Boo stabbed Bob Ewell in order to save the children, Atticus tells the sheriff there will have to be a trial. Although he owes his children's lives to Boo, Atticus cannot break free of the law's "guilty or not guilty." Boo, however, confounds and subdues the logic of the law. The sheriff urges the interests of a "higher" law—compassion. Scout concurs. As she did at the jailhouse, Scout gently indicates the limits of her father's law. By translating Atticus's literal prohibition against killing mockingbirds into a more powerful metaphorical one, she explains that Boo is like the mockingbird, only seeking to please, and it would be a sin to cause him harm. Together with the sheriff, Scout in effect makes Atticus party to a cover-up.

Boo not only exceeds the law's restrictive binarism, he is explicitly inarticulate. His story must be told by someone else. It is Scout who argues his case, takes him by the hand and walks him home. As she stands alone on the Radley porch, the victorious discoverer and interpreter of the "other scene," the narrator returns on the sound track in a wash of lush Southernisms set against Elmer Bernstein's delicate, emotion-laden score.

> The summer that had begun so long ago had ended and another summer had taken its place . . . and a fall . . . and Boo Radley had come out. I was to think of these days many times, of Jem and Dill and Boo Radley and Tom Robinson. And Atticus.
> He would be in Jem's room all night. And he would be there . . . when Jem waked up in the mornin'.

Back home, Scout crawls into her father's lap. The father can now be restored because the law has been subtly but firmly displaced.

The Narrator

As I have shown, Lee was a well-known public figure at the time of the film's release. The image that the public would have brought to *To Kill a*

Mockingbird of the author as a *literary* personage would have included not only biographical information about Lee, but a rich legacy of other works of the same genre. The reviewer for the *New York Times,* for instance, exclaimed thankfully that, in the novel, "Miss Lee has not tried to satisfy the current lust for morbid, grotesque tales of Southern depravity." [25] The genre to which he refers—and to which both *Mockingbird*'s certainly belong—is the "Southern Gothic." Many critics specifically compared Lee to other *women* writers working in this genre (e.g., Carson McCullers and Flannery O'Connor). One reviewer even condescendingly judges Lee on the basis of gender: "Miss Lee does write like a woman. . . . She paints Scout in warm tones and we like the child." [26] What is important is the contextualization of Lee and the book within a genre understood in its day as hospitable to women (if not altogether becoming) and tied firmly to a specific region.[27] Southern Gothic novels were also the source of a spate of films made in the late 1950s and early 1960s such as *God's Little Acre* (1958), *Cat on a Hot Tin Roof* (1958), *The Sound and the Fury* (1959), *Sanctuary* (1961), *Sweet Bird of Youth* (1962), and anything authored by Tennessee Williams or Truman Capote.[28]

In addition to preserving the first-person narration of the book, creating an "authorial presence," and foregrounding the work's status as an adaptation, the use of a narrator in the film version of *Mockingbird* introduces an extra dimension familiar to fans of the genre, a feverish preoccupation with words. The films of Tennessee Williams's works alone are filled with words lovingly lingered over; Burl Ives starting a roundelay of "men-dacity" in *Cat on a Hot Tin Roof,* or the contagious "dementia praecox" in *Suddenly Last Summer,* or Katharine Hepburn in the latter blissfully invoking "Sebastian and Violet, Violet and Sebastian," as she rises to madness in a byzantine iron-work elevator.

The opening moments of *To Kill a Mockingbird* are defined by Kim Stanley's slow, rolling emphasis as she tells us, "Maycomb was a tired . . . old . . . town," or when she describes how the ladies in the summer "were like soft teacakes with frostin's of sweat and sweet talcum." This sense of words as somehow special in themselves is restricted to the narrator. Scout never treats language like this. Nor—interestingly—does she ever express interest in becoming a writer. It is the woman narrator who binds the identification of Scout to Harper Lee. It is through her that we are instructed to read Scout as the central character, and through her voice that we are made aware of a narrating consciousness outside the film. The narrator is Scout grown up, but she is also the cinematic stand-in for Harper Lee, reiterating in the film the widespread assumption that the novel was partly autobiographical. Because of the narrator, we assume that Scout one day will choose to record her growing consciousness of injustice, choosing to become a woman who lingers over the rhythmic alliteration of "sweat and sweet talcum"—or a woman who leaves law school to write fiction.

There is nevertheless a price to be paid in choosing literature if not the law,

one the film makes clear. In accepting her father's liberalism (and consequently gainsaying radical change), Scout must forfeit the right to openly
speak her desire. The role of rebellious daughter is projected onto the discredited Mayella. Scout becomes nothing but words, luxurious words, but
only words. By accepting the substitution of language in place of her beloved
Atticus, Scout becomes the film's narrator—a bodiless woman. The choice of
literature, seen in this light, seems at first to be a compromise that borders on
collaboration.

What is notably absent from the film's adoration of language obtained
through a nurturing father is the figure of the mother. For Lacan, "division
from the mother" is necessary for the accession to language. In subsequently
passing through the Oedipus complex, the female subject is encouraged to re-
ject her mother, to "assume the burden of male lack as well as her own . . . by
defining the female body as the site of anatomical insufficiency . . . [and] the
female voice as the site of discursive impotence" (Silverman 1988, p. 123).
In doing so, the female subject accepts the negative patriarchal definition of
the feminine, just as tomboy Scout resoundingly rejects all things "girlish" as
she accedes to the "normative and normalizing desire for the father" (ibid.).
On the other hand, feminist writers have suggested a more positive reason
why women need to distance themselves from their mothers—the need to establish separate identities in the face of what Dorothy Dinnerstein has called
the "threat . . . of maternal omnipotence." [29] Silverman, for example, argues
that Kristeva's father-centered and "highly rationalized language must be
understood . . . as a defense against her desire for union with the mother,"
which "within the terms of her own analysis . . . would necessarily mean the
collapse of her subjectivity and the loss of her voice" (ibid., p. 113).

Whether Lee's elimination of the mother is a negative rejection of the feminine or a positive assertion of self in the face of a potentially overwhelming
identification with the mother, it is clear that the elision of the mother is fundamental to Lee's authorship.[30] In this sense we can situate the novel *To Kill a
Mockingbird* within the tradition of the Freudian "family romance" as described by Marianne Hirsch. In *The Mother/Daughter Plot,* Hirsch argues
that "the Freudian family romance pattern clearly implies that women need to
kill or to eliminate their mothers from their lives" in order to become writers
(1989, p. 56). "It is the mother's absence which creates the space in which the
heroine's plot and her activity of plotting can evolve. . . . To free the girl's
imaginative play, the mother must be eliminated from the fiction" (ibid.,
pp. 57, 56). As we've seen resoundingly in *Mockingbird,* this particular " 'female family romance' . . . is founded on the elimination of the mother and the
attachment to a husband-father" (ibid., p. 57). As Harper Lee said in the epi-
graph to this chapter, *To Kill a Mockingbird* is "a simple love story."

Actual mothers are notably absent from both the film and Lee's novel,
while fathers abound. Scout's mother has died before the story begins. May-

ella is surrounded by younger brothers and sisters, yet a mother is never mentioned. Dill's mother is somewhere up north, and Boo's offscreen mother dies somewhere in the course of the narrative, without ever being seen. The repression of the maternal assures that the maternal space within the film will be troubled and perverse. A neighbor lady offers occasional words of comfort, and Calpurnia, the black maid, enforces discipline, but the major potential mother figure besides Atticus is, oddly enough, Boo. Unlike father figures who attack children or pass judgment, Boo does motherly things—making toys, sewing Jem's trousers, watching over the children, protecting them from harm. Kuhn's "old dark house"—here associated with Boo—is "the site of unspeakable mysteries whose naming must yet be the condition of their solution"; it is located in the "both familiar and unfamiliar, reassuring and threatening" nature of the uncanny, and one finds there "nothing other than the riddle of the feminine, . . . [the] body of the mother" (Kuhn 1982, p. 10).

If Boo is what is at the heart of the repressed maternal space, then it is there that we can locate the most violent resistance to the father, particularly the father's power to castrate. Viewers frequently take Boo to be retarded or mentally ill. However, the book makes it clear that his condition is the result of overzealous punishment by his father. In many ways, Boo resembles Benjy from William Faulkner's *The Sound and the Fury,* another Southern Gothic with a 1930s setting, and one in which the threatened castration is literal. Boo is a man who, as a boy, assaulted his own father—a father described as highly principled, but cruel. Boo wields the knife again when he stabs Robert E. Lee ("Bob") Ewell to death.[31] Boo's revolt establishes resistance against the father as coming from the maternal space. Scout's endorsement of this rage when she takes Boo by the hand and shields him from Atticus's law attests to a common cause.[32] Scout—the woman in the process of creating her own story—also rejects the father's power to castrate. By becoming a writer, Scout can fix herself in time as a child, permanently "Scout," and avoid assuming the problematic feminine status of Jean Louise. But this is also why the adult Scout cannot be represented visually; in patriarchy, the non-castrated woman exists only as a discursive position. A voice.

Besides her love for her father, "Scout" (indicating this single persona constructed out of the character on screen, the voice-over narrator, and the author) seeks to heal the "wound" of symbolic castration through storytelling. Western tradition seeks to nail down being itself with words ("I think therefore I am," "the party of the first part," *Brown v. Alabama, Roe v. Wade*), but storytelling creates a space between the words that the reader can fill, potentially, with that which cannot be put into words: the "re-membered" plenitude offered by the mother's voice.[33] Scout's transformation of the literal into metaphor (Boo as the mockingbird) illustrates the crucial, undefinable space the maternal can preserve against the letter of the law. Oral storytelling being a preeminently feminine form, it is the *telling* of *To Kill a Mockingbird*

that allows Scout-the-author to reconstruct a self that incorporates child, adolescent (Mayella incorporated if not embraced), and woman/writer—to become, in effect, her own mother-in-language.

The resulting female subject is, perhaps necessarily, fragmented across
several "bodies" in the text: Scout, Mayella, the nameless, bodiless narrator,
and Harper Lee. A disjointed subjectivity, I would argue, is characteristic of
the experience of women in patriarchy. Here, it is through literature that
woman-as-(discursive)-subject is capable of reuniting the fragments of herself
declared irreconcilable by the Law.

By writing the novel, Harper Lee reunites the fragments of "woman" scattered by pressures of law and language and makes them all legitimate, valued
parts of her past. In the *film's* use of "Harper Lee, literary persona," however,
the woman-as-author serves a different purpose. I would argue that "woman's
authorship" in the film is foregrounded precisely because it affirms and con-
sents to the idolization of the father-as-representative-of-the-law. (This could
also be posed as one of the reasons for the film's continuing popularity—
popularity being a measure of a work's comforting endorsement of the status quo.) However, despite the film's containment of "female authorship"
through its appropriation of Lee's persona, I would now like to propose a rereading of the female narrator's voice-over from a feminist point of view.

With the body of the mother "missing," the adult female voice holds a
dramatically increased authority. Mary Ann Doane notes that it is rare for a
woman's voice-over to continue throughout a film,[34] but it is precisely the narrator's return at the end of *To Kill a Mockingbird* that imposes the sense of
closure and wholeness. It would be precisely here, in the narrator's physical,
voluptuous voice, that the woman's (the author's, and perhaps the mother's)
body might reinsert itself into the cinematic text.

Kristeva theorizes the semiotic as the eruption of the body into the symbolic. We can specify the semiotic here as the voice that surrounds and articu-
lates language.[35] Combined with the Southern Gothic's generic inclination to
play with words as things, Kim Stanley's specifically regional, feminine, *embodied* voice on the sound track fills the emptiness of the words-as-language
with a definite sensual pleasure. Stanley's (and Collin Wilcox's and Mary
Badham's) accent, enunciation, and vocal timbre (all the things that are so
hard to describe) call attention to that space *outside* of language and return us
to the body—here, undeniably, a *woman's* body. Where literary narrators
may seem androgynous, in film a voice-over must be em-bodied at every moment, gendered to a degree difficult to express in words. That is why I would
assert that all of the aspects Silverman identifies as limiting the authority of
the woman's voice in classical Hollywood cinema enrich it *as* a woman's voice
in *Mockingbird*.

Contemporary feminist writers have celebrated regional women's speech as
a form of language uncontained by dominant literary values and not subject to

grammatical dicta.[36] In what Molly Hite identifies as a black feminist tradition, the daughter's desire for the language of the father is reformulated in terms that do not necessarily exclude or devalue the mother.[37] For instance, in discussing Alice Walker's *The Color Purple*, Christine Froula describes Celie as "a woman reborn to desire and language" whose story "allegorizes not only women's need to be economically independent of men but *the daughter's need to inherit the symbolic estate of culture and language that has always belonged to the father.*"[38] Although the father's culture and language are not adopted without question or change, by depicting women as *entitled* to language and to the right to speak in a political sense, Froula suggests a position from which women can speak something other than their own exclusion under Oedipus. The language women speak in these works combines the oral tradition of their mothers with the "right to write" taken from their fathers. The film's voice-over (replete with accent, rhythm, warmth, and tone) makes the oral tradition sensually explicit, once again merging Kristeva's symbolic and semiotic, reasserting the body that continues to exist despite the law.

In the last shot of the film, Scout, having led Boo home, returns to Atticus's lap, as the narrator bestows her blessings on them all. In the background, highlighted and visible for the only time in the film, we see a framed portrait of a woman, the mother who was lost. The final image is wrapped in the woman's voice as the author embraces her creation—an image of father-daughter bliss within a symbolic system that enables her to speak her resistance to the law. However, the limited validation of the female voice does not encourage resistance to patriarchy. It can instead be seen as a way to preserve the father by covering over awareness of his inadequacy. And the disturbing cost of that may be not only the forfeiture of desire but infantilization.

As long as the mother is absented and the father idolized, the woman's "authorship" will underscore her acceptance of her exclusion as an adult subject. The approval of the father, representative of the Law, can be won only by renouncing desire. In *To Kill a Mockingbird*, female desire is displaced onto language and excluded from the image. "Scout" becomes a bodiless woman, her existence spread across the various women within and surrounding the text. However by recuperating her fragmented self through the process of storytelling, and by insisting on a regionalized and gendered voice that exceeds language, the woman *can* mark a small place for herself within patriarchy as a speaking subject—although that subjectivity is, admittedly, a highly qualified one.

Notes

Introduction

1. Ovid, *Metamorphoses*, book 3, trans. Frank Justus Miller (Cambridge, Mass.: Harvard University Press, 1985), pp. 151–59.

2. Ibid., p. 149.

3. For overviews, see E. Ann Kaplan, "Is the Gaze Male?" in Kaplan 1983, pp. 23–35, and Flinn 1986.

4. This urge was also articulated by visual mechanical reproduction apparatuses such as the daguerreotype and still photography, as well as in early silent films about daily life such as the Lumières' *Le repas de bébé*.

5. See J. P. Telotte, *Voices in the Dark: The Narrative Patterns of Film Noir* (Urbana: University of Illinois Press, 1989), on film noir as a genre that foregrounds crises in narrative, and Kaplan 1978a on issues of gender and genre.

Chapter 1

1. David A. Cook, *A History of Narrative Film* (New York: Norton, 1981), pp. 1–4.

2. Ibid., p. 5n.

3. C. E. McCluer, "Telephone Operators and Operating Room Management," *American Telephone Journal* 6, no. 2 (July 12, 1902), quoted in Rakow 1988, pp. 214–15.

4. By way of illustration, Anne McKay (1988, p. 198) mentions that in the first half of the century, "at the women's rights convention at Seneca Falls [in 1848], the organizers dared not preside over the meeting themselves, but delegated that honor to their husbands."

5. E.g., Mulvey 1975; Pam Cook and Claire Johnston, "The Place of Woman in the Cinema of Raoul Walsh," in Nichols 1985, pp. 379–87; Bergstrom 1979.

6. Emile Berliner, inventor of the disc-playing gramophone, echoed Edison in 1888, confidently stating that "future generations will be able to condense within the space of twenty minutes a tone picture of a single lifetime: five minutes of a child's prattle, five of the boy's exultations, five of the man's reflections, and five from the feeble utterances of the death-bed" (Gelatt 1955, pp. 62–63). Clearly, the voice the original inventors envisioned being recorded was conceived of as male.

7. All of these uses have since been realized through later sound technologies, primarily magnetic tape. These forms of voice are also predominantly forms of speech, as befits a "talking machine." The other major subject for sound recording is music, to which the voice is also closely tied through singing. In describing the maternal voice "as a sonorous envelope enclosing the newborn infant," the French theorist Guy Rosolato asserts that the "primordial listening experience" for the infant is the mother's voice, which serves as "the prototype for all subsequent auditory pleasure, especially the pleasure . . . [of] music" (Rosolato 1974, quoted in Silverman 1988, p. 84).

8. These operators were licensed through the Edison Speaking Phonograph Company ("The Evolution of Recordings: From Cylinder to Video Disc" [1978]).

9. Noël Burch notes: "It appears that in the earliest years of film-showing, at least one exhibitor set up rows of seats allowing spectators who wished to do so *to watch the projection rather than the film*." He adds that it was "quite general practice [to begin] every performance by a demonstration of the workings of the projector" (Burch 1979, p. 80; italics in original). Burch is, of course, speaking of Japanese cinema (as his source he cites Donald Richie and Joseph L. Anderson, *The Japanese Film: Art and Industry* [New York: Grove Press, 1960], who in turn cite Tanaka Junichirō, *Nihon eiga hotatsu* [Tokyo: Chuo-koron-sha, 1957]), but Stephen Heath observes much the same about early Lumière exhibitions ("The Cinematic Apparatus," in *Questions of Cinema* [Bloomington: Indiana University Press, 1981], pp. 220–21).

10. Heath, *Questions of Cinema*, p. 220; italics added.

11. "A single exhibition phonograph could earn as much as $1800 per week," according to Gelatt (1955, p. 28). This figure is comparable (given a 5:1 rate of exchange between the franc and the dollar) to the amount earned by the Lumières in France in the first film exhibitions in the 1890s. David Cook says that at "one franc per customer . . . the Cinématographe showings were earning an average of seven thousand francs a week, and motion pictures had become, overnight, an extremely lucrative commercial enterprise"—as the exhibition of phonographs had been twenty years earlier (*History of Narrative Film*, p. 11).

12. Cook, *History of Narrative Film*, p. 5n.

13. "Evolution of Recordings," p. 5.

14. Cook, *History of Narrative Film*, p. 5n.

15. In fact, a monopoly called the North American Phonograph Co., formed to license regional subsidiaries who would in turn rent equipment and provide service to customers, was built on the organizational model of AT&T ("Evolution of Recordings," p. 6).

16. Sears-Roebuck Catalogue, 1927. This offer is included in every ad on pp. 685–90.

17. Parr, Hicks, and Stareck 1976, Catalogue #114 (1906).

18. "Evolution of Recordings," p. 7.

19. For the differences between disc and cylinder reproduction, see Gelatt 1955, p. 68.

20. Parr, Hicks, and Stareck 1976, Catalogue #117 (1907); italics added.

21. Parr, Hicks, and Stareck 1976, Catalogue #118 (1909).

22. Walter Benjamin, "The Work of Art in the Age of Mechanical Reproduction," in *Film Theory and Criticism,* 2d ed., ed. Gerald Mast and Marshall Cohen (New York: Oxford University Press, 1979).

23. Parr, Hicks, and Stareck 1976, Catalogue #118 (1909).

24. Sears-Roebuck Catalogue, 1927, p. 685; italics added.

25. Parr, Hicks, and Stareck 1976, Catalogue #118 (1909).

26. Ibid.

27. Ibid.

28. And in contemporary advertising: "Is it Live or is it Memorex?"

29. Levin 1984, p. 55, quoting Jean-Louis Comolli, "Machines of the Visible," in *The Cinematic Apparatus,* ed. Teresa de Lauretis and Stephen Heath (New York: St. Martin's Press, 1980), p. 138.

30. David Alan Black, "Cinematic Realism and the Phonographic Analogy," *Cinema Journal* 26, no. 2 (Winter 1987): 39.

31. The political connotations of what Arnheim has to say about sound are, given the period in which *Radio* was written, a fascinating area for future study.

32. *The Random House College Dictionary* (1975); italics added.

33. In a recent article, David Alan Black quotes a 1920s music critic for the London *Sunday Times* on the congruence of the erotic and the experience of listening to the new electronic recordings: "We get from these records what we rarely had before—the physical delight of passionate music" (Black, "Cinematic Realism," p. 45).

34. Home recording did not become widely popular again until the introduction of the tape recorder in the 1950s.

35. "Because [the mother's] voice is identified by the child long before her body is, it remains unlocalized during a number of the most formative moments of subjectivity," Silverman asserts (1988, p. 76) and as an *objet (a)* its " 'otherness' is never very strongly marked" (ibid., p. 85).

36. Silverman is careful to stress that by using the term "fantasy" she "mean[s] to emphasize that trope's retroactivity rather than its fictiveness—to indicate its status as an after-the-fact construction or reading of a situation which is fundamentally irrecoverable, rather than to posit it as a simple illusion" (1988, p. 73).

37. Nancy Chodorow, *The Reproduction of Mothering* (Berkeley: University of California Press, 1978).

38. For an example of a Victorian lass and her user-friendly gramophone, see V. K. Chew's *Talking Machines 1877–1914: Some Aspects of the Early History of the Gramophone* (London: Her Majesty's Stationery Office, 1967), p. 24.

39. McKay is quoting Frederick Dolman, "Women Speakers in England," *Cosmopolitan* 22, no. 6 (April 1897): 679–80.

40. McKay is quoting Jennie Irene Mix, "The Listener's Point of View," *Radio Broadcast,* September 1924, p. 393.

41. McKay is quoting from John F. Rider, "Why Is Radio Soprano Unpopular?" *Scientific American,* October 28, 1928, p. 334.

42. McKay is quoting from Rider, p. 334.

Chapter 2

1. Fredric Jameson, *The Political Unconscious* (New York: Cornell University Press, 1980), p. 95.

2. Two films made in the black American cinema make substantial references to "Rain": *Dirty Gertie from Harlem U.S.A.* (1943) borrows the repressed clergyman from the first act of the play and the story's tropical setting, and much of the Nina Mae McKinney character in *Hallelujah!* (1929) seems to be based on Sadie Thompson and her conversion.

3. The change is so great, especially in regard to sexuality, that there is even a question of whether or not this Sadie Thompson is a prostitute. In his biography of Jeanne Eagels, Edward Doherty quotes her as arguing, upon first reading the play, "I don't want to be a prostitute. . . . The play doesn't really call me one. . . . I can't feel myself a prostitute. I don't want me to be cheap, sordid, vulgar" (*The Rain Girl: The Tragic Story of Jeanne Eagels* [Philadelphia: McCrae Smith, 1930], p. 183).

4. Perhaps the few titleless silent films are so celebrated because when silent film *is* capable of attaining a full closed, single-voiced, purely visual language, it becomes a poetic system. See Burch 1979, p. 79.

5. In the play, title 4 appears as "Was I doing you any harm, was I?" (Colton and Randolph 1936, p. 147), and title 5 condenses "You'd tear the heart out of your grand-mother if she didn't think your way and tell her you were saving her soul—you—you—you psalm-singing—!!" (p. 148).

6. This gesture is the visual equivalent of the business in the play where O'Hara tries to quiet Sadie. There he says, "Sadie—for God's sake!" (Colton and Randolph 1936, p. 145), and "Sadie—Sadie—come on—don't talk anymore" (p. 147).

7. In his book on Eisenstein, Yon Barna describes the painstaking care that went into Eisenstein and Prokofiev's collaboration on the score and the recording of the music for *Alexander Nevski.* According to Barna, Prokofiev "proposed experimenting with the microphones to produce deliberately distorted sound," recording instruments "so close to the microphone as to amplify the distortion" (p. 215). The 1988 *Nevski* tour and its substitution of a real orchestra was very much beside the point. See Yon Barna, *Eisenstein* (Bloomington: Indiana University Press, 1973).

8. Noël Burch, "Narrative/Diegesis—Thresholds, Limits," *Screen* 23, no. 2 (July–August 1982): 18; Walter Kerr, *The Silent Clowns* (New York: Knopf, 1975).

Chapter 3

1. Barthes acknowledges: "This cutting up, admittedly, will be arbitrary in the ex-treme; it will imply no methodological responsibility, since it will bear on the signifier, whereas the proposed analysis bears solely on the signified" (Barthes 1974, p. 13).

2. See also David Bordwell and Kristin Thompson's *Film Art: An Introduction* (Reading, Mass.: Addison-Wesley, 1979).

3. Richard Dyer, *Stars* (London: BFI Publishing, 1982).

4. The shot that ends act 2 does in fact show some horizontal obstacle at the top of the set, which the camera, rising on a crane, passes and uses for a wipe as it pans right toward the sea, having moved out of the set in a physically inexplicable way. Milestone uses a similar dolly-out, which also reveals the horizontality of the set, in the 1941 *Of Mice and Men*.

5. Bordwell, Staiger, and Thompson 1985, pp. 307, 308. In a chapter in his auto-biography entitled "We All Make These Schlemeil Pictures," William Gargan re-counts the tedium of filming a six-minute tracking shot. "We began one night at nine, and we finally satisfied Milly [Milestone] on the fifteenth take, at four the next morn-ing. Then we discovered at the next day's rushes there was a scratch on the entire nega-tive. Two days later we shot it again, and this time we got it on the fifth take. The scene exhausted close to a thousand feet of film, as opposed to not quite one hundred for an ordinary scene. And it exhausted a couple of actors—Crawford and me" (*Why Me?* [New York: Doubleday, 1969], p. 152).

6. For a detailed analysis of another film in terms of accent and vocal quality, see Marie 1980.

7. See, e.g., Lea Jacobs and Richard de Cordova, "Spectacle and Narrative The-ory," *Quarterly Review of Film Studies* 7, no. 4 (Fall 1982): 293–308.

8. Hanns Eisler, *Composing for the Films* (New York: Oxford University Press, 1947). "The spectator is always aware of the divergence [between the recorded voice and the flat screen], of the inevitable gap between the represented body and its voice. And for Eisler and Adorno this partially explains the function of film music: first used in the exhibition of silent films to conceal the noise of the projector (to hide from the spectator the 'uncanny' fact that his/her pleasure is mediated by a machine), music in the 'talkie' takes on the task of closing the gap between voice and body," Doane notes (1985b, p. 171). See also Lucy Fischer 1985b.

9. Dudley Andrew, "Dialogue," *Cinema Journal* 25, no. 1 (Fall 1985): 55–58.

10. The Kino International restoration of *Sadie Thompson* in fact has the film end-ing in just this way.

11. S. M. Eisenstein, V. I. Pudovkin, and G. V. Alexandrov, "A Statement" (re-printed in Weis and Belton 1985) is the most famous case for asynchronous sound. Rick Altman also mentions René Clair, Béla Balázs, and Rudolf Arnheim as promi-nent proponents of this position (Weis and Belton 1985, pp. 11–12).

Chapter 4

1. For her book of the same title, Kaja Silverman (1988) borrows Guy Rosolato's phrase from "La Voix: Entre Corps et langage" (1974), p. 79. On the mirroring rela-tionship of sound and image, see also Altman 1980b.

2. In a paper given at the 1987 Society for Cinema Studies Conference at Montreal, Maria La Place noted the rarity of men's screams in reference to war films. The horror film *White Zombie* (1932) is another exception. There the *only* characters who scream are men, a factor that helps contribute to the film's unsettling quality.

3. For instance, Donald Spoto refers to Alice's "coy cuteness" and "pretense of naivete" (1976, p. 20). Claude Chabrol and Eric Rohmer are even more frigidly judg-mental, describing Alice solely as "the fiancée of a detective [who] lets herself be picked up" by an artist. "He apparently tries to rape her," they snidely continue. "To

defend her virtue, which one would have thought to be less precious to her, she stabs him with a breadknife" (*Hitchcock: The First Forty-Four Films*, translated by Stanley Hochman [New York: Frederick Ungar Publishing, 1979], p. 21).

4. Subsequent to the writing of this chapter, Tania Modleski's excellent book on Hitchcock and feminist theory, *The Women Who Knew Too Much* (1988), was published. In her chapter on *Blackmail* (pp. 17–30), she makes many of the same points discussed here. Modleski also writes on *Notorious,* and while we are in agreement on the attractiveness of Alicia, the phonograph scene, a scene I find pivotal, is not central to her reading of the film.

5. One film in which Bergman's accent is mandated by the narrative as non-signifying is *For Whom the Bell Tolls* (1943), in which the tall, sturdy Swede plays a physically delicate Spanish schoolgirl.

6. Renov sees Hitchcock's "continuous manipulation of the most disruptive elements of classical cinema" (in *Notorious* in particular), as being "fueled by [a character's] desire to see and know" (Renov 1980, p. 30).

7. The film's titles give sole screenplay credit to Lucille Fletcher, "based on her famous radio play." The 22-minute radio version was "rebroadcast seven times between 1943 and 1948 and translated into 15 languages," according to Alain Silver and Elizabeth Ward, editors of *Film Noir: An Encyclopedic Reference to the American Style* (Woodstock, N.Y.: Overlook Press, 1979), p. 263.

8. In *Idols of Perversity* (New York: Oxford University Press, 1986), Bram Dijkstra states that Alice James's "condition was directly related to her desperate efforts to repress her own active, inquisitive nature in order to be more perfectly the infinitely tolerant, pliant woman she was expected to be" (p. 28). The historian Carroll Smith-Rosenberg describes the course feminine invalidism took in the nineteenth century, particularly the ways in which it could be bent to serve the active will of the seemingly passive woman, in *Disorderly Conduct: Visions of Gender in Victorian America* (New York: Knopf, 1985).

9. Lana F. Rakow cites several instances of allegations "that women talk a great deal, if not too much, on the telephone." Apparently Mark Twain was writing about " 'the woman user . . . her special love of the instrument and special ways of using it' " *in 1880* (Kramarae 1988, p. 208, quoting John Brooks, "The First and Only Century of Telephone Literature," in *The Social Impact of the Telephone,* ed. Ithiel de Sola Pool [Cambridge, Mass.: MIT Press, 1977], pp. 208–24).

10. D. W. Griffith's *The Lonely Villa* (1909) is built around a scene similar to the end of *Sorry, Wrong Number,* where a wife is in danger and her husband is far away on the other end of the line. The truly helpless character here though (especially in the short play the film is based on) is the husband. In the play, the audience watched while he listened to his family being murdered on the other end. The telephone thus became the signifier of his enforced passivity and impotence to control events.

11. Rakow notes that "the telephone has been used by some men to bring oppression through abusive and harassing calls into the most private spaces women occupy." She adds that this "kind of intrusion and violation," made possible by the telephone, "has been little noted or studied" (Kramarae 1988, pp. 224, 222).

12. The excessive, suffocating detail of the wedding fantasy in *Spiral Staircase* is noticeably similar to the almost von Stroheim–like deep-focus realism of the wedding

breakfast here. Robert Siodmak and Anatole Litvak have strikingly parallel careers and, at least in these films, similar styles as well.

13. An interesting example of the variety of uses these transitional devices can be put to, and the consequent ambiguity of point of view, is the scene where Leona calls her father. As the phone rings in his study, he picks it up. We hear Leona's voice, filtered. The camera pans around the room, sliding past Dad's various big game trophies stuffed and hanging on the wall, ending on a framed photo of Leona. As the camera wanders, Leona's voice fades out on the sound track, and all we can hear are her father's responses. It is only when we visually return to him and the telephone that we hear her filtered voice again. The camera movement in this scene is comparable to the introductory examination of Leona's bedroom: first, in the emphasis on camera movement, which relegates sound to an offscreen, secondary status, and second in the marked lack of character-generated point of view.

14. The poster illustration—a scene definitely not in the film—shows Henry viciously grabbing Leona's hand, causing her to drop the phone, while he prepares to slap her with the back of his hand.

15. See Sylvia Harvey, "Woman's Place: The Absent Family of Film Noir," in Kaplan 1978a, pp. 22–34, and Place 1978.

16. Joyce Nelson, "*Mildred Pierce* Reconsidered," in Nichols 1985, pp. 450–58. Pam Cook's article "Duplicity in *Mildred Pierce*," in Kaplan 1978a, pp. 68–82, is also an excellent examination of this film.

17. Although suffocating or strangling someone who is nothing but a voice has a perverse appeal, the acoustic figuration of suffocation might be ambiguous on the radio. Shooting Mrs. Stevenson would be ideal from a sound standpoint—a few shots and a scream would suffice. Stabbing her seems excessively violent and serves no immediate thematic purpose.

Chapter 5

1. Earlier, when we hear the powerful voices of marines singing somewhere offscreen, there is no attempt to link the cumulative voice-over to individual singers when we finally locate the men surrounding Sadie inside a bar. The power of the asynchronous male voice exceeds the diegetic interior in which Sadie is trapped.

2. The racial issue of denying any black actor authenticity or control—or the economic "star power" to insist on the unity of her/his voice and image (James Earl Jones as Darth Vader)—is quite comparable to the aural and visual dismemberment of women. In Otto Preminger's *Carmen Jones* (1954), *all* the voices were dubbed: Pearl Bailey's, Dorothy Dandridge's, Harry Belafonte's. . . .

3. "Whenever the female voice seems to speak most out of the 'reality' of her body, it is in fact most complexly contained within the diegesis," Silverman notes (1988, pp. 70–71). We see here that the same is true of ideology.

4. "Human vampire" and "gargoyle" (Molly Haskell); "spider woman" (Janey Place). See Molly Haskell, *From Reverence to Rape: The Treatment of Women in the Movies* (New York: Holt, Rinehart & Winston, 1974), p. 246; Place 1978a, p. 43. Richard Corliss calls *Sunset Boulevard* "the definitive Hollywood horror movie," with

Norma Desmond as "Dracula," Joe as the victim of her "jugular seductions," and the microphone she bats away at one point as this image-vampire's wolfbane. For Corliss and others, Norma Desmond can only be spoken of in mythical terms—as Dracula, Narcissus, Medusa. See Richard Corliss, *Talking Pictures: Screenwriters in the American Cinema, 1927–1973* (Woodstock, N.Y.: Overlook Press, 1974), pp. 147–50.

5. T. M. P., August 11, 1950, in *New York Times Film Reviews, 1913–1970: A One Volume Selection,* ed. George Amberg (New York: Arno Press, 1971), pp. 259–60.

6. Ibid., p. 260.

7. Several articles published in France focus on the unusual presence of death in the film: H. Guibert's "Le Mort qui parle," *Cahiers du cinéma,* no. 319 (January 1981): 35–39, and Y. Hersant's "Portrait de la star en singe mort," *Positif,* no. 271 (September 1983): 34–65.

8. French points out the parallels between the three main characters: "Norma, Joe, and Betty are drawn together because they are alike. The behavior of each is dictated by the savage, competitive, impersonal world they inhabit, a world in which mutual exploitation is the rule" (French 1978, p. 10).

9. For a revisionist reading of the myth of Medusa, see Hélène Cixous, "The Laughter of Medusa," *Signs* 1, no. 4 (1976): 875–93.

10. J. P. Telotte, *Voices in the Dark: The Narrative Patterns of Film Noir* (Urbana: University of Illinois Press, 1989), p. 34.

11. Holden's position as star is gently kidded when Norma rages about the stars of today when compared to "the Fairbanks's, the Gilberts, the Valentinos." She rhetorically asks, "And who've we got now? Some . . . nobodies." On the last word, the image cuts to Holden, himself one of those "new" stars. He smiles, shrugging, and says, "Don't blame me."

12. The presence of Henry Wilcoxin (named on the sound track) in the *Samson and Delilah* rehearsal indicates the greater longevity of male actors, as well as De Mille's ability to employ silent film cronies in his latest films if he so chose.

13. For Andrew Ross in *No Respect: Intellectuals and Popular Culture* (New York: Routledge, 1989), Norma Desmond's combination of emotional bravery and emotional excess have made her a camp icon, though it may be a form of appreciation "tinged with ridicule, derision, even misogyny" (p. 162). Like the other camp "queens of Hollywood" (Maria Montez, Carmen Miranda), Norma's "failed seriousness . . . is more often pathetic and risible than it is witty or parodic" (p. 162). Ross defines "the camp effect" as "when the products (stars, in this case) of a much earlier mode of production, which has lost its power to dominate cultural meanings, become available, in the present, for redefinition according to contemporary codes of taste" (p. 139). Norma Desmond as drag queen, demonstrates "how to *perform* a particular representation of womanliness," showing that "there is no 'authentic' femininity . . . only representations of femininity, socially redefined from moment to moment" (p. 161)—and Norma's moment has passed.

Chapter 6

1. A recently published study of the most frequently used literary texts in American high schools had *To Kill a Mockingbird* among the top ten, along with *Romeo and*

Juliet, Hamlet, and *The Adventures of Huckleberry Finn.* I have been unable to find any major articles written on the film in the past ten years.

2. *The Random House College Dictionary,* rev. ed. (New York: Random House 1975), p. 91.

3. While the narrator is a central, authoritative figure, the actress who plays the role does not receive screen credit. Although she had only made one film before *Mockingbird* (*The Goddess,* 1958), Kim Stanley's reputation as one of the major actresses of her generation is one that continues to the present day despite an extremely limited number of films.

4. Sarah Kozloff (1988, pp. 53–62) points out the similar narrator/child relationship in *How Green Was My Valley* (1941).

5. When "the voice-over is autobiographical and self-revealing," it frequently "takes the form of a temporal regression, a movement back to a prior moment in the speaker's life which accounts for his present condition" (Silverman 1988, pp. 52–53). Examples include the narrated flashbacks of *Double Indemnity* (1944), *D.O.A.* (1949), and *Sunset Boulevard* (1950). See also Kozloff 1988.

6. John Russell Taylor, *Sight and Sound,* 32, no. 3 (Summer 1963): 147. In fact, the film played a limited run in Los Angeles in December 1962 in order to qualify for Academy Award consideration before its general release in February 1963. The film received nine nominations including Best Picture and Best Director (Robert Mulligan), and won Oscars for Gregory Peck, Horton Foote's screenplay, art direction, and set decoration.

7. "Literary Laurels for a Novice," *Life,* May 26, 1961, pp. 78a–78b.

8. Ibid.; "Mocking Bird Call," *Newsweek,* January 9, 1961, p. 83; Joseph Deitch, "Harper Lee: Novellst of the South," *Christian Science Monitor,* October 3, 1961.

9. *Contemporary Literary Criticism,* vol. 12, ed. Dedria Bryfonski (Detroit: Gale Research Company, 1980), p. 340.

10. "Literary Laurels," p. 78a.

11. A photograph in *Life* shows "Miss Lee" working "at her father's law office where she wrote *Mockingbird*" (p. 78a).

12. Mary Badham's gestures and expression are strikingly reminiscent of Scarlet O'Hara's the morning after the rape scene in *Gone with the Wind.* She enacts the same kittenish suggestion of contentedness as Vivien Leigh in the earlier film.

13. *Time,* February 22, 1963.

14. Kinder 1985–86.

15. Editors of *Cahiers du cinéma,* "John Ford's *Young Mr. Lincoln,*" in Nichols 1976, p. 515.

16. Ibid.

17. Ibid.

18. Harper Lee was photographed in the balcony of the local courthouse for *Life.* While she mentions that she often watched her father work from there, it is not stated whether it was segregated at the time. Lee expressed overall satisfaction with the film's fidelity to the book (*The Motion Picture Guide,* vol. T–V, 1927–1983, ed. Jay Robert Nash and Stanley Ralph Ross [Chicago: Cinebooks 1987], p. 3470).

19. For a discussion of Griffith's Lincoln as maternal patriarch, see Mary Desjardin and Mark Williams, "Griffith as Auteur: Delineating the Creation of Myth in the Promotional Campaign and Film Text of *The Birth of a Nation*" (paper presented at the

University Film and Video Association / Society for Cinema Studies conference, Bozeman, Montana, July 1988).

20. "Mocking Bird Call," p. 83. Neither the book nor the film are narrated by a "tomboy"; both are narrated by an adult "offscreen."

21. "Literary Laurels," p. 78b.

22. A contemporary review identifies Ewell's daughter Mayella as the "Tobacco Road-ish 'victim'"—referring to Erskine Caldwell's definitive source of "white trash" iconography ("Tube," "*To Kill a Mockingbird,*" *Variety,* December 12, 1962).

23. Jane Gallop, *The Daughter's Seduction: Feminism and Psychoanalysis* (Ithaca: Cornell University Press, 1982), p. 71.

24. Annette Kuhn, "*The Big Sleep:* A Disturbance in the Sphere of Sexuality," *Wide Angle* 4, no. 3 (1980): 10.

25. Frank H. Lyell, *New York Times Book Review,* July 10, 1960, pp. 5, 18.

26. Edwin Bruell, *English Journal* (December 1964).

27. As the *Christian Science Monitor* identifies her, "Harper Lee: Novelist of the South."

28. Williams's prolific output alone also includes *Baby Doll* (1956), *The Rose Tattoo* (1956), *The Fugitive Kind* (1959), *Suddenly Last Summer* (with Gore Vidal) (1959), *Summer and Smoke* (1961), *Night of the Iguana* (1964), and, in the first half of the decade, *The Glass Menagerie* (1950) and *A Streetcar Named Desire* (1951). A list of important earlier film adaptations would also have to include Carson McCullers's *Member of the Wedding* (1952). The character of Scout and Jem's young friend, Dill, is reputedly based on Harper Lee's childhood friend Truman Capote.

29. Dorothy Dinnerstein, *The Mermaid and the Minotaur: Sexual Arrangements and Human Malaise* (New York: Harper Colophon, 1977), quoted in Hirsch 1989, p. 134.

30. The absence of the mother might also be autobiographical. Lee's actual family configuration is not repeated in the novel. Lee has a sister, for instance, who did complete law school.

31. It is Ewell's *legal* name, established at the trial, that connects the text's bad father and Harper Lee's ancestor.

32. And yet the adult woman *will not* confront the father directly; the author puts the knife in a man's hands.

33. Hirsch 1989 uses the term "re-member" in reference to Toni Morrison's *Beloved* when she discusses the need of memory to make one's self whole.

34. "When the voice-over is introduced in the beginning of a film as the possession of the female protagonist who purportedly controls the narration of her own past, it is rarely sustained" (Doane 1987, p. 150).

35. "The sounds the voice makes always exceed signification to some degree" (Silverman 1988, p. 44).

36. Alice Walker champions the recovery of regional speech in *In Search of Our Mother's Gardens* (New York: Harcourt Brace Jovanovich, 1983) and, in practice, in *The Color Purple* (New York: Harcourt Brace Jovanovich, 1983).

37. Molly Hite notes that "Walker's invention of what is effectively a *written* 'dialect' for Celie's 'letters' consciously continues the practice of Zora Neale Hurston and thus invokes a black feminist tradition. Walker is extremely aware of the risk such a

marginal discourse runs by being judged simply incorrect or primitive and plays on the implicit contrast with the dominant ('standard') dialect throughout *The Color Purple*" (i.e., Celie's unfettered, personalized speech compared with Nettie's colorlessly "correct" nineteenth-century language) (Hite, "Writing—and Reading—the Body: Female Sexuality and Recent Feminist Fiction," *Feminist Studies* 14, no. 1 (Spring 1988): 141 n. 19).

38. Christine Froula, "The Daughter's Seduction: Sexual Violence and Literary History," *Signs* 11, no. 4 (Summer 1986): 638, 641; italics added.

References

Claudia Gorbman's "Bibliography on Sound in Film," *Yale French Studies* 60 (1980): 269–86; and the invaluable annotated version (excluding music) reprinted in Weis and Belton 1985, pp. 427–45, are the definitive bibliographies of works on film sound to date. The books and articles listed below have been of particular help to me in this work.

Agee, James. 1958. *Agee on Film*. Toronto: McDowell, Obolensky.

Allen, Robert C. and Douglas Gomery. 1985. *Film History: Theory and Practice*. New York: Knopf.

Altman, Rick, ed. 1980a. *Cinema/Sound. Yale French Studies* 60 (1980).

———. 1980b. "Moving Lips: Cinema as Ventriloquism." *Yale French Studies* 60 (1980): 67–79.

———. 1985. "Psychoanalysis and Cinema: The Imaginary Discourse." Originally published in *Quarterly Review of Film Studies* 2, no. 3 (August 1977). Reprinted in Nichols 1985, pp. 517–31.

Arnheim, Rudolf. 1936. *Radio*. Translated by Margaret Ludwig and Herbert Read. Glasgow: Faber & Faber. Reprint. New York: Arno Press, 1976.

———. 1957. *Film as Art*. Reprint. Berkeley: University of California Press, 1966.

Bakhtin, M. M. 1981. *The Dialogic Imagination: Four Essays*. Translated by Caryl Emerson and Michael Holquist. Austin: University of Texas Press.

Balázs, Béla. 1952. *Theory of the Film: Character and Growth of a New Art*. Reprint. New York: Arno Press, 1972.

Barnouw, Erik. 1966–70. *A History of Broadcasting in the United States*. 3 vols. Oxford: Oxford University Press.

Barr, Charles. 1983. "*Blackmail:* Silent and Sound." *Sight and Sound* 52, no. 2 (Spring): 122–26.

Barthes, Roland. 1974. *S/Z*. Translated by Richard Miller. New York: Hill & Wang.

———. 1977. "The Grain of the Voice." In *Image-Music-Text*, selected and translated by Stephen Heath, pp. 179–89. New York: Hill & Wang.

Bazin, André. 1967. *What Is Cinema?* Vol. 1. Translated by Hugh Gray. Berkeley: University of California Press.

Baudry, Jean-Louis. 1985. "Ideological Effects of the Basic Cinematographic Apparatus." Originally published in *Film Quarterly* 28, no. 2 (Winter 1974–75): 39–47. Reprinted in Nichols 1985, pp. 531–43.

———. 1976. "The Apparatus." *Camera Obscura*, no. 1 (Fall): 104–26.

Belton, John. 1985. "Technology and Aesthetics of Film Sound." In Weis and Belton 1985, pp. 63–72.

Bergstrom, Janet. 1979. "Enunciation and Sexual Difference, Part 1." *Camera Obscura*, nos. 3/4 (Summer): pp. 33–69.

Bordwell, David, Janet Staiger, and Kristin Thompson. 1985. *The Classical Hollywood Cinema: Film Style & Mode of Production to 1960*. New York: Columbia University Press.

Burch, Noël. 1979. *To the Distant Observer: Form and Meaning in the Japanese Cinema*. Revised and edited by Annette Michelson. Berkeley: University of California Press.

Cameron, Evan William, ed. 1980. *Sound and the Cinema: The Coming of Sound to American Film*. Pleasantville, N.Y.: Redgrave Publishing.

Cameron, James. 1929. *Motion Pictures with Sound*. Foreword by William Fox. Manhattan Beach, N.Y.: Cameron Publishing.

———. 1930. *Encyclopedia on Sound Motion Pictures*. Manhattan Beach, N.Y.: Cameron Publishing.

Chion, Michel. 1982. *La Voix au cinéma*. Paris: Editions de L'Etoile.

———. 1985. *Le Son au cinéma*. Paris: Editions de L'Etoile.

Colton, John, and Clemence Randolph. 1936. *Rain*. 9th ed. Introduction by Ludwig Lewisohn. New York: Liveright.

Comolli, Jean-Louis. 1972. "Technique et ideologie." *Cahiers du cinéma* 241 (September–October): 20–24.

Cook, Pam. 1978. "Duplicity in *Mildred Pierce*." In Kaplan 1978a, pp. 68–82.

Dayan, Daniel. 1976. "The Tutor Code of Classical Cinema." Originally published in *Film Quarterly* 28, no. 1 (Fall 1974). Reprinted in Nichols 1976, pp. 438–51.

Doane, Mary Ann. 1984. "The 'Woman's Film': Possession and Address." In *Re-Vision: Essays in Feminist Film Criticism*, edited by Mary Ann Doane, Patricia Mellencamp, Linda Williams, pp. 67–82. Frederick, Md.: AFI/University Publications of America.

———. 1985a. "Ideology and the Practice of Sound Editing and Mixing." Originally published in *The Cinematic Apparatus*, edited by Teresa de Lauretis and Stephen Heath. New York: St. Martin's Press, 1980. Reprinted in Weis and Belton 1985, pp. 54–62.

———. 1985b. "The Voice in the Cinema: The Articulation of Body and Space." Originally published in Altman 1980a, pp. 47–56. Reprinted in Weis and Belton 1985, pp. 162–76.

———. 1987. *The Desire to Desire: The Woman's Film of the 1940's*. Bloomington: Indiana University Press.

Eisenstein, Sergei. 1957. *Film Form* [and] *The Film Sense*. Translated and edited by Jay Leyda. New York: Meridian Books.

"The Evolution of Recordings: From Cylinder to Video Disc." Anonymous pamphlet [1978].

Fielding, Raymond. 1980. "The Technological Antecedents of the Coming of Sound: An Introduction." In Cameron 1980, pp. 2–23.

Fischer, Lucy. 1985a. "*Enthusiasm:* From Kino-Eye to Radio Eye." Originally published in *Film Quarterly* 31, no. 2 (Winter 1977–78): 25–34. Reprinted in Weis and Belton 1985, pp. 247–64.

———. 1985b. "*Applause:* The Visual and Acoustic Landscape." Originally published in Cameron 1980, pp. 182–201. Reprinted in Weis and Belton 1985, pp. 232–46.

Flinn, Carol. 1986. "The 'Problem' of Femininity in Theories of Film Music." *Screen* 27, no. 6 (November–December): 56–72.

French, Brandon. 1978. *On the Verge of Revolt: Women in American Films of the Fifties*. New York: Frederick Ungar Publishing.

Freud, Sigmund. 1964. "Femininity." In *New Introductory Lectures,* translated and edited by James Strachey, pp. 99–119. New York: Norton.

Gelatt, Roland. 1955. *The Fabulous Phonograph: From Tin Foil to High Fidelity*. Philadelphia: Lippincott.

Gomery, Douglas. 1980. "Hollywood Converts to Sound: Chaos or Order?" In Cameron 1980, pp. 24–37.

Green, Fitzhugh. 1929. *The Film Finds Its Tongue*. New York: G. P. Putnam's Sons.

Heath, Stephen. 1978. "Difference." *Screen* 19, no. 3 (Autumn): 51–112.

Hirsch, Marianne. 1989. *The Mother/Daughter Plot: Narrative, Psychoanalysis, Feminism*. Bloomington: Indiana University Press.

Jacobs, Lea, and Richard de Cordova. 1982. "Spectacle and Narrative Theory." *Quarterly Review of Film Studies* 7, no. 4 (Fall): 293–308.

Kaplan, E. Ann, ed. 1978a. *Women in Film Noir*. London: BFI Publishing. Revised edition 1980.

———. 1978b. "The Place of Women in Fritz Lang's *The Blue Gardenia.*" In Kaplan 1978a, pp. 83–90.

———. 1983. *Women and Film: Both Sides of the Camera*. New York: Methuen.

Kinder, Marsha. 1985–86. "The Image of Patriarchal Power in *Young Mr. Lincoln* (1939) and *Ivan the Terrible, Part I* (1945)." *Film Quarterly* 39, no. 2 (Winter): 29–49.

Kozloff, Sarah. 1988. *Invisible Storytellers: Voice-Over Narration in American Fiction Film*. Berkeley: University of California Press.

Kramarae, Cheris, ed. 1988. *Technology and Women's Voices: Keeping in Touch*. New York: Routledge & Kegan Paul.

Kristeva, Julia. 1980. "Word, Dialogue, Novel." In *Desire in Language,* translated and edited by Leon S. Roudiez, Thomas Gora, and Alice Jardine, pp. 64–91. New York: Columbia University Press.

Kubie, Lawrence S., and Sydney Margolin. 1944. "The Process of Hypnotism and the Nature of the Hypnotic State." *American Journal of Psychiatry* 100, no. 5 (March): 611–22.

Kuhn, Annette. 1982. *Women's Pictures: Feminism and Cinema*. London: Routledge & Kegan Paul.

Lacan, Jacques. 1977. *Ecrits: A Selection*. Translated by Alan Sheridan. New York: Norton.

———. 1978. *The Four Fundamental Concepts of Psycho-Analysis*. Edited by Jacques-Alain Miller. Translated by Alan Sheridan. New York: Norton.

Levin, Tom. 1984. "The Acoustic Dimension." *Screen* 25, no. 3 (May–June): 55–68.

McKay, Anne. 1988. "Speaking Up: Voice Amplification and Women's Struggle for Public Expression." In Kramarae 1988, pp. 187–206.

Marie, Michel. 1980. "The Poacher's Aged Mother: On Speech in *La Chienne* by Jean Renoir." In Altman 1980a, pp. 219–32.

Maugham, W. Somerset. 1967. "Rain." In *Cakes and Ale* [1930], edited by Angus Wilson. Garden City, N.Y.: Doubleday.

Metz, Christian. 1982. *The Imaginary Signifier*. Translated by Ben Brewster. Bloomington: Indiana University Press.

———. 1985. "Aural Objects." Originally published in Altman 1980a, pp. 24–32. Reprinted in Weis and Belton 1985, pp. 154–61.

Modleski, Tania. 1988. *The Women Who Knew Too Much: Hitchcock and Feminist Theory*. New York: Methuen.

Mulvey, Laura. 1975. "Visual Pleasure and Narrative Cinema." *Screen* 16, no. 3 (Autumn): 6–18. Reprinted in Nichols 1985, pp. 303–15.

Nichols, Bill. 1976, 1985. *Movies and Methods*. 2 vols. Berkeley: University of California Press.

Parr, Leslie, Andrea Hicks, and Marie Stareck, eds. 1976. *The Best of Sears Collectibles, 1905–1910*. New York: Arno Press.

Place, Janey. 1978. "Women in Film Noir." In Kaplan 1978a, pp. 35–67.

Rakow, Lana F. 1988. "Women and the Telephone: The Gendering of a Communications Technology." In Kramarae 1988, pp. 207–28.

Read, Oliver, and Walter L. Welch. 1976. *From Tinfoil to Stereo: Evolution of the Phonograph*. 2d ed. Indianapolis: Howard W. Sams.

Renov, Michael. 1980. "From Identification to Ideology: The Male System of Hitchcock's *Notorious*." *Wide Angle* 4, no. 1: 30–37.

Rosolato, Guy. 1974. "La Voix: Entre corps et langage." *Revue française de psychanalyse* 37, no. 1 (January).

Sachs, Jacqueline, Philip Lieberman, and Donna Crickson. 1973. "Anatomical and Cultural Determinants of Male and Female Speech." In *Language Attitudes: Current Trends and Prospects*, pp. 74–84. Washington, D.C.: George Washington University Press.

Seymour, Henry. [1918]. *The Reproduction of Sound: Being a Description of the Mechanical Appliances and Technical Processes Employed in the Art*. London: W. B. Tattersall.

Silverman, Kaja. 1988. *The Acoustic Mirror: The Female Voice in Psychoanalysis and Cinema*. Bloomington: Indiana University Press.

Spoto, Donald. 1976. *The Art of Alfred Hitchcock: Fifty Years of His Motion Pictures*. New York: Hopkinson & Blake.

————. 1983. *The Dark Side of Genius: The Life of Alfred Hitchcock.* Boston: Little, Brown.

Swanson, Gloria. 1980. *Swanson on Swanson.* New York: Random House.

Vertov, Dziga. 1984. *Kino-Eye: The Writings of Dziga Vertov.* Edited and with an introduction by Annette Michelson. Translated by Kevin O'Brien. Berkeley: University of California Press.

Weis, Elisabeth. 1982. *The Silent Scream: Alfred Hitchcock's Sound Tracks.* Rutherford, N.J.: Fairleigh Dickinson University Press.

————, and John Belton, eds. 1985. *Film Sound: Theory and Practice.* New York: Columbia University Press.

Williams, Alan. 1980. "Is Sound Recording Like a Language?" In Altman 1980a, pp. 51–66.

Williams, Linda. 1984. "When the Woman Looks." In Doane, Mellencamp, and Williams 1984, pp. 83–99.

Williams, Raymond. 1977. *Marxism and Literature.* London: Oxford University Press.

Wills, David. 1986. "*Carmen:* Sound/Effect." *Cinema Journal* 25, no. 4 (Summer): 33–43.

Filmography

Sadie Thompson (1928)

Produced by Gloria Swanson; directed by Raoul Walsh; written by G. Gardner Sullivan, adapted from the story "Rain" by W. Somerset Maugham; photography, George Barnes, Robert Kurrle, and Oliver Marsh; art direction, William Cameron Menzies. Cast: *Sadie,* Gloria Swanson; *Sgt. Tim O'Hara,* Raoul Walsh; *Mr. Alfred Davidson,* Lionel Barrymore.

Rain (1932)

Produced by United Artists; directed by Lewis Milestone; written by Maxwell Anderson, adapted from the play by John Colton and Clemence Randolph and the short story by W. Somerset Maugham; photography, Oliver Marsh; sound, Frank Grenzbach; music, Alfred Newman. Cast: *Sadie,* Joan Crawford; *Sgt. Tim O'Hara,* William Gargan; *Mr. Davidson,* Walter Huston; *Mrs. Davidson,* Beulah Bondi; *Horn,* Guy Kibbee; *Ameena,* Mary Shaw.

Blackmail (1929)

Produced by John Maxwell for BIP; directed by Alfred Hitchcock; written by Alfred Hitchcock, Benn W. Levy, and Charles Bennett, adapted from the play by Charles Bennett; photography, Jack Cox; music, Campbell and Connelly; [no sound credit]. Cast: *Alice White,* Anny Ondra; *Frank,* John Longden; *Artist,* Cyril Ritchard.

The Spiral Staircase (1946)

Produced by Dore Schary for RKO; directed by Robert Siodmak; written by Mel Dinelli, adapted from the novel *Some Must Watch* by Ethel Lina White; photography,

Nicholas Musuraca; art direction, Albert S. D'Agostino and Jack Okey; sound, John L. Cass and Terry Kellum; music, Roy Webb. Cast: *Helen,* Dorothy McGuire; *Dr. Perry,* Kent Smith; *Prof. Albert Warren,* George Brent; *Mrs. Warren,* Ethel Barrymore; *Blanche,* Rhonda Fleming.

Notorious (1946)

Produced by Alfred Hitchcock for RKO; directed by Alfred Hitchcock; written by Ben Hecht; photography, Ted Tetzlaff; sound, John E. Tribby and Terry Kellum; music, Roy Webb. Cast: *Alicia Huberman,* Ingrid Bergman; *Devlin,* Cary Grant; *Sebastian,* Claude Rains.

Sorry, Wrong Number (1948)

Produced by Hal B. Wallis and Anatole Litvak for Paramount; directed by Anatole Litvak; written by Lucille Fletcher, adapted from her radio play; photography, Sol Polito; sound, Gene Merritt and Walter Oberst; music, Franz Waxman. Cast: *Leona,* Barbara Stanwyck; *Henry,* Burt Lancaster; *Sally,* Ann Richards; *Waldo Evans,* Harold Vermilyea; *Doctor,* Wendell Corey; *Mr. Cotterill,* Ed Begley.

Miss Sadie Thompson (1953)

Produced and directed by Curtis Bernhardt for Columbia Pictures; written by Harry Kleiner (the title is presented as "W. Somerset Maugham's Miss Sadie Thompson"); photography, Charles Lawton, Jr.; art direction, Carl Anderson; musical direction, Morris Stoloff; sound engineer, George Cooper. Cast: *Sadie,* Rita Hayworth; *Sgt. Phil O'Hara,* Aldo Ray; *Mr. Davidson,* Jose Ferrer; *Dr. Macphail,* Russell Collins.

Sunset Boulevard (1950)

Produced by Charles Brackett; directed by Billy Wilder; written by Billy Wilder, Charles Brackett, and D. M. Marshman, Jr.; photography, John F. Seitz; art direction, Hans Dreier and John Meehan; editorial supervision, Doane Harrison; sound, Harry Lindgren and John Cope; music, Franz Waxman. Cast: *Norma Desmond,* Gloria Swanson; *Joe Gillis,* William Holden; *Max von Mayerling,* Erich von Stroheim; *Betty Schaeffer,* Nancy Olson; *Artie Green,* Jack Webb; Cecil B. De Mille as himself.

To Kill a Mockingbird (1962)

Produced by Alan J. Pakula; directed by Robert Mulligan; written by Horton Foote, Jr., adapted from the novel by Harper Lee; photography, Russell Harlan; art direction, Henry Bumstead; sound, Waldon O. Watson, Corson Jewett, Charles Cohn, and James Curtis; musical score, Elmer Bernstein. Cast: *Atticus Finch,* Gregory Peck; *Scout,* Mary Badham; *Jem,* Philip Alford; *Dill,* John Megna; *Tom Robinson,* Brock Peters; *Mayella Ewell,* Collin Wilcox; *Bob Ewell,* James Anderson; *Rev. Sikes,* Bill Walker; *Calpurnia,* Estelle Evans; *Boo Radley,* Robert Duvall. Narrated by Kim Stanley.

Index

207

Compositor:	G & S Typesetters, Inc.
Text:	10/12 Times Roman
Display:	Helvetica Light, Helvetica, & Helvetica Bold
Printer:	Malloy Lithographing, Inc.
Binder:	John H. Dekker & Sons